RECORDKEEPING REQUIREMENTS

RECORDKEEPING REQUIREMENTS

The First Practical Guide to Help You Control
Your Records . . . What You Need to Keep and
What You Can Safely Destroy!

Donald S. Skupsky, JD, CRM

Information Requirements Clearinghouse
Denver, Colorado

Information Requirements Clearinghouse
5600 South Quebec Street, Suite 250C
Englewood, Colorado 80111
(303) 721-7500

Printed in the United States of America
98 97 96 95   7 6 5

Library of Congress Cataloging in Publication Data
Skupsky, Donald S.
    Recordkeeping Requirements

    Bibliography: p.
    Includes index.
    1. Business records—Law and legislation—United States.
    2. Business records—United States. I. Title.
KF1357.5.S59 1988   346.73'0664   88-13335
ISBN 0-929316-21-5   347.306664

CONTENTS

APPENDIXES

Foreword

For years people worked in offices surrounded by asbestos and other hazardous substances and didn't know they had a problem. Thanks to the Occupational Safety and Health Administration, we now know! For years people used unsafe drugs and harmful consumer products and didn't know they had a problem. Thanks to the Food and Drug Administration and the Consumer Products Safety Commission, we now know! And for years people worked in offices surrounded by records and didn't know they had a problem. Thanks to Donald Skupsky, you will soon know about this problem, too!

Certainly, records are not life threatening or potentially harmful to people. Yet, records can do incredible damage to an organization and could indeed hasten its demise, if they are not properly created, maintained, or destroyed.

In *Recordkeeping Requirements*, Donald Skupsky shows you the record problems you didn't know you had. He explains the difficulty in dealing with conflicting laws, ambiguous laws, or even non-existent laws. He cites examples of organizations that failed to confront the issues and paid the price.

But . . . there is more. This book not only tells you what the problems are (although that in itself would be a significant contribution given the dearth of information on the subject), it provides detailed information on how to solve them. In clear, understandable fashion you are told the steps that are necessary to establish a legally acceptable records management program . . . a program that will not only assist you in managing your organization and your valuable information more effectively, but will help you avoid fines, bankruptcy, or even jail. Now you can determine what records to keep and what records can safely be destroyed.

Recordkeeping Requirements is a landmark work. It is important reading for all managers striving to improve their organization's records program and comply with the law, and it is certainly *required* reading for all managers who thought that records management was an "option."

Ira A. Penn, CRM, CSP
Editor
Records Management Quarterly

Preface

In the early 1980's, while working with some oil companies in Denver as an associate of Austin Associates Consultants, Inc., I was asked to determine how long these companies should keep their records. Now we all keep lots of records and some for a long time, but petroleum companies, particularly, seem to keep everything forever because "it may be needed someday."

I found it frustrating that even after law school and several years of records management experience, getting the answer to that question turned out to be extraordinarily complex and time consuming. No good sources of information were available, the government indexes to their own requirements were a disaster, and the research materials were located all over the law library. Law libraries don't keep most state regulations and, as I later found, some state regulations aren't even published.

In 1984 I formed my own company, Information Requirements Clearinghouse, to pursue my goal of making the legal requirements for recordkeeping available to those needing the information. The net result of this initial effort was the acclaimed loose-leaf service *Legal Requirements for Business Records*. My initial expectation was that one, five-hundred page loose-leaf would be ample for this service. To my great surprise—because of the staggering number of existing legal requirements and annual revisions encountered— the service is now over 2500 pages long in four volumes.

While *Legal Requirements for Business Records* is invaluable for large companies with in-house records managers or legal counsel to analyze and implement these requirements, I have always felt the need to place this information in the hands of the small and medium-sized businesses who need it desperately but don't have the resources to gather and analyze it. *Recordkeeping Requirements* answers this need for small and medium-sized organizations.

Much of the information has been derived from my previous research and writings in the field. A lot of new and updated information has been added to better address the needs of the intended audience. Because this type of information must be customized to meet specific needs of an organization, I am also writing a series of companion workbooks to help you customize the information from this book to better meet the needs of your organization.

An effort such as this can never proceed in a vacuum. I am very grateful and appreciative of my wife, Lorraine, who supported me in this endeavor, and prepared the marketing and distribution plan for the book. I wish to also thank Toni Mote, my administrative associate, for her dedication in typing and revising this manuscript.

Finally, I would like to thank the reviewers who provided helpful comments and recommendations to ensure the accuracy, readability, and acceptance of this book: William Benedon, CRM, Corporate Director, Management Support Services, Lockheed Corporation; Mark Langemo, Ed.D., CRM, Professor, College of Business and Public Administration, University of North Dakota; Gail Pennix, CRM, Manager, Corporate Information Management, Hewlett Packard Company; Jerry D. Sheely, President, Colorado National Bank Boulevard; Thomas Wilds, CRM, Information Management Consultant, Thomas Wilds & Associates, Inc.; Jean Yancey, Small Business Consultant, Jean Yancey Associates.

Special thanks to Ira A. Penn, CRM, CSP, Editor, *Records Management Quarterly* who both reviewed the book and prepared the Foreword and to Donald R. Rose, PhD, MBA, Technical Writer, who served as technical editor.

Introduction

Intended Audience

All of us are plagued with recordkeeping requirements. Records must be kept to verify payments, prepare income tax returns, verify benefits under warranties, manage employees, develop products, satisfy the needs of customers, ensure compliance with contracts, and many other reasons.

This book was written primarily to help the small (up to a few hundred employees) and medium-sized (a few hundred to a few thousand employees) organizations, both public and private, deal with these difficult records problems. Most do not have the resources or internal expertise to undertake the extensive research needed to determine their recordkeeping requirements. Yet, each must comply with a myriad of laws if they want to continue operation, protect the public and their employees from harm, verify compliance with federal and state regulatory programs, and avoid fines, penalties, and other adverse consequences. While we should keep records primarily because they are needed by our organizations, the law often causes us to keep more records for longer periods of time.

This book should appeal to business owners and managers of smaller organization with little or no experience in this area, as well as to lawyers, accountants, records managers from larger organization who need a handy reference. The text is presented in non-technical, laymen's language with detailed appendixes containing the full text of key statutes and regulations and summary charts for many other state requirements.

Scope

This book provides most organizations with the information they need to determine their recordkeeping requirements. Requirements for general business activities such as tax, employment, contracts, litigation, etc. are covered in great depth.

Companion workbooks are
available from the
publisher to help customize
and expand the
information presented here
to better meet the needs of
your organization. An
Order Form is provided at
the back of this book for
your convenience.

This book does not cover, however, the unique recordkeeping requirements for companies engaged in special industries such as manufacturing, petroleum, transportation, communications, or utilities, or other special activities.

You may need to contact those state or federal administrative agencies which regulate your industry or special activity for additional requirements applicable to your situation. The additional effort can be small, because *Recordkeeping Requirements* provides most of the needed information.

Research Methodology

This book is based upon the research findings of Information Requirements Clearinghouse (Denver, Colorado) as published in its three-volume loose-leaf service entitled *Legal Requirements for Business Records*. This service provides the full text of federal and state recordkeeping requirements plus extensive research indexes. More than 2800 sections of federal law (with from one to approximately 400 different requirements in each section) and over 1500 sections of state law are addressed in this 1500-page service which is updated annually. Mr. Donald S. Skupsky, JD, CRM, author of *Recordkeeping Requirements, Records Retention Procedures, and Legal Requirments for Microfilm, Computer and Optical Disk Records* is also the editor of *Legal Requirements for Business Records*.

Organization

This book has six parts plus an extensive appendix.

Part A provides the background for recordkeeping requirements. Chapter 1 describes real-life case studies of companies who either failed to recognize the importance of controlling their records in advance and paid the price, or those who established effective programs and averted disaster. Chapter 2 identifies the scope of your recordkeeping responsibilities, including the agencies that regulate your organization, the applicable state laws, the status of so-called "private records", and your responsibility for records belonging to others or acquired by acquisition or merger. Chapter 3 provides the legal justification for a records management program. Chapter 4 alerts you to the consequences of failing to comply with the laws in the hope it will motivate you to install a records management program or at least continue reading this book. Chapter 5 presents a unique strategy for dealing with the many different laws (even those you may inadvertently fail to consider) and explains how to implement a program to meet the needs of your organization and protect it against adverse consequences.

Part B identifies the factors which determine how long you must keep your records. Chapter 6 describes the six considerations for records retention and provides a basic strategy for complying with each. Chapter 7 tells you how to handle your records when the laws do not state how long to keep them. Finally, Chapter 8 explores the complexities of keeping records currently covered by a statute of limitations and the risks in the event of litigation.

Part C explains the specific records retention requirements for many of the records found within your organization. Chapter 9 discusses the retention periods for records maintained for tax purposes. Similarly, Chapter

10 explains the retention of personnel or employment records. Chapter 11 covers general business records such as those establishing your organization, contracts, general manufacturing records, client records, and others. Finally, Chapter 12 lists hundreds of common business records, the minimum and maximum records retention requirements found throughout the United States, and the typical retention periods for your use.

Part D explains how to establish a legally acceptable records retention program. Chapter 13 identifies those components of a program which prepare you to respond to the concerns raised by the courts in case decisions. Chapter 14 recommends procedures for developing and operating a records retention program and customizing the information contained in this book to better meet your needs. Chapter 15 reviews those special circumstances which allow records to be destroyed as part of a regular records retention program or as part of a one-time records destruction or microfilming program.

Part E addresses the various types of record media— paper, microfilm, computer records, and digitized records— and the requirements for their admissibility in evidence and acceptance by regulatory agencies. Chapter 16 discusses the admissibility of original records in evidence. Chapter 17 addresses the admissibility of microfilm and duplicate records in evidence plus the specific microfilm requirements of the Internal Revenue Service and state revenue departments. Chapter 18 reviews the admissibility of computer records in evidence plus the requirements of the Internal Revenue Service and state revenue departments for computerized accounting systems. Finally, Chapter 19 addresses the admissibility of records in evidence produced from digitized images created with electronic imaging systems, and discusses the legality of this technology under existing laws.

Part F is designed for those who must perform additional legal research to uncover the requirements for their specific industries or activities. Chapter 20 introduces the concept of legal research and suggests a desirable working relationship with your attorneys. Chapter 21 describes the sources of recordkeeping requirements and provides research strategies. Chapter 22 explains a proven method for organizing your legal research and presenting it to your attorneys for review.

The appendixes compile the various laws and sources for your reference. The full text of the most important laws addressed in this book, as they relate to recordkeeping requirements, are reproduced. State requirements, especially for tax and statutes of limitations, have been summarized in charts for your convenience. A glossary, bibliography and index facilitate your use of this book.

How To Use This Book

Everyone should read Parts A through C before making recommendations to your organization. Chapter 12 is particularly valuable in helping you identify the appropriate records retention periods.

Part D can then help you to customize the records retention program to meet the unique needs of your organization. If you use or plan to use technologies such as microfilm, computer, or electronic imaging systems, you will find Part E very valuable in examining the legality of these technologies and the procedures necessary to ensure their acceptance as evidence or by regulatory agencies.

Finally, while this book was developed to meet the needs of a great many different organizations, it is not possible to answer every question about the legal requirements of recordkeeping. Some organizations will need to perform additional research in order to uncover those requirements related to their specific industries or activities at both the federal and state level. Part F provides the appropriate research methodology to quickly and effectively identify those requirements.

PART A INTRODUCTION TO RECORDKEEPING REQUIREMENTS

Chapter 1   Some Endure Misfortune While Others Plan Ahead

You probably expect this book to give you some "quick and dirty answers" to a growing dilemma: what to do with all those records that have accumulated over the years? Well, rest easy, this book has the answers — probably, more than you ever wanted to know. But they may not be "quick and dirty ones."

This book provides answers to the records problems you face today. Your predecessors and counterparts, however, were not so lucky. Many ignored the inevitable and paid the price.

Thankfully, we can learn from those who had records problems; they either did not know or did not want to know what the law expected of them and their records. Their stories flow through the business pages of prominent newspapers and magazines. Judges chastise their indiscretions in court opinions throughout the country. The rest of us may be no better or worse—we just haven't gotten into trouble, yet!

Even the smallest organization, using *Recordkeeping Requirements*, can determine what records you need to keep and what you can safely destroy. The law expects much of us in terms of the management of records. It often specifies what records we must keep and how long we must keep them. Other legal events, such as litigation, a government investigation or audit, can abruptly thrust our records to the forefront.

If you need more motivation, just read about those who learned too late.

CASE STUDY 1: Selective Destruction of Records

See *Carlucci et al v. Piper Aircraft Corporation*, Case Nos. 78-8370-CIV-JCP to 78-8372-CIV-JCP, United States District Court, Southern District, Florida, as reported in 102 Federal Rules Decisions 472, St. Paul: West Publishing Company, 1984.

Clara Carlucci and others (plaintiffs) initiated a lawsuit in 1978 to recover damages resulting from the deaths of three men who perished in the crash of a Piper Cheyenne II at Shannon, Ireland, in 1976. The plaintiffs alleged various design defects which caused the pilot to lose control and crash.

The plaintiff, to prepare the case, subpoenaed various documents from Piper Aircraft (defendant) relative to the design and testing of the aircraft. Despite repeated requests by both the plaintiff and the judge, Piper failed to provide the plaintiffs with the information. The judge appointed a Special Master in 1983 to review the discovery process and determine why the appropriate records had not been provided to the plaintiff.

Two employees in the Flight Test Department told the Special Master that they, at the request of their supervisor, had selectively "purged" hundreds of records that might be "detrimental" to Piper in future lawsuits. Piper claimed that these records were destroyed under document retention procedures but offered no evidence demonstrating that these procedures were followed by its employees.

William J. Campbell, Senior District Judge, after reviewing the evidence, entered a default judgment against Piper Aircraft Corporation in the amount of $10 million because of the selective destruction of records, without even considering the merits of the case:

> . . . I conclude that the defendant engaged in a practice of destroying engineering documents with the intention of preventing them from being produced in law suits. Furthermore, I find that this practice continued after the commencement of this law suit and that documents relevant to this law suit were intentionally destroyed. . .

> I am not holding that the good faith disposal of documents pursuant to a *bona fide*, consistent and reasonable document retention policy cannot be a valid justification for failure to produce documents in discovery. That issue never crystallized in this case because Piper has utterly failed to provide credible evidence that such a policy or practice existed . . .

> . . . The policy of resolving law suits under merit must yield when a party has intentionally prevented the fair adjudication of the case. By deliberately destroying documents, the defendant has eliminated plaintiffs' right to have their case decided on the merit. Accordingly, the entry of a default is the only means of effectively sanctioning the defendant and remedying the wrong . . .

The Carlucci case serves as a milestone decision about the destruction of records. The courts will not tolerate the selective destruction of records in anticipation of litigation, especially after litigation starts. While we can be guided by judicial attitudes, it is sad that the ax fell on Piper for the same practice of selective destruction or purging of records followed by most organizations in the United States. Most of us selectively destroy records as part of a "search and destroy mission" without the guidance of a proper record retention program.

Upon closer review of this case, the facts do not support a conclusion that Piper did anything wrong, they only support the conclusion that what Piper did "looked wrong." Piper did have a records retention program, although it did not establish this point in court, and did maintain the official company set of flight test records in the Engineering Department. The records destroyed in the Flight Test Department consisted of valueless duplicate copies held only in the event test results became lost when sent back to the Engineering Department (the department requesting the tests).

Piper's major indiscretion was its inability to document to the court that records were destroyed in the regular course of business under an approved records retention schedule and that records maintained in the Flight Test Department were valueless duplicate copies that could have been appropriately destroyed at any time. Instead, their so-called "program" appeared to the court as a "sham" and the judge never looked beyond it to the merits of the case. Piper currently faces similar issues in other litigation and courts could continue to rule against Piper in these cases, too.

CASE STUDY 2: Keeping Records Too Long

In the 1940's and 50's, various state and federal laws mandated the use of fire retardants, especially in public buildings such as schools, hospitals, and government office buildings. Some government contracts even required its use. Responding to the demand, Manville Corporation (formerly Johns Manville) manufactured products from asbestos, the best fire retardant available at that time.

Subsequently, a number of individuals developed a lung disease (later diagnosed as asbestoses) which they claimed was caused by asbestos products manufactured by Manville. They either had worked as employees in a Manville–operated asbestos products plant or had been exposed to asbestos in their work environment. The nature of this disease is such that symptoms may take as long as twenty or more years to appear. By the time researchers determined the link between asbestos and health problems, the damage had been done. And because asbestos had been installed in buildings, the damage continued.

Many of those harmed by asbestos products either sued Manville directly for damages or made claims against other companies, who in turn filed suit against Manville for reimbursement. By the early 1980's, observers estimated the potential asbestos claims against Manville amounted to billions of dollars. Since the company's net worth was only $1.9 billion dollars and it did not have the resources to pay the claims, Manville filed Chapter 11 bankruptcy to protect itself from creditors until the claims could be resolved. One of this country's largest and most profitable companies placed itself under the protection of the courts rather than face certain ruin.

How does this tragic story of human suffering and product liability relate to your records? During the litigation process before and after filing Chapter 11, the courts compelled Manville to turn over relevant records to private litigants and other companies alike. Manville ultimately assembled 16 million documents relating to these lawsuits and Chapter 11 issues. The cost in human resources and dollars to assemble the documents was staggering.

Although Manville had a records retention program, its files still contained many records that legally could and should have been destroyed. Some of these records were kept too long. More importantly, buried among the millions of documents were internal memos and documents which the plaintiffs claimed confirmed other evidence about the potential dangers of asbestos and Manville's responsibility.

Little was known about the dangers of asbestos in the 1940's and 50's. The deleterious effects of asbestos became evident only after its use for twenty to thirty years. The regulations of the Occupational Safety and Health Administration for asbestos and other hazardous substances in the work place were imposed only in recent times.

The discovery of these memos and documents created the impression or constituted an admission that Manville "knew" or "should have known" that asbestos was dangerous. Whether Manville actually knew the danger was never clearly demonstrated. Certainly, nobody knew the danger when the asbestos products were first manufactured.

The internal memos and documents may have been just speculation incorporated into "memos to the file" rather than actual findings. Or perhaps they contained information which was taken out of context during litigation. While the internal memos may have indicated that Manville should have stopped manufacturing or installing asbestos products at an earlier date, they may never have found their way to the proper authorities inside Manville. Regardless of why these documents came into existence, there they were, in Manville's files, and powerful ammunition in the hands of the plaintiffs.

See Black's Law Dictionary, West Publishing Company, St. Paul, Minnesota. "Strict Liability" may be defined a liability without fault. "Negligence" may be defined as "the omission to do something which a reasonable man, guided by those ordinary considerations which, ordinarily regulate human affairs, would do, or the doing of something which a reasonable and prudent man would not do." "Recklessness" may be defined as "the state of mind accompanying an act, which either pays no regard to its probably or possibly injurious consequences, or which, though foreseeing such consequences, persists in spite of such knowledge."

In our society, a manufacturer who produces a product which proves to be dangerous and causes harm to others will be held responsible. Minimally, the legal system requires the manufacturer to pay damages under a "negligence" theory if fault is shown, or under a "strict liability" theory if the product was inherently dangerous, even if fault is not shown. When a manufacturer knew or should have known of the danger and failed to alert the public or stop manufacturing the product, the legal system imposes a much higher level of damages for this apparent "reckless" conduct, including punitive damages.

In Manville's case, the basic damages for injury to others and for property damage would have been high anyway, but the internal memos and documents helped confirm the impression of recklessness and drove the potential claims and risks of punitive damages even higher.

Manville is emerging from Chapter 11 under a court approved settlement. The agreement dilutes Manville's stock and requires the company to pay $2.5 billion into a trust fund over the next 25 years to cover the claims of current and future victims. The company must also operate a warehouse at its own expense to provide the claimants access to the 16 million pages of asbestos–related documents.

CASE STUDY 3. Failure to Maintain Required Records

The United States Department of Labor fined General Dynamics Corporation $615,000 in 1987 for failing to report illnesses and injuries. The Occupational Safety and Health Administration requires employers to maintain records about work-related injuries and illnesses and report these occurrences. Regulatory agencies have the right to enter your facilities, inspect your records, and, if they find you have failed to comply with the law, assess fines and penalties.

Many activities, products, and industries are regulated by various state and federal regulatory agencies. You are required to comply with their recordkeeping requirements.

CASE STUDY 4: Failure to Preserve Records During a Tax Audit

See Yoffe et al v. United States, Case No. 3993, United States Circuit Court of Appeals, First Circuit, as reported in 153 Federal Reporter, 2d Series 570, St. Paul: West Publishing Company, 1946.

The United States Internal Revenue Service suspected that YK Associates did not properly report its revenues and that it could owe additional tax. The company had been liquidated in 1936 and one of its partners kept the company's records in the basement of his office building. The basement flooded in the summer of 1938, causing substantial damage. While throwing away hopelessly damaged merchandise, some employees apparently also discarded the old books and records of the company.

The judge chastised the company for failure to exercise a reasonable level of care for records subject to tax audit.

> . . . Such seemingly careless concern for records at a time when they were being requested by the revenue agents would clearly support the inference that the information contained therein would be harmful to the defendants.

The requirement to protect records subject to litigation, government investigation or audit, has been reiterated in hundreds of court cases since that time.

CASE STUDY 5: Proper Destruction of Records

See INA Aviation Corporation v. United States, Case No. 75-C-1086, United States District Court, Eastern District, New York, as reported in 468 Federal Supplement 695, St. Paul: West Publishing Company, 1979.

The plaintiffs filed suit against the United States government (defendant) for personal injuries and property damage resulting from an airplane crash. Plaintiffs contended that the flight controllers employed by the Federal Aviation Administration failed to advise the pilot of weather problems prior to the crash. When plaintiffs subpoenaed certain weather records used by the flight controllers to advise pilots, the defendant claimed that these records were not available because they had been destroyed under the records retention practices approved by the Federal Aviation Administration.

In this case, the defendants had kept all of the weather records requested under the subpoena. Certain specialized records known as "traces" were destroyed within 20 or 60 days after they were created, following recordkeeping procedures established by the Federal Aviation Administration. Because the subpoena did not mention or hint at traces, they were destroyed without bad intent. The records provided to the plaintiffs were responsive to the subpoena and the court did not view the destruction of the traces as inappropriate:

> . . . Defendant contends that all papers potentially relevant to an accident cannot be saved, that FAA employees who are not lawyers cannot be expected to anticipate plaintiffs' counsel's legal theories, that plaintiffs' requests for records were ambiguous at best and failed to put FAA personnel on notice at the time that the traces should be retained, and finally that where weather reports are recorded in a log included among the documents preserved for plaintiffs' case, destruction of the traces is satisfactorily explained. As a matter of law, we are inclined to agree with the defendant that plaintiffs' request for the retention of pertinent documents did not provide notice that the traces should be retained. We conclude that there is no showing that the governments' destruction of the traces was intentional . . .

If the subpoena had been specific enough to cover the traces, the decision might have been different.

CASE STUDY 6: Proper Destruction of Records

See Vick v. Texas Employment Commission, Case No. 74-1525, United States Court of Appeals, Fifth Circuit, as reported in 514 Federal Reporter, 2d Series 734, St. Paul: West Publishing Company, 1975.

Vick (plaintiff) in an unemployment compensation hearing contended that the Texas Employment Commission (defendant) inappropriately denied her benefits because of her sex. The plaintiff subpoenaed various commission records in order to support her claim of sex discrimination, only to find that these records had been destroyed.

The defendant had indeed destroyed records of the plaintiff's original unemployment hearing under its own regulations for the destruction of inactive records. These records were destroyed in accordance with the defendant's records retention program and before it received any notice of the filing for this lawsuit.

> . . . Records on Vick were destroyed before trial, apparently pursuant to Commission regulations governing disposal in inactive records . . . There was indication here that the records were destroyed under routine procedures without bad faith well in advance of Vick's service of Interrogatories.

CASE STUDY 7: You and Your Records

The case studies explored in this chapter demonstrate what can happen to organizations that fail to make recordkeeping a priority and maintain a legally acceptable records program. This book can help you avoid similar problems and prevent the recordkeeping problems of your organization from appearing as Case Study 7 in the next edition.

CONCLUSION

CHAPTER 1

☐ Some organizations do not realize the importance of controlling and managing their records until they get into trouble.

☐ Some organizations inappropriately or selectively destroy records—a practice which can be very harmful in litigation.

☐ Some organizations tend to keep records too long or fail to control internal memos and documents—hurting themselves in litigation.

☐ Some organizations fail to keep the records required by law and then suffer fines and penalties.

☐ Some organizations fail to preserve and protect records during litigation, government investigation or audit, and suffer severe consequences.

☐ Some organizations follow proper records retention practices, comply with subpoenas to produce records during litigation, and suffer no adverse consequences.

Chapter 2 The Scope of Your Recordkeeping Responsibilities

Your organization must follow the recordkeeping requirements for documenting its activities. This chapter helps you identify these regulated activities, the jurisdictions that exercise control, the ownership of records, and your responsibility for records belonging to someone else.

REGULATED ACTIVITIES

The United States federal government, state and local government entities, and other countries have an interest in your organization's activities. Most are primarily interested in collecting taxes. Your accounting, sales, and tax records, for example, are important to these government entities in determining the amount of tax due.

Employment and personnel records are also important to government entities. Government has developed a wide variety of laws to protect employees, ensure the payment of proper wages, protect the health and safety of employees, and eliminate discrimination. While you maintain employment records primarily to better manage your employees, government looks to these records to monitor your activities and enforce compliance with the law.

The third major area of government regulation relates to your specific industry. Some requirements deal with public health and safety, fraudulent or discriminatory business practices, and other concerns for the general welfare such as protecting the public from dangerous products, air and land pollution, and property damage. Government also regulates security exchanges, insurance, mail order, lending, housing, product labeling, foreign trade, foreign currency transactions, and immigration.

The law generally views doing business as a privilege rather than a right. In order to transact business and exercise other privileges such as employing others, government requires that you follow its rules. Failure to follow these requirements may subject you to fines, penalties, and other adverse consequences, such as losing the privilege of doing business.

This book provides the recordkeeping requirements for those business records generally found within an organization. You can determine the requirements for specific industries or activities with the help of *Records Retention Procedures* available from the publisher. An order and inquiry form has been provided at the back of the book for your convenience.

To understand the requirements for recordkeeping, therefore, it is necessary to determine which of your organization's activities are regulated by a government entity. Start by asking your legal counsel and colleagues for the names of regulatory agencies with which they have contact. You should also review the functions of each department within your organization and the various types of products manufactured and sold.

BUSINESS LOCATIONS OR JURISDICTIONS

You are required to comply with the law in every location or jurisdiction in which you do business. Within the United States, you must follow the requirements of the United States federal government as well as those for each state in which you are legally "doing business."

The concept of "doing business" depends on the type of activity being conducted. You are generally doing business in a state if any of the following conditions are met:

- You have an office in that state,

- You have employees in that state, or

- You have property in that state (even if it is for a short time, such as a truck or railroad car moving through the state)

On the other hand, you are probably not doing business in a state under these conditions or circumstances:

- Your product is being sold by an independent sales person, or

- You conduct your business solely by telephone or mail and do not perform any activities which clearly indicate that you are "doing business" in the state, other than shipping products into the state by common carrier (e.g., U.S. Postal Service, private mail carrier, or private freight company).

Unfortunately, the legal distinction between an "independent contractor" and an employee is not always clear. In its simplest terms, an independent contractor is one who performs work according to his own methods, without being subject to the control of an employer except as to the result of the work. A sales person, for example, is considered an independent contractor if he sells products for a number of different organizations and has contact with your organization only for placing orders, servicing orders, resolving problems, obtaining quotes and obtaining sales literature.

An employee, on the other hand, is someone who performs services for another person under the condition that the employer has a right to control and direct the employee not only as to the result but also as to the details and means by which the result is accomplished. Whenever a sales person sells only your products or is under the direct control of your organization, that person is probably an employee.

If the sales person has some characteristics of both an employee and an independent contractor, the law will probably construe that person to be an employee and you will be considered as doing business in that state.

See Chapter 8 for additional discussion on product liability.

The generally accepted opinion is that if you or your employees only have contact with a state by telephone, public mail, or freight carrier, you are not doing business in that state and are not required to collect the state sales tax or keep any sales tax records for that state. In most states, however, the recipient of your products is required to pay a "use tax" for the privilege of using your product within the state without having paid sales tax—but that is their concern and not yours. You may still be liable for injury and damage caused by your product shipped into a state in which you may not technically be "doing business."

Remember, even if you are not doing business in a state, you are still subject to the requirements of the United States federal government for all matters under its control, including employment advertising, product labeling, manufacturing, product testing, taxes, and environmental protection.

Most local governments (county, city, township) do not specify recordkeeping requirements. Many, however, collect sales, occupational privilege, and property taxes. You should check with the local governments where you are doing business to see if any special recordkeeping requirements exist.

You must also comply with the rules for recordkeeping in every country in which you do business. When doing business in Canada, for example, you must comply with the requirements of the Canadian federal government as well as those for each province in which you do business. Except for some of the industrialized western countries, most other countries do not have a systematic recordkeeping requirements for organizations doing business within their borders. You may be subject to the discretion of local bureaucrats or be required to produce any record at any time requested by the host government.

Because recordkeeping requirements in international markets may be difficult if not impossible to determine, many U. S. organizations develop recordkeeping programs designed to comply primarily with U. S. rules. When specific requirements of a foreign country are known, the organizations add the rules for recordkeeping in that country.

RECORDS NOT REQUIRED BY LAW

You will certainly be held responsible for those records required to be created and maintained by the law. Few people realize, however, that you will also be held responsible for the manner in which you maintain and destroy records, even those records not required by law.

Court cases have repeatedly stated your obligation to protect records which may be relevant to future litigation. These records can be destroyed but only in the regular course of business and under an approved records retention program. The courts do not accept the argument that since you had no obligation to create these records, you can do anything you want with them. On the contrary, judges have treated litigants quite harshly when records which did not have to be created in the first place were destroyed because the organization had concerns that these records might fall into the wrong hands or be subject to subpoena and litigation.

In a similar vein, courts have become skeptical of organization-sponsored efforts to prevent the creation of certain sensitive documents. While you certainly do not have to create records unless there is a legal requirement to do so, a systematic attempt to prevent the creation of written documents may be viewed with suspicion by the courts as an attempt to compromise the rights of others.

COMPANY VERSUS PRIVATE RECORDS

Many individuals or groups within an organization maintain what they mistakenly believe to be their own "personal" or "private" records. Some reasons for maintaining these records are:

- The lack of confidence in the organization's records system, often resulting from previous bad experiences,

- The convenience of having records close at hand or in a convenient form,

- The desire to maintain "self-serving" or "self-protecting" memos, away from the view of others, which document problems within the organization or provide an alibi for a problem, or

- The mistaken belief that a record, such as a calendar book, actually is personal.

The perceived need for personal or private records often leads to personal filing systems and the haphazard destruction of records. Regardless of why the records were created in the first place, *private or personal records are the property of the organization, not the individual.*

Well established principles of employment and agency law make your organization responsible for the acts of its employees and agents for work performed within the scope of employment. All records created by your employees or agents within the scope of your business will be considered the records of your organization. All records located at your facilities or located anywhere else but related to your organization belong to your organization.

Organization records include almost all personal copies of records, convenience copies, and even the self-serving, protective type documents. Only those records obviously outside the scope of employment, such as the schedule for your club softball team, will be considered personal or private records.

See Chapter 16 for the legal requirements for admitting records into evidence.

The rules governing the admissibility of records into evidence require that:

- Records must be made at or near the time of the event,

- Records must be made by or from a person with knowledge of the event,

- Records must be kept in the regular course of business,

- Records must be kept because it is the regular practice of the business to keep these records, and

- Testimony must be provided by the custodian of the records or other qualified witness showing the above requirements have been met.

In most cases, personal or private records are not admissible as evidence by the organization creating them because one or more of these criteria cannot be met. For example, self-serving or protective memos are seldom created within the regular course of business and are not sufficiently trustworthy to be admitted as evidence. Similarly, because the procedures by which private records were created are not documented, the custodian of the records may not be able to testify about the methods used to create them (unless the author is available to testify). So, some of the organization's records created outside normal channels may not be admissible as evidence and could not support the organization during litigation.

On the other hand, these same records are subject to subpoena by an adverse party in litigation. The records will not just be introduced as mere evidence, but will constitute an "admission"— a statement against the interest of the organization creating them. While evidence must be weighed in terms of its trustworthiness, an admission is given greater weight and considered as if it was a "fact" or "the truth." The party creating the records assumes responsibility for their content and "admits" that the information therein is true. As a result, many of these self-serving or protective type memos can be used effectively by adverse parties to bolster their position and improve their chances in litigation.

During antitrust litigation, for example, the Department of Justice frequently has subpoenaed calendar books maintained by individuals within organizations. The correlation of travel schedules for key individuals in several organizations, recorded in calendar books, may indicate meetings or the possibility of meetings to illegally fix or set prices. Even though an individual may purchase and even own the calendar book, the contents will be considered the organization's record because it relates to business matters. Records such as calendar books, travel itineraries, and personal notes can be subpoenaed and introduced into evidence as an admission to support the claims of an adverse party.

Finally, persons maintaining private or personal records generally either fail to destroy them or destroy them selectively, outside the scope of an approved records retention program. The legality of the entire organization's records retention program can be compromised by the actions of a few individuals.

See Chapter 13 for the components of a legally acceptable records retention program.

Because personal or private records cannot help you during litigation, yet may be subpoenaed in litigation and used against you, these records should be controlled by the records management program. Convenience or personal copies should be discouraged or totally prohibited. The records program should cover all original and duplicate copies, including "personal copies," and audits should be conducted to ensure that all copies of records scheduled for destruction have in fact been destroyed.

RECORDS HELD IN A CUSTODIAL OR FIDUCIARY CAPACITY

You hold records in a "custodial" capacity if you maintain them for someone else and in a "fiduciary" capacity when you handle financial matters and maintain the related records on behalf of somebody else.

Your organization may maintain various records that belong to clients. Law firms, accounting firms, engineering firms, and other service organizations such as hospitals often maintain large volumes of client records.

These records may consist of records received from, developed for, or maintained on behalf of clients. When you do not own records in your possession, you may not modify or destroy them, or even microfilm and then destroy them, without permission.

Records which meet the following criteria are generally not the property of your organization or business:

- *Official records that are received from the client for use during a specific case, activity, or project.* Accounting firms, for example, use the client's original receipts and canceled checks to prepare accounting records and tax returns. Commercial records centers, as another example, maintain and preserve records for clients on a fee basis.

- *Records prepared for and maintained on behalf of clients.* Lawyers frequently serve as corporate secretaries and maintain minutes of board meetings on behalf of corporations.

- *Records in the organization's possession that the client regularly relies upon for additional copies or for reference purposes even though the client has received all copies to which it is entitled.* The continual reliance by a client upon records in another organization's possession could create a "new reality"—the records are in fact maintained in a custodial capacity. Engineering firms, for example, regularly provide copies of engineering drawings to clients for a number of years, even though the clients have all the copies to which they are entitled.

In all these cases, the organizations creating, receiving, or maintaining the records act in a custodial or fiduciary capacity on behalf of their clients and must exert reasonable efforts to protect the records from damage or destruction.

When managing records belonging to another, you must ensure that the records can be located within a reasonable time, protect the records from unauthorized use or distribution, and protect the records from destruction. It is often best to keep client's records separated from your records. Otherwise, it becomes difficult to locate them when required and to protect them according to the higher standard required for property belonging to someone else. You could keep these records in separate folders or separate areas of the filing system. Regardless of the filing method, the records should be clearly identified as the property of a client.

Records and property belonging to someone else should be used only for purposes authorized by their owner. You must prevent access to them by unauthorized persons until the owner gives permission. Similarly, records belonging to another should not be turned over to a third party without the permission of the owner, except under a court-ordered subpoena. If you give unauthorized persons access to these records, you may be liable for conversion of property or invasion of privacy.

Finally, records belonging to another cannot be destroyed without the permission of the owner. Although records may be microfilmed to improve access or protect them, the original records cannot be destroyed without the permission of the owner.

To obtain permission, send a registered letter to the owner advising that the records will be destroyed within a specific time period (e.g., 30 days). Arrangements can then be made to return the records to the owner upon request. The post office will obtain a signature for a registered letter indicating that the letter has been received. If no response is received from the registered letter in the required time, the records can be destroyed under an approved records retention program with minimal risk.

RECORDS FROM FORMER ORGANIZATIONS: ACQUISITIONS AND MERGERS

Organizations sometimes dissolve by choice, other times as a result of business failure. The board of directors (for a corporation), general partners (for a partnership), or owners (for a sole proprietorship) are *personally* responsible for records related to the dissolved organization. For example, you may be responsible for maintaining records required by regulatory agencies or records required to support old tax returns. Because a dissolved organization has no assets, you can be sued or fined personally for violations of the legal requirements for these records.

When a new organization emerges through merger or acquisition, the legal responsibility for records becomes more complex. In most cases, the surviving organization obtains all property and other assets of the previous organization and assumes responsibility for all debts and other obligations. The surviving organization then becomes responsible for maintaining the records of the former organization. This is often a difficult task because the recordkeeping habits of the former organization often differ significantly from the procedures used by the surviving one. Under these circumstances, maintain the inactive records of the former organization in their original form, but prepare a separate records retention schedule to cover their destruction. Merge active records with the surviving organization's active records and maintain them according to the surviving organization's records management program.

If the former organization remains responsible for the debts and obligations (and maybe even the records), its board of directors, partners, or owners may be personally liable for the records. The terms of the acquisition agreement should be reviewed carefully to determine the status of these debts and obligations, since records are rarely mentioned specifically.

To reduce potential problems from mergers and acquisitions, it is recommended that a clause be included in all such contracts which specifically addresses the responsibilities of each party for records. This is particularly important when a subsidiary or a part of another organization is involved. Without a specific clause in the contract dealing with records, it may be very difficult to determine who has the responsibility for maintaining the records of the entities involved in the acquisition or merger.

CONCLUSION   **CHAPTER 2**

☐   You must comply with the laws for all business activities regulated by the government.

☐   You must comply with the law in every location or jurisdiction in which you do business.

☐   You must properly maintain records and comply with the requirements for the destruction of records, even when you are not required to create those records in the first place.

☐   Records created within your organization's property or within the scope of employment are the property of the organization, not the individual.

☐   Records held by you in a custodial fiduciary capacity are not the property of your organization and must be handled with special care.

☐   Records belonging to a former organization may either be the responsibility of the surviving or the former organization, depending upon the terms of the acquisition or merger.

Chapter 3   Why You Should Develop a Legally Acceptable Records Management Program

Even if you run your business efficiently, paper tends to accumulate in file cabinets, records storage areas, and valuable office space. Hence, you must give special attention to the destruction of records. Many records retention and microfilm programs have been developed with the specific intent of either eliminating paper records or reducing the amount of storage space required.

The elimination of valueless information within a records retention program improves the organization's ability to handle the valuable information. By getting rid of the junk, we reduce the chances of filing errors and speed the retrieval of the information needed every day. A well managed records retention and microfilming program also lowers costs.

Unfortunately, management may not be sufficiently motivated by the advantages of a records management program. Some managers may feel that the records problem will "go away by itself" or that it represents such a minor problem that even modest expenditures for improvement are not warranted.

The legal reasons for developing an effective records program are compelling. The following section highlights the legal reasons why you should commit to a records management program, and emphasizes the need for immediate action.

LITIGATION PROTECTION

A good records management program protects the organization in case of litigation. The program ensures that records that should exist, do in fact exist, and that records that should not exist, do in fact not exist. It also ensures that records prepared by the organization can readily be admitted into evidence to support the organization's claims. A records management program also puts you in charge of records previously maintained outside the scope of normal business activities and which may later prove detrimental in litigation.

One attorney relates an embarrassing incident about records subpoenaed by an adversary in litigation. When the judge called upon him to explain why subpoenaed records had not been produced, he explained in great detail that they had been properly destroyed prior to litigation under the company's records retention program. The other attorney then addressed the court and indicated that he had received copies of the requested records from a former employee of the defendant. It seems the former employee, upon retirement, took a set of the records to his home. Even though the attorney sincerely believed that the subpoenaed records had been properly destroyed under the records retention program, the program failed to identify some duplicate copies. This weakness severely hurt the organization in the case. Large organizations, in particular, have problems controlling copies of records.

Legal counsel often has difficulty locating records in defense of the organization's position. Unfortunately, people often do not know where the records are, how they are organized, or whether they have been destroyed. Employees sometimes maintain "personal" files in credenzas or remove them from the office to their homes.

Searching for the information takes a lot of time and money. The preparers of many records may no longer be employed by the organization and their successors have no idea as to how the records were maintained. Even the most thorough and costly of searches may not detect some of the most crucial information needed by the organization that created it.

A well managed records management program helps to identify records needed to support your side of the case as well as those requested by your adversary. The program significantly reduces the time and cost of locating information and identifies the information relevant to the case. Similarly, records that should not be available will have been properly destroyed. Those personal copies, and other records, often created outside the control of most organizations, will not exist to haunt you.

The protection afforded by an effective records management program not only reduces the costs of litigation but can have a major impact on the outcome.

LEGAL COMPLIANCE

A good records management program also ensures compliance with the multitude of laws affecting records retention, microfilm, computer data, and other records matters. The federal government alone has issued over ten thousand laws affecting recordkeeping. Although not all of these rules apply to your organization, you are responsible for complying with those that do. The fifty states and territories plus some foreign countries have issued their own rules for recordkeeping—compounding the problem even more.

See Part F, Chapter 20 through 22 for a description of adequate legal research.

The number of recordkeeping rules facing an organization is awesome. How can you know that your organization complies with all these laws affecting your records? The answer is to do your research with the help of this book.

See *Legal Requirements for Business Records, Information Requirements Clearinghouse, Denver, Colorado (2500 pages) for detailed research covering federal and state requirements for records, including the full text of thousands of relevant laws. An inquiry form is available in the back of this book.*

A good records management program includes legal research to determine your records retention, microfilm, computer system, and other record requirements. You can be confident that most legal requirements have been met if your records management program includes adequate legal research.

Up to now, only large organizations have had the resources necessary for this type of coverage. Most small and medium-sized businesses have relied on incorrect advice, guessed at what the rules were, or (and much worse) ignored the problem. This book goes a long way toward providing the information previously available only to large organizations.

While the next chapter vividly describes the consequences of failing to meet the legal requirements for your records, the remainder of this book details what it takes to comply.

CONCLUSION

CHAPTER 3

☐ A good records management program improves efficiency, provides better access to valuable information, and often saves money while providing peace of mind.

☐ A good records management program protects an organization in case of litigation by ensuring that those records that should exist, do exist; that records that should not exist do not exist, and that records needed by your organization are readily available.

☐ A good records management program includes adequate legal research to evaluate the myriad of rules and determine your requirements.

Chapter 4 Consequences of Your Failure to Comply with the Law

See John M. Fedders and Lauryn H. Guttenplan, "Document Retention and Destruction: Practical, Legal and Ethical Considerations," *The Notre Dame Lawyer, Volume 56, Number 1, October 1980.*

The preceding chapter discussed a number of reasons why you should develop a legally acceptable records management system. You should also understand what could happen when a records retention program fails to meet legal requirements. The consequences can be catastrophic.

LOSS OF RIGHTS

An organization can lose some of rights when it fails to maintain appropriate records, can not find them, or fails to properly destroyed them. If, for example, Company A does not have the records to prove that Company B owes it $5,000, then it will be difficult and probably impossible to win a lawsuit compelling Company B to pay. In addition, many tax laws and other government regulations require proof that certain actions have been performed or conditions of an agreement complied with. The lack of supporting records becomes an enormous disadvantage and may preclude you from exercising certain rights.

LOSS OF TIME AND MONEY

Records provide an efficient means to prove your case in litigation or government investigation. Without them, your organization must depend upon the testimony of witnesses. Testimony, however, is time consuming, expensive, and sometimes less credible than records. It distracts your employees from their duties and diverts their skills and talents into non-productive channels.

OBSTRUCTION OF JUSTICE

For federal obstruction of justice statutes see 18 USC 1503 (Influencing or Injuring Officer, Juror, or Witness Generally); 18 USC 1505 (Obstruction of Proceeding Before Department, Agencies, and Committees); 18 USC 1510 (Obstruction of Criminal Investigations). See also Fedders, supra note 9, pp. 28-30.

The law holds you responsible for the deliberate destruction of documents when litigation, government investigation or audit is pending or imminent, and you may be held liable for obstruction of justice. While the law is clear regarding your responsibilities while litigation, government investigation or audit is pending (currently in progress) and imminent (about to happen), it is somewhat unclear regarding your responsibilities when these events are "foreseeable."

Some court decisions indicate that the individual must possess a specific criminal intent to be convicted of obstruction of justice. Other decisions indicate that the individual's intent is irrelevant if the act nonetheless interferes with a judicial process. Still other decisions indicate that the defendant need only have known or believed that the successful destruction of documents would likely thwart a judicial proceeding.

Even if the destruction of documents does not, in fact, obstruct the proceeding, the courts may still hold the individual who destroyed the records liable for obstruction of justice.

The major issue related to obstruction of justice is whether the particular proceeding was foreseeable or not. To reduce the chances of criminal prosecution under the obstruction of justice statutes, you should stop destroying records at the slightest hint of litigation or government investigation. A careful review of the situation may then permit you to destroy some records without risk of a criminal penalty.

CONTEMPT OF COURT

A court can hold an individual or organization in contempt for disobeying a court order, including a subpoena to produce records ("Subpoena Duces Tecum"). Contempt of court is committed whenever a court or administrative tribunal (with subpoena powers) orders documents produced and the party defies the order by failing to produce them or deliberately destroys the requested documents. Penalties can include imprisonment and fines.

ADVERSE INFERENCE IN LITIGATION

Certain presumptions or inferences may arise in litigation when relevant records have been destroyed:

See *Corpus Juris Secundum*, The American Law Book Company, Brooklyn, NY, 1983, 31A C.J.S. Evidence 153, pp. 388-390 for full descriptions of and citations to numerous state and federal cases addressing adverse inferences at trial for destroying records. Also see Rule 37(b)(2)(A) below, Federal Rules of Civil Procedure for similar provisions in the federal courts.

> The unexplained and deliberate destruction of relevant documentary and other evidence or the manipulation or alteration of such evidence, gives rise to an inference that the matter destroyed or mutilated is unfavorable to the spoliator . . The inference arising from the destruction of evidence ordinarily will not dispense with the necessity for the introduction by the other party of some secondary evidence as to the contents of the documents . . . it merely diminishes the force of the spoliator's evidence and enhances the probative value of [the evidence produced] by his opponent . . . When evidence is willfully destroyed, the court will view the evidence presented in the light most unfavorable to the wrongdoer . . . The inference cannot operate when there is positive evidence of the contents of the instrument destroyed, and it is, like other inferences, ordinarily rebuttable by satisfactory explanation . . . An unfavorable inference can arise only against one who actually destroyed or was privy to the destruction of the evidence, and only in cases where the destruction or mutilation was in bad faith for the purpose of suppressing evidence. No unfavorable inference arises when the evidence was lost, destroyed, or mutilated by accident or without the fault of the party in possession of it.

It is critical that an organization establish controls to stop the destruction of all documents when a judicial proceeding or government investigation is pending, imminent and perhaps, foreseeable. The destruction of any documents relevant to a court proceeding may give rise to an adverse inference. The inference may be rebutted, however, by showing that the destruction of records was performed under the retention program without any intent to destroy potential evidence. If the judicial proceeding or government investigation was pending, imminent or even foreseeable when the records were destroyed, even if destroyed under an approved records retention program, the organization may still be held accountable.

SANCTIONS

If an organization fails to produce documents under a discovery order without a satisfactory explanation, the court can subject it to criminal penalties for obstruction of justice or contempt of court, or to an adverse inference which is often harmful in litigation.

The federal courts can also apply the following sanctions for failure to comply with the discovery order; state courts have similar provisions.

Rules of Civil Procedure, Rule 37, United States District Counts.

Rule 37. Failure to Make or Cooperate in Discovery: Sanctions

(b) Failure to comply with order . . .

(2) Sanctions by court in which action is pending. If a party or an officer, director, or managing agent of a party or a person designated under Rule 30(b)(6) or 31(a) to testify on behalf of a party fails to obey an order to provide or permit discovery, including an order made under subdivision (a) of this rule or Rule 35, or if a party fails to obey an order entered under Rule 26(f), the court in which the action is pending may make such order in regard to the failure as are just, and among others the following:

(A) An order that the matters regarding which the order was made or any other designated facts shall be taken to be established for the purposes of the action in accordance with the claim of the party obtaining the order;

(B) An order refusing to allow the disobedient party to support or oppose designated claims or defenses, or prohibiting him from introducing designated matters in evidence;

(C) An order striking out pleadings or parts thereof, or staying further proceedings until the order is obeyed, or dismissing the action or proceeding or any part thereof, or rendering a judgment by default against the disobedient party;

(D) In lieu of any of the foregoing orders or in addition thereto, an order treating as a contempt of court the failure to obey any orders except an order to submit to a physical or mental examination . . .

In lieu of any of the foregoing orders or in addition thereto, the court shall require the party failing to obey the order or the attorney advising him or both to pay the reasonable expenses, including attorney's fees, caused by the failure, unless the court finds that the failure was substantially justified or that other circumstances make an award of expense unjust.

See Chapter 1 for *Carlucci et al v. Piper Aircraft Corporation*, 102 Federal Rules Decisions 472 (1984), United States District Court, Southern District Florida.

Rule 37(b)(2) was used by a federal court in 1984 in the case of Carlucci vs. Piper Aircraft Corporation (1984) to penalize Piper Aircraft because of the selective destruction of relevant documents prior to and during pending litigation. The judge in this case prohibited the defendants from introducing evidence in support of their defense, issued a directed verdict in favor of the plaintiffs, and imposed a judgment of ten million dollars.

CONCLUSION   **CHAPTER 4**

☐ You may lose certain rights if records are not properly maintained or improperly destroyed.

☐ The time and money required to prove your case in the absence of appropriate records can be significant.

☐ You are responsible if documents are deliberately destroyed when litigation, government investigation or audit is pending, imminent and, in some cases, foreseeable.

☐ You may be in contempt of court for disobeying a court order to produce documents or if you deliberately destroy requested documents.

☐ The courts may adversely infer that documents you destroyed were unfavorable to your case if these documents were inappropriately destroyed for the purpose of suppressing evidence.

☐ The courts may also impose sanctions for failure to comply with discovery orders such as imposing a default judgment or eliminating claims which support your position.

Chapter 5   A Strategy for Managing Your Records and Complying with the Law

Meet the needs of your business, follow established records management principles, follow the guidelines presented in this book, apply the law in a reasonable manner, accept a reasonable level of risk, and your organization will comply with most applicable recordkeeping requirements.

THE BASIS FOR MANY RECORDKEEPING REQUIREMENTS

While the fear of legal repercussions may motivate some people to develop a good recordkeeping program, meeting your organization's needs for records should be the principal objective. We all need records to perform our individual responsibilities. We must also comply with the law.

Drug manufacturers, for example, maintain records of drug testing to ensure that new products brought to market are effective and safe. The testing process also provides useful information about the manufacturing process and how to produce the drugs in the most economical manner. So even though the Food and Drug Administration has developed specific recordkeeping requirements for the testing of drugs, drug manufacturers would still maintain many of these same records whether or not the regulatory requirements existed.

Similarly, telephone companies need information about the location of telephone cables, the costs of providing telephone services, and customer information. These records would be created and used on a regular basis even if the Federal Communication Commission did not have specific recordkeeping requirements. In fact, the Federal Communication Commission recognized in 1986 the reality that telephone companies would maintain records simply because they were needed by their businesses, regardless of whether regulations existed or not. The new regulations eliminated most recordkeeping requirements in the telephone industry, with little or no impact on the records actually maintained by the individual telephone companies.

See 47 CFR Part 42 for the current regulation adopted in 1986. An 18 month retention period for telephone toll records remains because the Department of Justice requested this information.

Where once about 700 different requirements existed, almost none exist today. And yet, the telephone companies maintain most of the same records as were previously mandated by law.

You can readily identify those records needed for your business activities because you could not conduct business without them. The law often requires you to keep these same records. Why does this phenomenon occur?

Regulatory agencies depend upon the public to maintain records to verify compliance with the law. The Internal Revenue Service, for example, requires you to keep records of your income and expenses so that they can determine whether you computed and paid the proper amount of tax. Similarly, the Equal Employment Opportunity Commission monitors employment records to prevent discrimination based upon race, sex, and age.

Federal and state laws specify, often in great detail, records management practices. The law promotes uniform recordkeeping practices, making them easier to audit and enforce. There may also be a presumption that organizations do not understand records management as it relates to their own business needs.

It is ironic, however, that businesses would still prepare 80 to 90 percent of the required records even if the laws did not exist. To this extent, the laws merely reflect reality.

Federal agencies and almost every state provide an opportunity for the public to comment on proposed statutes and regulations. We are all aware of the intense lobbying efforts undertaken to ensure that the views of interested parties are considered by the legislature before passing new legislation. The public brings considerable pressure on legislators and regulatory agencies to devise laws which inflict the least hardship and burden on those affected. Most people accept laws in the recordkeeping area which reflect current practices. When requirements vary from these practices, the outcry is vigorous. So, for this reason, too, new legislation and regulation, especially in the recordkeeping area, tends to reflect generally accepted practices.

See Appendix A for the text of the Office of Management and Budget regulations related to the Paperwork Reduction Act of 1980.

Congress passed the Paperwork Reduction Act of 1980 to reduce the burden of recordkeeping placed upon the public by the federal government. One provision of the Act requires the Office of Management and Budget to review the recordkeeping burden imposed by federal regulatory agencies. The public is also invited to comment on each aspect of the proposed new regulation, including the recordkeeping requirements.

Keep in mind that some recordkeeping requirements deviate from generally accepted practices. This often occurs in new areas of regulation where the public interest has not been previously defined or, frequently, when a government agency requires records to be kept for long periods to meet its needs rather than yours. The Occupational Safety and Health Administration, for example, requires organizations to keep medical records of employees exposed to hazardous substances for the term of employment plus thirty years in order to monitor exposure problems which take many years to manifest. While most responsible employers would keep the records for lengthy periods of time, few would voluntarily keep them thirty years. Exceptions such as these constitute only a small percentage of all recordkeeping requirements. But the law sometimes requires you to keep records for periods longer than you need for normal business purposes.

THE COMPONENTS OF THE STRATEGY

Meet Your Needs First

Records should be kept primarily to meet the needs of your organization rather than legal requirements. Set up your files, microfilm, and computer systems to support the business. If you respond to the needs of the organization, you will meet many of the legal requirements for your records.

See *Legal Requirements for Business Records: Federal Requirements*, **Information Requirements Clearinghouse, Denver, Colorado. An inquiry and order form is found at the back of this book.**

More than 3,500 sections of federal law contain provisions about recordkeeping. A section may be one page or many pages of the Code of Federal Regulations or the United States Code and may specify up to 400 different recordkeeping rules. So, the number of federal rules applicable to records may be tens of thousands. The fifty states and territories contribute additional thousands of rules, differing from state to state.

As a practical matter, it is virtually impossible to identify, analyze, and properly apply all the laws affecting your records. You may never find some rules and incorrectly apply others. While large corporations can dedicate the resources to locating and applying these recordkeeping rules, most small- and medium-size organizations cannot.

Follow Records Management Principles

The best method of ensuring that your organization follows proper procedures for its records is to develop a records management program. The Association of Records Managers and Administrators defines "records management" as follows:

See *Developing and Operating a Records Retention Program*, **Association of Records Managers and Administrators, Prairie Village, Kansas.**

See Appendix C for the full text of Revenue Procedure 81-26.

> The systematic control of all records from creation or receipt through processing, distribution, maintenance and retrieval, to ultimate disposition.

The process includes forms design, filing systems, microfilm, data processing, inactive storage, and records retention.

The established principles for developing and operating a records management program generally correspond with the procedures required by law. The Internal Revenue Service, for example, specifies numerous procedures in Revenue Procedure 81-26 controlling the use of microfilm for tax purposes. Even if an organization was not familiar with this regulation, it would comply with almost every provision by merely following accepted practices for microfilm programs.

Your organization probably will not uncover all the relevant laws pertaining to its records, even after extensive legal research. If you follow standard records management practices, however, your organization will probably select retention periods close to the mandate of the law and avoid adverse legal consequences in judicial or administrative proceedings.

Follow the Guidelines Presented in This Book

This book was developed after the careful analysis of thousands of laws affecting records. It reflects existing legal requirements and established judicial positions. The guidelines are broad enough to fit the general needs of most organizations, and the needs of others with some customization.

Apply the Law in a Reasonable Manner

You will need to read some of the laws in full in order to interpret the requirements and understand the nuances as they apply to your records. While this book analyzes and digests the most common requirements, specific requirements applicable to your particular industry must be located and understood.

You may also want to read the full text of the several significant laws found in the Appendix. Some people think it takes a law degree to read and analyze laws. While a legal background can help, the laws are there to be read by everyone. It is true that different people interpret laws differently. In fact, attorneys often interpret the same law differently; that is the basis for our adversary system of justice. No one answer is necessarily right, although some answers may be more legally correct than others.

The law does require, however, that you interpret and apply the law in a "reasonable" manner. Given a particular fact and the law, you are expected to act as a "reasonable person" would act in the same circumstance.

How do you determine what is reasonable? In a trial, the judge may decide what is reasonable after carefully reviewing the facts. If a jury has been impaneled, it will be asked to do so. Because different people interpret the same law differently, the issue should not be which interpretation is right but, rather, did you make a reasonable effort to properly interpret and apply the law to your records. You have great latitude in reading the law and interpreting it, especially for laws related to recordkeeping requirements.

Government publishes laws and regulations to provide notice to the public so that their requirements can be enforced. Without adequate notice, you cannot be penalized for failure to comply. When the language of the law is ambiguous, however, the public may not have received proper notice. If you read the law and interpret it one way while the agency interprets it differently, how can you be punished for not complying?

The obligation to clearly write the law and provide adequate notice should be placed upon government. When the law is ambiguous or subject to multiple interpretations, the public should not be penalized provided they have attempted to comply and acted reasonably based upon their interpretation.

To simplify the interpretation of a complex law, divide it into a series of phrases or concepts separated by connector words such as "and," "or," "if" and "then." For example, the Uniform Rules of Evidence permit the introduction of duplicate records into those courts which have adopted this rule:

See Chapter 16 for an analysis of the Uniform Rules of Evidence and the admissibility of duplicates in evidence.

Rule 1003. Admissibility of Duplicates.

A duplicate is admissible to the same extent as an original unless (1) a genuine question is raised as to the authenticity or continuing effectiveness of the original or (2) in the circumstances it would be unfair to admit the duplicate in lieu of the original.

Analyze this section by separating the various phrases into an outline and then simplify the language wherever possible. Outlining helps to analyze the law; the details can be reconsidered later:

A duplicate is admissible in evidence, UNLESS

- the trustworthiness of the original is questioned, OR

- it would be unfair to admit the duplicate in place of the original.

See Chapter 16 for the admissibility of original records in evidence under the Uniform Rules of Evidence and Chapter 17 for the analysis of the UPA.

This method works particularly well for long, complex laws like the 100-word requirement for admissibility of original records in evidence under the Uniform Rules of Evidence or the 100-word Uniform Photographic Copies of Business and Public Records as Evidence Act (UPA).

Any records program based upon a reasonable interpretation of the law should be acceptable to the courts and government agencies. Ambiguity should generally be interpreted against the government agency seeking enforcement, because the ambiguous language was prepared by the government itself. In case of a technical violation of the law, you might expect a "slap on the wrist"or a small fine or penalty, provided that you made a reasonable attempt to comply.

Remember, you always take some risks with records because many laws are almost impossible to find. But if you act reasonably in developing your records program, you will often be in compliance.

Determine Your Risk Level

You may encounter multiple requirements covering your business activities and the locations in which you do business. Some of the laws may address the same issues such as taxes, others may address the same records but for different purposes. Payroll records are often required for both income tax purposes and monitoring wage levels and discrimination. A study, for example, revealed more than 900 different recordkeeping requirements for one organization doing business in 14 states.

Technically, you are required to comply with every law applicable to your organization. Failure to comply exposes you to fines, penalties, and other losses of rights. As a result, many organizations attempt to develop a recordkeeping program designed to comply with all applicable laws.

See Appendix B for statutes of limitation related to written contracts.

While this approach may seem to protect the organization from risk, it is extremely time-consuming and expensive. Some laws, especially for those states in which you are only marginally doing business, do not conform with the norms or standards followed elsewhere in the country.

More than 90 percent of the states and territories, for example, have established statutes of limitations of ten years or less, while Indiana (20 years), Kentucky (15 years), and Ohio (15 years) have set longer periods.

See Chapter 8 for analysis of records retention requirements during the statute of limitations period.

If you conduct business in one of these three states, you may choose to maintain contract records for the longest period for which the statute of limitations applies. This ensures a uniform recordkeeping system without distinction between the states in which you are doing business. On the other hand, this approach can create a recordkeeping burden greater than is otherwise necessary. By keeping contract records for the longest statute of limitations period you do, in fact, ensure that all records are kept long enough, but you end up keeping some records too long and increase your costs and your risks in case of litigation.

By following most of the legal requirements for your records, you obviously will not comply with some. While the fines and penalties for noncompliance can hurt, the costs and benefits of this approach may be extremely attractive, while the risks are generally minimal.

The following criteria may help you determine which legal requirements *not* to follow:

- *Exclude those requirements that are significantly out of line with norms or standards.* In the above example, because the statute of limitations period for three states is 50 percent longer than for other states, do not consider those laws for recordkeeping purposes.

- *Ignore individual state requirements only for those states in which you do little or no business.* While you might be conducting a small amount of business in some states which have particularly burdensome rules, the volume of business may not justify imposing their longer requirements on all of your records. Prudence dictates that you meet the requirements of those states where your organization does a significant amount of business because the adverse consequences of noncompliance are great.

Some organizations choose to comply with most (50 percent) or a preponderance (up to 80 percent) of the legal requirements. Most people accept the premise that it takes approximately 20 percent of the time to perform 80 percent of the work; the remaining 80 percent of the time is required to do the remaining 20 percent of the work. The cost or risk versus the benefits often favors an approach which attempts to consistently follow 80 percent of the requirements. In most cases, this should be viewed as a reasonable attempt to comply with the law especially since the law is so complicated and many organizations fail to make even a reasonable effort.

You act "recklessly" if you do not try to comply with the law.

Your organization is subject to fines and penalties if it fails to comply with certain laws. These risks must be weighed against the advantages of developing a program that meets most requirements, but not all. The risk, however, should be planned rather than haphazard. You should establish criteria for determining which requirements you can reasonably follow and which create a burden on your organization. Whenever you fail to properly consider the legal requirements for records, however, the fines and penalties can be potentially large because you "recklessly" failed to comply with the law.

THE STRATEGY DEFINED

You can still manage to comply with most requirements by simply meeting the needs of your organization and following established records management principles. Even if you did not know the law or failed to apply it properly to your records system, you would still accidentally comply with many laws by following this strategy:

Meet the needs of your business, follow established records management principles, follow the guidelines presented in this book, apply the law in a reasonable manner, accept a reasonable level of risk, and your organization will comply with most applicable recordkeeping requirements.

CONCLUSION   **CHAPTER 5**

☐ Most recordkeeping requirements reflect current business practices.

☐ Meet the needs of your organization when developing a record system.

☐ Follow established records management principles when developing a records system.

☐ Follow the guidelines presented in this book when developing a records system.

☐ Apply the law in a reasonable manner. You do not have to be an attorney to understand the law.

☐ Determine the level of risk that is comfortable for your organization.

☐ Meet the needs of your business, follow established records management principles, follow the guidelines presented in this book, apply the law in a reasonable manner, accept a reasonable level of risk, and your organization will comply with most applicable recordkeeping requirements.

PART B   DETERMINING THE LEGAL RETENTION PERIODS FOR RECORDS

Chapter 6   Six Legal Considerations for Records Retention

This chapter identifies those considerations affecting the time records must be retained for legal purposes. You, of course, are in the best position to determine the second critical factor used to determine the records retention period—how long to keep records to meet your own needs.

In some cases, the law clearly states the legal requirements and these can be directly applied. If you operate in several states, however, you can encounter multiple requirements; you must then determine which, if not all, of these laws to follow. On the other hand, a variety of laws may apply to your records which either do not state a specific retention period or merely give a legal consideration, such as a statute of limitation. These, too, must be considered when developing the overall records retention program.

The records retention period may be viewed as follows:

The period of time during which records must be maintained by an organization because they are needed for operational, legal, fiscal, historical, or other purposes. Records should be destroyed after the termination of the retention period.

See *Developing and Operating a Records Retention Schedule,* Association of Records Managers and Administrators, Prairie Village, KS, glossary.

While you may not be familiar with the term "records retention period" or "records retention program," we all recognize that records lose their usefulness over time. We may be tempted, unfortunately, to participate in "search and destroy missions" to get rid of the unnecessary records. We may also have heard that tax records can be destroyed after seven years or that personnel records must be kept forever.

This seven year retention myth for tax records is dispelled in Chapter 9.

If you could devote the time to carefully analyze the thousands of laws affecting records, you could precisely determine how long you are legally obligated to maintain old records, and therefore, when they could be safely destroyed. Since only the largest organizations can devote the time to extensive analysis, you must use a more simplified approach to reach acceptable conclusions.

There are six categories of laws or legal considerations that could affect the records retention period for your records:

Each of these six considerations are described briefly below and then fully explained in subsequent chapters. Chapter 7 expands upon Considerations 1 and 2 dealing with the situation where a specific records retention period is not stated in the law. Chapter 8 further explains Consideration 4 as it relates to statutes of limitations. Chapter 9 explores Consideration 5 as it relates to the limitation of assessment for your tax records. Chapters 10 through 12 apply a number of these considerations to other records found within your organization.

- Consideration 1. The absence of a legal requirement for certain records.

- Consideration 2. The requirement to keep records for which no retention period is stated.

- Consideration 3. The requirement to keep records for a specified retention period.

- Consideration 4. A statute of limitations or limitations of action period which determines when a legal action or lawsuit can be initiated.

- Consideration 5. A limitation of assessment period which sets the period of time your taxes may be assessed and tax records audited.

- Consideration 6. Pending or imminent litigation, government investigation or audit affecting certain records.

Sometimes the records retention period is controlled by more than one legal consideration.

CONSIDERATION 1. The Absence of a Legal Requirement Affecting Your Records

Although some records need not be created in the first place, courts have taken the position that these as well as required records should be destroyed only under an approved records retention program. See Chapter 13 for details about the proper destruction of records.

Some people mistakenly believe that all records are controlled by legal requirements. This is not true. In fact, many records created and used by organizations are not covered by any law—federal, state, or local. Organizations create these "internal" records purely to support the conduct of their business.

See Chapters 20 to 22 for an analysis of adequate legal research.

You can safely conclude that legal requirements do not exist for certain records only after completing adequate legal research. Granted, some recordkeeping requirements are extremely difficult to locate even by an experienced researcher. Failure to conduct adequate legal research, however, is never a valid excuse for not finding records requirements. On the other hand, while "ignorance of the law is no excuse," the inability to find the law after reasonable legal research just may be.

When you find that no legal requirements exist for certain records, select the records retention period which best serves the needs of the organization. The actual retention period can, therefore, be as short as a few weeks or months, or extend several years.

Some people, being conservative, keep these records for three years for reasons discussed below, treating them the same way as records required to be maintained but for which the law does not give a specific retention period. This practice offers a protective blanket for those situations where a legal requirement may exist but could not be found after adequate legal research. It would also be reasonable to simply not consider any legal retention period for these records and keep them only as long as needed by your organization.

CONSIDERATION 2. The Requirement to Keep Records for Which No Retention Period is Stated

Many requirements to keep records do not specify how long they must be kept. In this situation, you need to keep these records only for a "reasonable" period of time. While the definition of "reasonable" varies according to your perspective, a strong argument can be made that it is always reasonable to keep records for three years if the law does not specify a different retention period.

See Chapter 7 for the detailed legal analysis supporting the "three-year presumption."

The Paperwork Reduction Act of 1980, statutes in four states, records retention standards established by the majority of the recordkeeping requirements in federal laws, and realistic business practices support this three-year presumption. This is, however, a "three-year presumption" and not a "three-year fact".

CONSIDERATION 3. The Requirement to Keep Records for a Specified Retention Period

Many laws containing recordkeeping requirements do state a specific retention period. Here is an example from the U.S. Department of Labor regulations implementing the Fair Labor Standards Act:

See U.S. Department of Labor Wage and Hour Division regulations implementing the Fair Labor Standards Act. 29 CFR § 516.5. Appendix E contains the full text of this law.

PART 516—RECORDS TO BE KEPT BY EMPLOYERS

§516.5 Records to be preserved 3 years.

Each employer shall preserve for at least three years: (a) *Payroll records*. From the last date of entry, all payroll or other records containing the employee information and data required under any of the applicable sections of this part . . .

The Internal Revenue Service requires employers to maintain records supporting employment taxes for a period of four years:

Text from the U.S. Internal Revenue Service tax regulations related to employment tax. 26 CFR § 31.6001-1.

PART 31—EMPLOYMENT TAXES AND COLLECTION OF INCOME TAX AT SOURCE

§31.6001-1 Records In General.

(e) *Place and period for keeping records. . .*

(2) Except as otherwise provided in the following sentence, every person required by the regulations in this part to keep records in respect of a tax (whether or not such person incurs liability for such tax) shall maintain such records for at least four years after the due date of such tax for the return period to which the records relate or the date such tax is paid, whichever is the latter . . .

The Department of Labor requires you to keep payroll records for three years; the IRS specifies four years. When confronted with differing requirements for records retention, generally keep the records for the longest period stated. This ensures that you meet the requirements of each and every law.

CONSIDERATION 4. A Statute of Limitations Period Which Determines When a Legal Action or Law Suit Can Be Initiated

"Statutes of limitations" or "limitations of action" are laws prescribing the time period during which a legal action or lawsuit may be initiated. Once the statute of limitations ends, no further legal action can be brought for a specific matter.

Records are the principal form of evidence used in litigation, either to defend a party's position or to show that the other party acted improperly. Court rules permit one party to subpoena the records of the other and use them effectively to pursue his claims.

This issue is complicated and requires careful consideration. Chapter 7 provides detailed strategies as well as potential pitfalls in retaining or destroying records before the statute of limitations expires.

While a statute of limitations may relate to matters for which records have an important role, the statute of limitations itself does not require that records be kept. During the period of time defined by the statute of limitations, you may or may not want to keep records, according to your judgment as to the possibility and severity of adverse claims.

A typical statute of limitations that may impact on recordkeeping requirements for contracts reads as follows:

California Code of Civil Procedure § 337.

CHAPTER 3. THE TIME OF COMMENCING ACTIONS OTHER THAN FOR THE RECOVERY OF REAL PROPERTY

§337. Four years: Written contract . . .

Within four years: 1. An action upon any contract, obligation or liability founded upon an instrument in writing . . .

In California, for example, a court action can be brought within four years of the breach of a contract to compel performance, recover damages, or to collect payments due. While an organization need not maintain records during the statute of limitations period, you may want records in order to defend your claims in case of litigation.

The courts are quite emphatic that records should not be destroyed either just before or during litigation with the intent to deliberately harm the other person by depriving him of information relevant to his claim.

See Chapter 9 for the recordkeeping requirements for tax records including the application of the limitation of assessment.

CONSIDERATION 5. A Limitation of Assessment Period That Determines the Period of Time Your Taxes May Be Assessed and Tax Records Audited

A "limitation of assessment" is similar to a statute of limitations except that it specifically refers to the period of time that the tax agency can determine the taxes owed. Under most circumstances, if the agency fails to act within the limitation of assessment period, the taxes are the amount stated on your tax return.

The tax agency, on the other hand, has the right to audit your records at any time prior to the termination of the limitation of assessment period (and beyond if you agree to an extension of the limitation of assessment period). Unlike a statute of limitations, if you do not have tax records during this period to support your tax return, you can be fined or penalized, your claims for deductions or your characterization of income may be disallowed, and your taxes calculated according to the tax agency's own formula, rather than your calculations.

Most states require the assessment to be completed within three years after the return was filed or the return was due, whichever is later. A typical provision is found in New York:

See Consolidated Laws of New York, Tax Law, § 1083.

Article 27. Corporate Tax Procedure and Administration.

§1083. Limitations on assessment.

(a) General.—Except as otherwise provided in this section, any tax . . . shall be assessed within three years after the return was filed . . .

Most states have exceptions to this general rule. For example, taxes can be assessed for a six year period if you understate your income by 25 percent or more. This period can be extended indefinitely if you file a false return, fail to file, or agree to extend the assessment period (audit).

While the statute of limitations does not require you to maintain records, a limitation of assessment implies that records must be kept. Most states specify that you must support your tax return with records, and tax agencies can impose fines and penalties for non-compliance. Since a limitation of assessment indicates the period of time during which you could be audited, it also establishes the period of time during which you should maintain tax records.

CONSIDERATION 6. Pending or Imminent Litigation, Government Investigation or Audit Affecting Certain Records

Even after the legal retention period has been determined, you may be required to keep records for a longer period because of litigation, government investigation or audit. The courts have consistently concluded that pertinent records must be maintained while these actions are pending or imminent. While most people expect to keep pertinent records while matters are in progress, few realize that they must also keep them while the matters are "imminent"—close to being initiated.

A lawsuit is considered imminent when you have been advised by the other party that a lawsuit will be initiated or have reasons to believe, based upon investigations and overtures, that the other party is preparing or seriously considering the lawsuit. Similarly, a government investigation is imminent when you receive notice that your organization will soon be investigated.

When litigation or a government investigation or audit is pending or imminent, do not destroy relevant records until the matter is complete. Retain and protect these records until it is clear that they will no longer be needed for these actions. The courts impose severe consequences where records have been destroyed in violation of a court order or to deliberately obstruct justice.

You can, in some instances, obtain permission from the court or government agency to destroy relevant records before the action ends. Otherwise, your legal counsel should determine which records are unrelated to the matter. Most often you will simply have to keep the records until the matter has been completed. Finally, the courts or government agency may required you to maintain the records for a period of time after the action has concluded as part of the settlement order or in case other similar matters should arise.

CONCLUSION   **CHAPTER 6**

☐   The legal requirements related to the retention of your records can be determined through adequate legal research.

☐   When no legal requirements exist for certain records, you may destroy these records after they are no longer needed for business purposes or after three years.

☐   When a legal requirement to keep records does not specify a retention period, the records can generally be safely destroyed after three years.

☐   When a legal requirement specifies the retention period, you may destroy the affected records only after the specified period.

☐   A statute of limitations or a limitations of action describes the time period during which someone can initiate a legal action or lawsuit. You are not required to keep records during this period, but you should carefully analyze your need for them and the ramifications of destroying records before the end of the period.

☐   A limitation of assessment is the period of time your taxes may be assessed and your tax records audited. You are generally required to keep records during this period and could be subject to fines, penalties, and higher taxes if you destroy them before the period expires.

☐   You are required to keep records when litigation or a government investigation or audit is imminent or pending, even though the normal retention period has ended.

Chapter 7   When the Law Does Not State a Specific Retention Period

This chapter deals with the analysis of two types of legal considerations related to records retention:

- *The absence of a legal requirement for certain records.* Even after a reasonable effort to locate records requirements, the researcher may be unable to find a law that addresses certain records. Some researchers have been told by a government agency that it is either "getting out of the records retention business" or reducing the number of published records retention requirements. In both cases, researchers feel uncomfortable and tend to establish overly-long retention periods "in case they missed something." Some recommendations and background related to these issues are discussed below.

- *The requirement to keep records without a stated retention period.* A large number of statutes and regulations contain phrases such as "the following records shall be maintained . . ." Although you must keep records accordingly, you do not have enough information to determine how long the record must be maintained—days, months, years, or forever! Unfortunately, many attorneys and non-attorneys alike, interpret this requirement to mean that records must be kept "permanently" because permission is not given for their destruction. Some strategies to deal with these situations are provided in the remainder of this chapter.

A REQUIREMENT TO KEEP RECORDS FOR WHICH NO RETENTION PERIOD IS GIVEN

You will encounter statutes and regulations which state that certain records must be maintained, but fail to provide a specific retention period. This is typical; in fact, many federal and state statutes and regulations do not state retention periods.

Paperwork Reduction Act of 1980

Recordkeeping requirements are generally imposed so that government agencies can determine whether organizations are complying with the law under particular federal or state programs. This information collection and monitoring process often imposes substantial financial burdens on the public.

The Paperwork Reduction Act of 1980, 44 USC Chapter 35, Coordination of Federal Information Policy.

The United States Congress passed the Paperwork Reduction Act in 1980 to minimize and control the burdens associated with the collection of information by federal agencies. This statute empowers the Office of Management and Budget (OMB), Executive Office of the President, to develop regulations implementing the Act and to monitor progress.

See Appendix A for the Office of Management and Budget regulation *Controlling Paperwork Burdens on the Public*, **5 CFR 1320, 1983 that implements the Paperwork Reduction Act of 1980.**

The implementing regulation became effective for federal agencies May 2, 1983. After that date, all federal agencies must obtain OMB approval before burdening the public with rules about the preparation of reports, applications, questionnaires, or other methods of collecting and maintaining information. No paperwork burden can be imposed upon the public until the regulation has been approved by OMB and has been assigned an official OMB identification number.

The following excerpt from the regulation describes the guidelines followed by the OMB in evaluating paperwork requirements for records retention:

§ 1320.6 General Information Collection Guidelines

Unless the agency is able to demonstrate that such collection of information is necessary to satisfy statutory requirements or other substantial need, OMB will not approve a collection of information: . . .

(f) requiring respondents to retain records, other than health, medical, or tax records, for more than three years . . .

Retention periods longer than three years can be justified in certain circumstances; but, this represents a very small number of records, perhaps fewer than 10% of the records maintained by most organizations.

Legal counsel should review these conclusions before you establish a three-year retention period. Note that the OMB regulations do not apply to federal statutes, although few recordkeeping requirements appear in federal statutes, or to state statutes and regulations.

In the situation where an agency fails to state a specific retention period, we can assume that it did not request a retention period longer than three years or they failed to justify a longer retention period under the OMB regulations. *The absence of a specific records retention period implies that the period is no longer than three years and that records can be safely destroyed after that time.*

Uniform Preservation of Private Business Records Act (UPPBRA)

See Appendix H for the *Uniform Preservation of Private Business Act (UPPBRA)* **adopted by Illinois, Maryland, New Hampshire, and Oklahoma.**

Four states have adopted the "Uniform Preservation of Private Business Records Act." Although the wording may differ slightly in the four states, the essence of Section 2 of the uniform law has been preserved as follows:

Sec. 2. Period of Preservation

The section in brackets was considered optional, although all four states kept the essence of that provision.

Unless a specific period is designated by law for their preservation, business records which persons by the laws of this state are required to keep or preserve may be destroyed after the expiration of three years from the making of such records without constituting an offense under such laws. [This section does not apply to minute books of corporations nor to records of sales or other transactions involving weapons, poisons, or other dangerous articles or substances capable of use in the commission of crimes.]

The UPPBRA states that a three-year retention period shall apply whenever a law does not specify a retention period and that destruction under this law will not constitute an offense. Destruction in less than three years, however, may subject the organization to some risks.

Other Considerations

Finally, where states have not adopted the UPPBRA, no specific law exists creating a similar three-year records retention presumption. You assume a greater risk in relying on the three-year records retention presumption when the laws of the state do not specify a records retention period.

An effective argument can be made, however, that because the law does not provide a specific retention period, the records need only exist at some measurable period of time —for example, one day, one month, one year, or five years— to meet the "letter of the law." However, maintenance of the records for only one day clearly fails to meet the "spirit of the law"—its underlying purpose to ensure that certain information is maintained for agency review. Courts would certainly require you to hold records long enough to permit the state to monitor compliance with its regulations and assess the impact of it laws—a "reasonable" period of time.

How long then must records be maintained when the law requires their maintenance but does not specify a retention period? The answer is that these records should be kept for a "reasonable period of time" (rather than permanently). What is considered "reasonable?" Based upon the previous discussion about federal records and the existence of specific state laws in four states, a three-year records retention period seems to be reasonable.

In fact, it may not be necessary to keep all records for three years. An organization can assess the risk of maintaining some records less than three years. Where the risk is low or nonexistent, keep these low risk records only long enough to meet operating needs and then destroy them. Some organizations are comfortable retaining these records for the current year plus two years (CY+2); others an even shorter period of time.

THE ABSENCE OF A LEGAL REQUIREMENT AFFECTING CERTAIN RECORDS

See Part E, Chapter 20 to 22, for details related to adequate legal research.

Some records are not covered by any legal requirements and some legal requirements cannot be found even after adequate legal research. If you fail to conduct or document adequate legal research, however, you will not have a valid excuse for not finding some records requirements.

Since it is practically impossible to find all the legal requirements and it is reasonable to expect that no legal requirements exist for some types of records, how should you determine the records retention period for those records for which no legal requirements have been found?

First, you (perhaps, in coordination with legal counsel) can determine that since no records maintenance requirements exist, there is no legal requirement to keep the records. Maintain the records only as long as they meet the needs of the organization and then destroy them. The risk that you missed a legal requirement during research may be minimal compared to the cost of further research. This is, in general, the best approach to follow when you have performed adequate legal research.

Second, you can maintain the records for three years. When no records requirements have been found after a reasonable research effort, three years appears to be a reasonable retention period. You must, however, document your search effort and the assumptions used to set the three year retention period. Then, if you missed a legal requirement during the search, you can show the judge or regulatory agency that your organization made a good faith effort to comply with the law.

Still other will select a retention period slightly longer than the period the records are needed by the organization, but, yet, shorter than three years.

CONCLUSION   **CHAPTER 7**

☐   Many federal requirements for recordkeeping do not specify records retention periods.

☐   Under the federal Paperwork Reduction Act of 1980 and the Office of Management and Budget regulations, a presumption exists that records required to be kept can be destroyed after three years when applicable regulations do not specify otherwise.

☐   Four states have adopted specific legislation that permits the destruction of records after three years unless the law states a different records retention period.

☐   When you are required to keep records under a law which does not state a recordkeeping period, you must keep those records only for a reasonable period of time such as three years.

☐   You will not find recordkeeping requirements for every record within your organization, even after adequate legal research. Some requirements are extremely difficult to locate while other requirements sought may not exist.

☐   When no legal requirement exists for certain records, maintain them only as long as they serve the needs of the organization.

☐   When no legal requirements have been found for certain records, but you are concerned that the research overlooked a requirement, you will act reasonably if you destroy these records after a three year retention period.

Chapter 8   When Statutes of Limitations and Litigation Affect Records

Lawyers traditionally have advised us to "retain records forever in case we are sued." This mistaken advice sometimes thwarts the development of an effective records retention program. Recent increases in litigation and the use by adversaries of discovery to obtain relevant documents makes this advice more harmful than helpful to some organizations.

STATUTES OF LIMITATION OR LIMITATIONS OF ACTION

Louisiana uses the term "prescription" when referring to a statute of limitations.

"Statutes of limitations" or "limitations of action" prescribe the time periods during which legal actions or lawsuits may be initiated. Under these laws, people bring contemplated legal actions within a reasonable time after a problem arises and prevent hardships resulting from the passage of time. This period of time is generally sufficient for the plaintiff to decide that legal action is appropriate yet short enough that the defendants and other parties will have the information necessary to support their positions.

The statute of limitations period usually starts when a specified action occurs. The statute of limitations for contracts, for example, usually begins with a breach or violation of the terms of the contract; the period for personal injury begins when an individual or property is injured. The statute of limitations period may be tolled or stopped when a party is incapacitated by serious injury or age (i.e., most states will toll the statute of limitations until a child reaches age 18), or the defendant has fled the jurisdiction of the court (in a criminal matter). Once the statute of limitations time passes, however, no future legal action may be brought related to the incident in question except for fraud—but no program should be designed to accommodate fraud.

EFFECT OF DISCOVERY AND SUBPOENAS ON RECORDS

Once a legal action has been initiated under the statute of limitations, either party, under the rules of discovery, has the opportunity to uncover relevant information in the possession of the other party. Discovery includes the right to inspect documents, perform tests on products, conduct depositions of witnesses, and obtain responses to written interrogatories or questions.

The scope of discovery related to the production of records for federal cases is as follows:

Rule 34, Rules of Civil
Procedure, United States
District Courts

Rule 34. Production of Documents and Things and Entry Upon Land for Inspection and Other Purposes

(a) Scope.

Any party may serve on any party a request (1) to produce or permit the party making the request, or someone acting on his behalf, to inspect and copy, any designated documents (including writings, drawings, graphs, charts, photographs, phonograph records, and other data compilations from which information can be obtained . . .)

The rules of discovery also permit records to be obtained from persons who are not a party to the legal action.

The request to produce documents is usually accompanied by a "subpoena duces tecum," an order to appear in court and produce documents. The subpoena spells out the scope of the records to be produced. Some parties write the subpoena as a broad statement covering all records in an attempt to expand the opportunity to uncover relevant information. The court reserves the right, however, to narrow the scope of the subpoena in order to reduce hardship, clarify the type of information required, and prevent one party from unfairly rummaging around in the records of another looking for potentially useful information.

The party producing the records may request compensation from the court for producing documents. Compensation is usually limited to approximately ten cents per page copied and is often not provided. In recent cases, litigants have received inadequate compensation or none at all to offset the sizable costs of producing documents benefiting the opposing party.

Failure to Produce Documents Required by Discovery

If an organization fails to produce documents under a discovery order, the court can subject it to criminal penalties for obstruction of justice or contempt of court, or to an adverse inference which is often harmful in litigation.

See Chapter 1 for Carlucci
et al v. Piper Aircraft
Corporation, 102 Federal
Rules Decisions 472 (1984),
United States District
Court, Southern District
Florida. See Chapter 4 for
Rules of Civil Procedure,
Rule 37, United States
District Court and other
adverse consequences for
failure to comply with the
law.

The federal and state courts can also impose sanctions for failure to comply with discovery orders. For example, Rule 37(b)(2) was used by a federal court in 1984 in the case of Carlucci vs. Piper Aircraft Corporation (1984) to penalize Piper Aircraft because of the selective destruction of relevant documents prior to and during pending litigation. The judge in this case prohibited the defendants from introducing evidence in support of their defense, issued a directed verdict in favor of the plaintiffs, and imposed a judgment of ten million dollars.

The Impact of a Records Retention Program on Discovery

The failure to produce documents in response to a court order can effectively be overcome through the introduction of evidence indicating that the records had been destroyed in the regular course of business under an approved records retention program and prior to litigation. This evidence should include testimony regarding the records retention program, documentation regarding procedures and approved schedules, and documentation showing a systematic destruction of records over a period of time.

See Chapter 6, Consideration 6. See also Chapter 1 for Carlucci, Ibid. Senior District Judge William J. Campbell concluded on page 485 of the opinion that "the defendant engaged in a practice of destroying engineering drawings with the intent of preventing them from being produced in lawsuits . . ." This opinion concurs with many other judicial opinions that the selective destruction of records prior to litigation with the intent of preventing potentially harmful records from being available during litigation is construed as a deliberate violation of the rights of the other party in discovery.

When you destroy records before the start of litigation, under an approved records retention program, they are no longer available to the adverse party. You also avoid the significant costs of searching the archives and reproducing the documents. You are cautioned, however, that the courts can treat you harshly if you selectively destroy records prior to litigation with bad intent or systematically destroy records once litigation is pending or imminent.

WHEN RECORDS MAY BE DESTROYED BEFORE THE END OF THE STATUTE OF LIMITATIONS

Because a statute of limitations only impacts the period of time during which a legal action may be brought and does not specify a legal retention period, you can destroy records even while the statute of limitations is in effect. Do not, however, destroy records while litigation, government investigation or audit is pending (has already started) or imminent (about to start). You can destroy records at all other times under an approved records retention program designed to meet the legitimate business needs of the organization.

Many attorneys advise their clients to keep records during the full statute of limitations period so that the records will be available in case of litigation. That attitude, however, assumes that the records will be more helpful than harmful during litigation. Often, the opposite proves to be true—records are effectively used by adverse parties to pursue their cases against the record holders.

The risks of keeping records for the full statute of limitations period must, therefore, be weighed against the advantages of destroying them. Similarly, the disadvantages of not having records needed by the organization in litigation must be weighed against the costs and inefficiencies associated with maintaining valueless records. The following questions should be considered in making the decision:

- What are the chances of litigation?

- In case of litigation, which party would have the burden of proof?

- When does the statute of limitations take effect?

The chances of litigation and potential consequences should be evaluated carefully by legal counsel. Generally, litigation is initiated within a relatively short time of the event (i.e., usually within one or two years). You should first attempt to resolve the conflict through direct negotiations with the other party. When all else fails and litigation is the last resort, plaintiffs seldom wait longer than two years before initiating a lawsuit. Most records are kept at least that long to meet the needs of the business and so are also available for litigation.

The plaintiff has the burden of proof—going forward with the evidence—during the trial and convincing a judge or jury that its case is stronger than the one presented by the defendant. The defendant presents evidence either to weaken the case of the plaintiff or to strengthen its own.

If either party lacks sufficient information to pursue its case, the rules of discovery permit relevant information to be subpoenaed from the other party. If, however, the party receiving the subpoena previously destroyed records in the regular course of business under an approved records retention program, the requesting party is at a disadvantage.

Finally, while some statutes of limitations specify a period during which litigation must begin, other statutes (such as those related to product liability or defects in design or construction of improvements to real property) may expose an organization to unlimited liability because a legal action can be brought at any time. For example, a product liability suit must be initiated in most states within two or three years of the injury, but this can occur at any time after the product was manufactured. The type of activity determines the period of liability under the statute of limitations.

General Guidelines for Destroying Records Prior to the Conclusion of the Statute of Limitations

Here are some guidelines for deciding whether or not records can be destroyed before the termination of the statute of limitations. *These guidelines are only for purposes of discussion and do not represent recommended retention periods. Only you can determine the retention periods that best serve your organization.*

- *Litigation is pending or imminent.* Do not destroy records while litigation is pending or imminent because their destruction could result in fines and penalties for obstruction of justice or contempt of court, and could result in adverse consequences in the litigation.

- *Your organization will be the likely plaintiff in litigation.* Records should be kept for all or most of the statute of limitations period if your organization is likely to be the plaintiff in the litigation. Records are usually critical to fulfilling your burden of proof and enabling you to successfully prove your case.

- *The other party will be the likely plaintiff and has little information.* When it is likely that another party will initiate the litigation, your organization must assess whether or not that party will have the necessary information to fulfill its burden of proof. If it has been determined that the other party may need to subpoena your records to obtain sufficient information to pursue its case, certain records may then become candidates for destruction in the regular course of business under an approved records retention program.

Please note that selective destruction of records in anticipation of litigation may be more harmful to an organization than their use by an adverse party in litigation. Never selectively destroy records. Destroy only entire groups or classes of records in the regular course of business under an approved records retention schedule to meet legitimate business needs such as reducing costs and improving efficiency.

- *Records related to activities involving small sums of money.* Records related to sales contracts or other activities involving small sums of money can usually be destroyed in a short period of time, even though the statute of limitations period may be longer (e.g., normally four years for sales contracts under the Uniform Commercial Code). Even if your organization became involved in litigation at a later time, your risk might be minimal compared to the cost of storing these records for longer periods of time. Some sales receipts (perhaps without all the supporting documentation) might be kept to respond to future insurance claims or tax audits.

Product and Construction Records

See Chapter 11, *Contracts and Agreements and Manufacturing Records* for details.

Records retention decisions are more difficult for manufacturers and distributors of products and for those who design and construct improvements to real property. Most states specify that the statute of limitations for personal injury begins at the time the injury occurs. The injury can occur years after the product has been manufactured and distributed. The manufacturer and distributor may be responsible throughout the life of the product for defects in design and manufacturing or errors in the instructions for using the product. Records may be needed until the product is no longer being used. Architects, engineers, and contractors are similarly exposed for work related to the design and construction of improvements to real property.

Some states restrict the statute of limitations for both product liability and construction to a specified period from the date of manufacture or substantial completion of the construction, respectively. Trade associations are working with state legislatures and congress to develop more uniform statutes in these areas.

The restrictions imposed by some states on the statute of limitations period generally do not help manufacturers or distributors of nationally used products because most states do not restrict liability. Construction companies are generally liable only in those states in which they build and can, therefore, determine the scope of their liability.

Finally, a distinction must be made between the liability for personal or property injury and that for breach of contract. While the statute of limitations for personal injury may be unlimited in duration in many states, contractual obligations are limited under the statute of limitations for written contracts to a specified period following the breach of contract. You can, therefore, safely purge some records from the project files after the contractual obligations cease to exit while maintaining others in case of product- or construction-related injury. Note, however, that you may need to retain information about subcontractors or component manufacturers if questions about their defects in manufacture or design should arise.

CONCLUSION   **CHAPTER 8**

☐ A statute of limitations or limitations of action determines the time period during which a legal action or lawsuit may be initiated.

☐ The court procedure rules for discovery allow one party in litigation to subpoena records in the possession of the other.

☐ Failure to produce documents in response to a court order or subpoena could result in severe criminal penalties for obstruction of justice or contempt of court, or severe sanctions or adverse inferences which could cause you to lose your case.

☐ Failure to produce documents in response to a court order can effectively be overcome by introducing evidence showing that the records in question were destroyed in the regular course of business prior to litigation under an approved records retention program.

☐ Since a statute of limitations is not a requirement to keep records, records can be destroyed before the end of the statute of limitations period.

☐ When determining whether records should be destroyed prior to the end of a statute of limitations period, consider the chances of litigation, which party has the burden of proof, and the exact time period when the statute of limitations applies.

☐ Records should not be destroyed before the conclusion of the statute of limitations period if litigation is pending or imminent, or if your organization will be the likely plaintiff in litigation.

☐ You might consider destroying records prior to the conclusion of the statute of limitations period and before litigation starts if the other party will be the likely plaintiff and has little information, the records are for activities involving small sums of money, or disposal carries with it the risk of only small adverse consequences.

☐ When records will be destroyed prior to the end of the statute of limitations period, the records retention schedule should show that it is the organization's policy to destroy entire classes of records as a group.

☐ Some records, such as those related to manufacturing or construction, may have to be kept indefinitely because the statute of limitations could begin to run at any time in the future after an injury occurs.

PART C RECORDS RETENTION REQUIREMENTS FOR YOUR RECORDS

Chapter 9   Requirements for Tax Records

Your organization probably maintains many accounting records for long periods of time. These records may consist of canceled checks, check stubs, invoices, vouchers, and general ledgers. During the first year or so after creation, accounting records serve as operational records to ensure payments have properly been received or disbursed. Occasionally, these records have a longer term value when disputes over payment or performance of services arise. As a practical matter, however, most accounting records are maintained beyond one year primarily for tax purposes; some may be retained for other purposes such as contracts or insurance.

See Appendix C for federal tax requirements and Appendix D for state tax requirements.

This chapter reviews the principal federal tax laws affecting the maintenance and retention of tax records. You should also carefully review the appropriate laws for the states in which you do business to determine their impact on the records retention period.

MYTHS REGARDING TAX RECORDS

You may have been told some myths by your tax advisors about tax records. The most common myth is that tax records must be kept for seven years. As you will learn in this chapter, only one minor provision in the tax laws specifies a seven year period and it has to do with credits or refunds for the overpayment of income tax resulting from bad debts. Even this provision does not require records to be kept. All other tax provisions specify six years or less for the typical assessment or audit period.

How did the seven year myth arise? If you ask your advisors for their source of this information, they will probably answer "I don't know" or "we have always done it this way." Some may say that the longest retention requirement for tax purposes is six years and add one more year to include the year during which the tax return is filed. Maybe the myth comes from the Bible:

Leviticus 25:8-10 and 39-41

You shall count off seven weeks of seven years—seven times seven years—so that the period of seven weeks of seven years gives you a total of 49 years. Then you shall sound the horn loud; in the seventh month on the tenth day of the month, the Day of Atonement—you shall have the horn sounded throughout your land and you shall hallow the fiftieth year. You shall proclaim the release throughout the land for all its inhabitants. It shall be a jubilee for you: Each of you shall return to his holding and each of you shall return to his family . . . And if thy brother be waxen poor with thee and sell himself unto thee, thou shalt not make him to serve as a bondservant. As a hired servant, and as a fiddler, he shall be with thee; he shall serve with thee unto the year of jubilee. Then shall he go out from thee, he and his children with him, and shall return unto his own family, unto the possession of his fathers shall he return.

These passages urge society to declare a jubilee every seven times seven years and relieve the debtor of those debts being paid back through hired services. Unfortunately, the Internal Revenue Service does not celebrate jubilees. This chapter separates myths from facts.

BASIC RECORDS REQUIREMENTS FOR TAX RECORDS

Regulations promulgated by the Internal Revenue Service do not give specific periods for the retention of tax records except for employment tax records, some excise tax records, and a few other miscellaneous records. Instead, the regulations caution taxpayers to maintain accurate records in support of their tax returns.

26 CFR 1.6001-1. See Appendix C for other federal tax requirements.

§ 1.6001-1 Records.

(a) . . . any person required to file a return of information with respect to income, shall keep such permanent books of account or records, including inventories, as are sufficient to establish the amount of gross income, deductions, credits, or other matters required to be shown by such person in any return of such tax or information.

The phrase "permanent books of account or records" motivates some organizations to maintain all records pertaining to tax matters "permanently" or "forever." The law does not support this position. The IRS must act within the time specified in its regulations. You cannot be required to produce tax records or be assessed penalties for not having the records after the time has lapsed. The term "permanent," as used in this regulation, refers to the ability of the records to last for long periods rather than referring to the required retention period.

The tax laws are quite unusual. Our legal system considers a person innocent until proven guilty. Our tax system, however, considers a person guilty and subject to the full amount of tax unless proven "innocent" by establishing appropriate deductions, evidenced by full and complete records. Substantial tax benefits and deductions can be disallowed unless supported by records. Tax records, then, must be maintained for the time necessary to support tax returns and tax payments but need not be maintained beyond the time when the IRS can legally assess taxes or require you to produce records.

LIMITATION OF ASSESSMENT FOR TAX RECORDS

Except as otherwise provided by law, the limitations of assessment stated in the tax regulations set the period during which the IRS can assess your taxes. Related statutes of limitations restrict the time during which taxpayers can demand refunds or credits, or during which the IRS can collect taxes previously assessed. Most states have adopted these same limitations of assessment and statutes of limitations:

26 USC 6501(a). See Appendix C for other federal tax requirements.

Except as otherwise provided in this section, the amount of any tax imposed by this title shall be assessed within three years after the return was filed (whether or not such return was filed on or after the date prescribed) or, if the tax is payable by stamp, at any time after such tax became due and before the expiration of 3 years after the date on which any part of such tax was paid, and no proceeding in court without assessment for the collection of such tax shall be begun after the expiration of such period.

If the IRS does not audit the taxpayer's return or specify a tax different from the amount stated in the taxpayer's return within the three year period (after the tax return was filed or the tax was due, whichever occurs later), it may be barred from further action against the taxpayer for that specific tax return. The period of assessment may extend to six years if:

26 USC 6501(e)

- you understate gross income, estate, gift, or excise tax by an amount in excess of 25%,

- you fail to declare constructive dividends, or

- you operate a personal holding company.

These exceptions make it prudent to check with your tax advisor for any that might apply to your organization.

26 USC 6501(c)

Finally, the period for assessing taxes can be extended indefinitely if you file a false return, willfully attempt to evade tax, fail to file a return, or extend the period by mutual agreement. The potential for this unlimited assessment period, however, does not affect the retention of your tax records—a retention period should never be based on the commission of a crime such as fraud.

Abbreviations used for tax retention periods:
  ACT: active
  ACY: active plus current year
  ATX: active plus filing date of tax return
  CY: current year
  TAX: filing date of tax return

 Figure 12.1 adopts the retention period of "current year plus four years (CY+4)" for tax records to simplify computing the time period. This period also corresponds to the retention requirement for employment tax and payroll records discussed later in this chapter.

If you properly determine the tax owed, report the correct amount of gross income, and do not commit fraud, you usually do not have to keep supporting records longer than three years after filing the tax return (with some exceptions)—the "filing date of tax return plus three years (TAX+3)".

Some use a simpler retention period—although a few months longer—of the "current year plus four years (CY+4)" to simplify computing the start of the retention period. Records are kept for the tax year (CY) in which they were created, the full year in which the tax return was filed (one year), plus the limitation of assessment period (three years). The retention period CY+4 relieves you of the burden of tracking the month in which the tax return was filed; it also corresponds to the common practice of destroying records only at the end of the year (CY).

When using either retention period—CY+4 or TAX+3—you can destroy all accounting records supporting the tax return and the tax return at the end of the retention period, in the regular course of business under the records retention program.

Still others opt for a much longer retention period—the "filing tax return plus six years (TAX+6)" or, more simply, "current year plus seven (CY+7)—in case they mistakenly understate their income by 25% or more. Since this type of error should not occur in a legitimate organization that operates a good accounting system, only use this longer retention period if it reflects the needs of your organization and your assessment of risk.

Additional statutes of limitations exist which might affect the period during which all or some of the tax records are maintained:

26 USC 6502   • Collection of tax by IRS after assessment—six years

26 USC 6511   • Claim for credit or refund for overpayment of tax—two or three years

26 USC 6531   • Criminal prosecution—three or six years

26 USC 6532   • Legal proceeding to recover taxes or refunds—two years

These statutes of limitations should not affect the retention periods. In practice, most organizations pay their estimated taxes during the tax year and pay any additional amounts with the return. Once the tax has been assessed or the period for assessment has lapsed, the rules state that the tax amount has been precisely determined and can no longer be litigated.

Taxpayers usually initiate claims for credits or refunds within a short period of time following the assessment of tax. Some records supporting these claims may therefore be necessary for the period these claims for credits or refunds are outstanding. Other records, after appropriate review, may be destroyed under the records retention program.

SPECIAL RECORDS RETENTION PROBLEMS

Some special situations influence the records retention program for tax records: capital gains or losses, depreciation of capital property, voluntary extension of audit period, excise taxes, employment taxes, and state taxes.

Capital Gains or Losses

See abbreviations on previous page.

When your organization acquires or sells property (buildings, equipment, fixtures, etc.), it may incur capital gains or losses based upon the difference between the purchase and sale price. The taxpayer must first prove the "basis"—the purchase price plus the cost of any improvements to the property—to determine the amount of the capital gain or loss. Because property may be owned for many years, records which prove the purchase price must be kept for the full period of ownership and then for the normal three-year from the date the tax return was filed—ATX+3 (ACT+TAX+3) or, more simply, ACY+4 (ACT+CY+4).

If the taxpayer is unable to prove the purchase price after the property has been sold, the IRS assumes the purchase price was zero. The IRS then assesses taxes based upon the full amount of the sale price, as opposed to the difference between the sale price and the purchase price ("basis"). For example, a building purchased for $250,000 to which the new owner added a $100,000 air conditioning system and then sold thirty years later for $750,000 would usually be subject to tax on the $400,000 appreciation minus improvements. If the taxpayer did not maintain records to prove the purchase price and improvements, the full $750,000 would be subject to tax.

It would be inappropriate to maintain all records supporting capital acquisitions for the lifetime of the assets. Your organization should segregate the records supporting costly capital acquisitions from the less expensive capital acquisitions and keep records only for those costing more than a specified dollar amount (such as $1,000, $5,000, or $25,000). The IRS does not usually audit or protest the basis of less expensive capital acquisitions such as office furniture. A listing of lesser capital acquisitions with their purchase price generally suffices. Most accounting records, including records supporting small capital purchases, can be safely destroyed after the shorter CY+4 period. Records supporting significant capital acquisitions should be maintained in paper or microfilm form for as long as necessary to prove the purchase price or basis for capital gains.

Depreciation

Depreciation for tax purposes is an amount the taxpayer deducts each year to reflect the loss of value over time of property or equipment used for business purpose. Depreciation schedules maintained by the taxpayer show the purchase price, the annual charges for depreciation, and the undepreciated value of the equipment. The sale of property or equipment requires a calculation of any capital loss or gain incurred after the original purchase price is reduced by the amount of depreciation. Fully depreciated property has a taxable basis equal to zero and any sale price received for it is fully taxable.

See abbreviations on page 55.

The depreciable life for property varies according to the IRS regulations, which then become your guide as to how long to keep acquisition records. Keep purchase, sale, repair, and depreciation records until the property is sold and then for the retention period for the year in which you file the return—ATX+3 (ACT+TAX+3) or, more simply, ACY+4 (ACT+CY+4).

Credit or Refund for Overpayment of Taxes Resulting from Bad Debts

See Internal Revenue Service, 26 CFR § 301.6511(d)-1(a) in Appendix C.

The Internal Revenue Service generally honors a claim for credit or refund for a period of three years from the time the tax return was filed or within two years from the time the tax was paid, whichever of these periods expires last. Where the credits or refunds arise from an overpayment of tax due to bad debts, you can file the claim up to seven years from the date of filing the tax return. You may, then, retain documentation of bad debts for up to seven years. However, most organizations recognize the reality of bad debts or worthless securities within a few years and seek refunds earlier.

The rules do not require you to keep bad debt records for seven years; they give you up to seven years to recognize the bad debt as uncollectable. Perhaps this provision of the tax laws forms the basis for the seven year myth.

Voluntary Extension of Audit Period

If you refuse to extend the
audit period when
requested, IRS can
disallow your deduction or
characterization of income,
refuse any disputed items,
or determine your taxes
using their own formulas.

Most organizations cooperate with the IRS by extending the period of assessment or audit beyond the three year period when asked. If a subsidiary has been audited, the assessment period may be extended for the entire organization by agreement. So, periodically meet with your tax advisor before destroying tax records to determine whether or not the assessment period has been extended and what, if any, other factors apply for retaining certain records for longer periods of time.

Employment Taxes, Excise Taxes, and Other Taxes

See 26 CFR 31.6001-1 in
Appendix C for
employment tax
requirements. Also see
Chapter 10 for further
discussion on payroll
records.

Special requirements for excise taxes, employment taxes, and other taxes affect the retention period for certain tax records. For example, employers are required to maintain records supporting the employment tax for at least four years after the due date of the tax or the date the tax is paid. Since employment tax is paid and due during each calendar year, the retention period of current year plus four years (CY+4) should be followed. The retention period for excise tax records can range from two to six years depending upon the product being regulated. These requirements should, therefore, be carefully reviewed before establishing the records retention period for these records.

State Taxes

See Appendix D for state
tax requirements.

Most states use the federal income tax return as part of the state return. So, the federal return and supporting documentation must be maintained for whatever period is required for state tax returns. Some states have limitations of action similar to the federal government; others specify a retention period of four to six years, especially for sales tax records. Review the requirements of each state in which you do business and establish appropriate records retention periods.

MICROFILM AND COMPUTER SYSTEMS FOR TAX RECORDS

See Chapter 17 for IRS
microfilm requirements
and Chapter 18 for IRS
computer requirements.

The Internal Revenue Service has issued regulations controlling microfilm and computers systems used for tax records. Most state revenue departments defer to these Internal Revenue Service requirements, but often have their own requirements for sales and other taxes.

Generally, when you develop a good microfilm or computer system to meet your business needs, you simultaneously meet the requirements of the Internal Revenue Service and state revenue departments. Review the requirements, nonetheless, to ensure complete compliance with the few unusual provisions.

CONCLUSION **CHAPTER 9**

☐ The United States Internal Revenue Service requires you to maintain records to support your tax return but does not state the form or retention requirements for these records.

☐ The Internal Revenue Service is barred from auditing you or assessing your taxes after the termination of the limitation of assessment period.

☐ Most tax records must be kept for three years from the date of filing (TAX+3) or, more simply, four years from the end of the year in which the records were created (CY+4).

☐ Some organizations maintain all tax records for a longer period of six years from the date of filing (TAX+6) or, more simply, seven years from the end of the year in which the records were created (CY+7) just in case they mistakenly understate their income by 25 percent or more.

☐ Employment tax records must be kept for four years from the end of the calendar year (CY+4), since employment tax is paid throughout the year.

☐ Records related to the purchase, sale, improvement, and depreciation for property such as buildings, equipment, and fixtures must be kept from the time of purchase to the time of sale plus the retention period for the tax records for the year of sale—ATX+3 (ACT+TAX+3) or, more simply, ACY+4 (ACT+CY+4).

☐ Tax records must be maintained when the taxpayer agrees to a voluntary extension of the audit period.

☐ State requirements for tax records generally follow the federal limitation of assessment period, but some states have a specific retention period of four to six years, especially for sales tax records.

☐ You must follow the requirements of the Internal Revenue Service and state revenue departments for microfilm and computer systems for your tax records.

Chapter 10   Requirements for Employment Records

Your organization maintains employment records in order to process personnel actions and to comply with the myriad of legal requirements imposed by both federal and state law.

Legal requirements for employment records in the United States are found primarily in regulations implementing a variety of Congressional acts or statutes. State statutes and regulations generally parallel their federal counterparts with a few variations. You should review the legal requirements for those states in which your organization does business. This chapter focuses upon the major federal laws that affect personnel records and their records retention requirements.

FEDERAL LAWS AFFECTING PERSONNEL RECORDS

See Appendix E for the text of the recordkeeping provisions in the laws discussed below.

Federal employment laws specify standards of conduct for employers and empower federal agencies to implement these laws through regulations. Some of the more significant statutes and implementing regulations affecting employment records are as follows:

Equal Employment Opportunity Commission, 29 CFR 1627

- Age Discrimination and Employment Act of 1967.

  This law prohibits discrimination in the work place based upon age. Employers are required to maintain information about payrolls, job applications, promotions, job orders, testing, and advertising.

Equal Employment Opportunity Commission, 29 CFR 1602.

- Civil Rights Act of 1964, Title VII.

  Title VII of the Civil Rights Act prohibits discrimination against employees in the work environment for reasons of race, color, national origin, or sex. The resulting regulations administered by the Equal Employment Opportunity Commission set requirements for hiring, promotion, demotion, transfer, termination, rates of pay or compensation, and selection for training or apprenticeship.

29 USC Chapter 18

- Employee Retirement Income Security Act (ERISA).

  This law establishes the guidelines for employee benefit and pension plans. The law requires you to file a summary of the plan with the

Department of Labor and sets forth the statute of limitations during which an employee may bring a civil action against an employer for failure to comply with the approved plan.

Equal Employment Opportunity Commission, 29 CFR 1620

• Equal Pay Act.

The Equal Pay Act seeks to prevent wage discrimination between the sexes who perform the same work. Recordkeeping requirements include those covered by the Fair Labor Standards Act (discussed below) plus any records that describe or explain the basis for paying different wages to employees of different sex.

Department of Labor, Wage and Hour Division regulations: 29 CFR 516

• Fair Labor Standards Act (FLSA).

This law is designed to ensure that employers pay minimum wages and overtime to employees. Records specified include payroll, collective bargaining agreements, employment contracts, wage rates, work schedules, and time cards.

Internal Revenue Service, 26 CFR 31.6001-1

• Federal Insurance Contribution Act (FICA).

This regulation implements the recordkeeping requirements of the Social Security Program and specifies the types of records employers must maintain documenting contributions to social security.

Internal Revenue Service, 26 CFR 31.6001-4

• Federal Unemployment Tax Act (FUTA).

This regulation implements the recordkeeping requirements for unemployment tax payments.

Occupational Safety and Health Administration, 29 CFR 1904 and 1910

• Occupational Safety and Health Act (OSHA).

This act is designed to ensure the health and safety of employees in the work place. Its implementing regulations require employers to maintain a log of injuries and illnesses, employee medical records, and records of exposure to toxic or harmful substances.

RECORDS RETENTION REQUIREMENTS

The federal laws related to employment records generally specify overlapping requirements. For example, the regulations implementing each of the following laws specify retention requirements for payroll records: the Fair Labor Standards Act, Federal Insurance Contribution Act, Federal Unemployment Tax Act, Civil Rights Act, Equal Pay Act, and Age and Discrimination Employment Act. The overlap of the regulations for these laws means you must analyze all of them to determine the longest retention period applicable to your personnel records. Generally, use the longest federal retention period found.

Payroll Records

Payroll records usually include information such as the name, social security number, hours worked, compensation rate, deductions, and total wages paid to each employee. These records are often derived from time sheets or time cards maintained on a daily basis. Various laws require payroll records to be maintained to accomplish specific goals:

- The regulations implementing the Fair Labor Standards Act require you to maintain payroll records to ensure that employees receive minimum wages and appropriate overtime pay.

- The regulations implementing the Civil Rights Act, The Equal Pay Act, and The Age Discrimination and Employment Act require you to maintain payroll records to ensure no discrimination exists in the wages paid employees.

- The regulations implementing The Federal Insurance Contribution Act and the Federal Unemployment Tax Act require you to maintain payroll records to ensure that the appropriate employment taxes are withheld and paid to the federal government.

  Because FICA and FUTA regulations specify the longest retention periods, you should keep payroll records for at least four years. This retention period also meets the requirements of other federal regulations and all state statutes of limitations related to wages.

Employment Applications and Other Pre-Employment Records

Employment applications and other pre-employment records such as job applications, resumes, and advertising should be retained one year under the Age Discrimination and Employment Act. This period also suffices for the Equal Opportunity Commission under Title VII of the Civil Rights Act. These records need be maintained for only 90 days for temporary positions.

Employment Actions

These records document promotions, demotions, transfers, selection for training, layoffs, recalls, or other related employee actions. Surprisingly, the recordkeeping regulations under the Age Discrimination and Employment Act, containing the longest legal requirements, require you to keep these records for only one year from the date of the personnel action. This requirement runs contrary to the commonly held perception that employee records should be kept "forever."

As a practical matter, while the detailed documentation of specific actions need be retained only one year, most organizations maintain summary records of personnel actions much longer, using them as guides in setting salary rates, pension benefits, and future promotions. Personnel files can, therefore, be purged on a regular basis under an approved records retention program.

Some organizations keep detailed employment records for long periods, such as six years, out of a concern for litigation arising from alleged discrimination under the Civil Rights Act and other laws. The decision to maintain records in case of litigation versus the right to destroy them should be carefully reviewed by your legal counsel. Keep in mind, though, that personnel action records do not have to kept forever.

Injuries and Illnesses

The Occupational Safety and Health Administration requires employers to maintain a summary log and detailed records regarding each occupational injury and illness for 5 years from the end of the current year (CY+5).

Employee Medical Records and Hazardous Exposure Records

The Occupational Safety and Health Administration requires you to keep employee medical records while the employee is active (term of employment) plus 30 years (ACT+30). Health insurance claims, however, can be destroyed at the discretion of the employer.

Whenever employees have been exposed to toxic or other harmful substances, the employer must maintain a record of the exposure for 30 years, including the identity of the substance to which the employees were exposed plus information about the methods used to determine the degree of exposure. Detailed environmental monitoring records and material safety sheets can be destroyed at an earlier period if you keep adequate summary records. Other specific health and safety requirements apply to noise, fire protection, and specific activities such as mining.

Some organizations are very concerned about potential litigation arising from the exposure of their employees to hazardous substances. While the federal government has identified some hazardous substances, these organizations worry that the federal government may add, perhaps retroactively, additional substances to the list—such as happened when asbestos was declared hazardous years after it was first manufactured by Manville. Some attorneys suggest that "strict liability" principles might apply, making employers liable for damages unless a totally safe working environment can be demonstrated.

A defensive strategy adopted by some organizations is to maintain records of facilities, employee schedules, work locations, and other information for long periods of time. While these actions might reflect the advice of legal counsel concerned about future litigation, the specific legal retention requirements issued by OSHA are more limited.

Employee Pensions and Benefits

The regulations implementing the Age Discrimination and Employment Act specify that employers must maintain pension and benefit plans, seniority system plans, and merit pay plans for the time the plan is in effect plus one year (ACT+1). This requirement applies specifically to the plans, and not the employment service or contribution records which determine the eligibility of an individual to participate or benefit from the plan.

The Employee Retirement Income and Security Act does specify the statute of limitations during which an employee can bring a civil suit against an employer for not properly applying the plan. A suit under this provision could be brought, for example, if the employer fails to credit the employee for years of service or for his contributions, or fails to distribute the appropriate benefits under the plan. The law specifies that the employee must bring an action within three years of learning about a breach of the employer's fiduciary responsibility under the plan, if the employee had been informed about the employer's actions (e.g., through annual reports related to the employer's contribution to the employee's pension plan). The statute of limitations is extended to six years from the time of the breach if the employee had not been informed of the employer actions leading to the breach. Finally, the employee can bring a legal action at any time in case of fraud or concealment by the employer.

The affect of these statute of limitations periods is that if an employer fails to properly credit an employee for years of service or payments, the employee has up to six years (absent fraud) to sue the employer. Since when the employee actually knew about the problem may be difficult to determine, the records related to pension or benefit plan activities should be maintained for six years to be safe under the ERISA statute of limitations. As a practical matter, however, employers usually maintain summary records of contributions, years of service, and benefits accrued for a long, but "indefinite" period, in order to administer the plans, rather than to meet legal requirements.

CONCLUSION

CHAPTER 10

☐ Legal requirements for personnel records are generally governed by federal statutes and regulations.

☐ Federal statutes and regulations require employers to maintain records in order to prevent discrimination against employees, ensure proper minimum wage and overtime pay, ensure proper payment of social security and unemployment tax, and protect the health and safety of employees in the work place.

☐ Payroll records should be kept for four years in order to meet the requirements of the Federal Insurance Contribution Act and the Federal Unemployment Tax Act.

☐ Employment applications and other pre-employment records such as job applications, resumes, and advertising should be retained for one year under the Age Discrimination Employment Act.

☐ Detailed records documenting employment actions such as promotions, demotions, transfers, selection for training, layoffs, and recalls should be retained for one year under the Age Discrimination and Employment Act. As a practical matter, organizations generally maintain summary records of personnel actions while the employee is active. Some organizations maintain detailed records of employment actions for six years in response to the statute of limitation found in the Civil Right Act.

☐ A summary log and detailed records regarding occupational injury and illness should be retained for the current year plus 5 years (CY+5), according to the regulations of the Occupational Safety and Health Administration.

☐ Employee medical records should be retained for the term of employment plus 30 years (ACT+30) under regulations of the Occupational Safety and Health Administration but health insurance claims can be destroyed at the discretion of the employer.

☐ Records of employee exposure to hazardous substances should be retained for 30 years from the date of the exposure.

☐ Employee pension plans should be kept while the plan is in effect plus one year (ACT+1) under the Age Discrimination and Employment Act.

☐ Detailed records of employer contributions and payments under retirement or benefit plans should be kept for 6 years under the Employee Retirement Income and Security Act and summary records of contributions, years of service, and benefits should be retained for a long, but indefinite period in order to administer the benefit plan.

Chapter 11   Requirements for General Business Records

This chapter discusses the legal requirements for some common business records other than tax or personnel records. In some cases, specific legal requirements determine retention periods while in others legal considerations influence retention periods.

BUSINESS ORGANIZATION

The establishment of business organizations such as corporations, partnerships, and limited partnerships is generally governed by state law. A corporation, for example, is incorporated in one state and may be licensed to do business in others. Your organization must meet the requirements of the state in which it was founded as well as the states in which it does business. If the law is not met, the state has the right to prevent you from doing business there.

The typical laws presented below require records to be kept but do not state how long to keep them. How long then should organization records be kept for corporations and partnerships?

Corporations

The "three year rule" previously discussed in Chapter 7 may also apply here because no retention period is stated. The Uniform Preservation of Private Business Records Act, however, specifically excludes board minutes. On the other hand, most organizations would feel uncomfortable keeping these important records for only three years.

The articles of incorporation and bylaws for a corporation are generally filed with the Secretary of State for the state of incorporation. These are "permanent" public records and you can obtain certified copies of these records from the state at any time. Your copies are, therefore, for convenience only.

The other records generally specified in the law, such as minutes of board or shareholder meetings and records of shareholders, are needed by the corporation to conduct its business. The minutes of meetings remind the organization of decisions made in the past and protect the board and officers from personal liability by showing that their actions were specifically approved by the corporation through the formal meeting process.

Board minutes for small or privately held corporations show that the corporation actually functions as a corporation rather than as a private business. The absence of board minutes can lead to the suspicion that the corporation is a "sham" and should not be protected by the limited liability protection granted corporations.

The statute of limitations for shareholder suits are generally limited to three years after the breach by the corporation.

While a three year retention period may be justified for general corporate records for which there is no specific requirement, most businesses maintain these records for long periods of time. Meeting records kept for ten years or so would be sufficient to show how the resolutions and activities of the board shape current operations. Shareholder records, on the other hand, should be kept only so long as the information is current or active plus about three years to provide for any shareholder suit alleging a failure in the corporation's responsibilities, such as failure to pay dividends or notify shareholders of annual meetings.

Two typical laws related to recordkeeping for corporations are presented below:

California Corporations
Code § 1500

TITLE 1. CORPORATIONS

CHAPTER 15. RECORDS AND REPORTS.

§ 1500. Books and records of account; minutes of meetings; share register; form.

Each corporation shall keep adequate and correct books and records of account and shall keep minutes of the proceedings of its shareholders, board and committees of the board and shall keep at its principal executive office, or at the office of its transfer agent or registrar, a record of its shareholders, giving the names and addresses of all shareholders and the number and class of shares held by each. Such minutes shall be kept in written form. Such other books and records shall be kept either in written form or in any other form capable of being converted into written form.

Delaware Code Annotated
§ 224

TITLE 8. CORPORATIONS

CHAPTER 1. GENERAL CORPORATION LAW.

§ 224 Form of records.

Any records maintained by a corporation in the regular course of its business, including its stock ledger, books of account, and minute books, may be kept on, or be in the form of, punch cards, magnetic tape, photographs, microphotographs or any other information storage device, provided that the records so kept can be converted into clearly legible written form within a reasonable time. Any corporation shall so convert any records so kept upon the request of any person entitled to inspect the same. When records are kept in such manner, a clearly legible written form produced from the cards, tapes, photographs, microphotographs or other information storage device shall be admissible in evidence, and accepted for all other purposes, to the same extent as an original written record of the same information would have been, provided the written form accurately portrays the record.

Partnerships

Partnership laws generally specify that the partnership agreement be available for review by the partners. Most partners, out of self interest, keep copies of the agreement anyway, regardless of the law.

Most states have requirements for partnerships such as those found in the partnership laws California and Delaware:

California Corporation Code § 15019

TITLE 2. PARTNERSHIPS

CHAPTER 1. UNIFORM PARTNERSHIP ACT.

§ 15019. Partnership books; right to inspect.

The partnership books shall be kept, subject to any agreement between the partners, at the principal place of business of the partnership, and every partner shall at all times have access to and may inspect and copy any of them.

Delaware Code Annotated § 1519

TITLE 6. COMMERCE AND TRADE

SUBTITLE II. OTHER LAWS RELATING TO COMMERCE AND TRADE.

CHAPTER 15. PARTNERSHIP

§ 1519. Partnership books.

The partnership books shall be kept, subject to any agreement between the partners, at the principal place of business of the partnership, and every partner shall at all times have access to and may inspect and copy any of them.

CONTRACTS AND AGREEMENTS

Four kinds of written contract requirements may affect your organization:

- Government contracts

- Sales contracts under the Uniform Commercial Code

- Contracts related to improvements to real property

- All other written contracts

Contracts are distinguished according to whether they involve government, sales, or improvements to real property instead of being classified by subject matter, such as employment, consultant, royalty, or equipment. Some organizations treat all contracts alike and retain them for the longest period appropriate, with an eye toward the statute of limitations and the recordkeeping burdens when records are kept for long periods of time.

Government Contracts

See Appendix F for the text of the Federal Acquisition Regulations related to recordkeeping requirements for federal contract records.

The United States federal government requires that government contract records be maintained for three years from the date of final payment (ACT+3). This provision appears in both the published requirements of all federal agencies and the written contract between the agency and the contractor. The law defines the requirements for microfilm and computer records, plus the following additional records retention periods:

- 4 Years: accounts receivable, invoices, freight bills, purchase orders, material transfers, travel expenses, canceled checks, accounts payable, payroll, work orders, receipt and inspection reports, production records, etc.

- 2 Years: labor cost distribution documents, petty cash records, time cards, paid employment checks, store requisitions, etc.

You should check your written contracts with the federal government to determine if there are any deviations from this retention period.

State and local government entities can establish their own retention period, but in most cases they have adopted the same active plus three year (ACT+3) retention period. You should read your state contracts for any deviations or contact your state agency.

Sales Contracts

The Uniform Commercial Code has been adopted by all states to regulate commercial transactions between merchants. Since merchants are individuals regularly engaged in the purchase and sale of goods, the Uniform Commercial Code governs transactions between groups such as wholesalers and retailers and between subcomponent and component manufacturers. These merchants sell products to other merchants who, in turn, sell to consumers. Purchases by consumers or other end users are generally not covered by the Uniform Commercial Code.

Transactions covered by the Uniform Commercial Code are governed by a four year statute of limitations except for South Carolina (six years), Wisconsin (six years) and Colorado (three years). In case of breach, either party may sue the other within the specified time after the breach. Records related to these sales contracts need only be kept for the period of time the contract is active plus four years (ACT+4), unless you do substantial business in the three states mentioned.

Because the statute of limitations begins with the breach, it is safe to destroy records supporting the implementation of the contract four years after creating them. Typical supporting records are proof of shipment, equipment specifications, and other information demonstrating compliance with the contract.

The wording of the statute of limitations provision of the Uniform Commercial Code is as follows:

§ 2-725. Statute of Limitations in Contract for Sale.

(1) An action for breach of any contract for sale must be commenced within four years after the cause of action has accrued. By the original agreement the parties may reduce the period of limitation to not less than one year but may not extend it.

(2) A cause of action accrues when the breach occurs, regardless of the aggrieved party's lack of knowledge of the breach. A breach of warranty occurs when tender of delivery is made, except that where a warranty explicitly extends to future performance of the goods and discovery of the breach must await the time of such performance the cause of action accrues when the

breach is or should have been discovered.

(3) Where an action commenced within the time limited by subsection (1) is so terminated as to leave available a remedy by another action for the same breach such other action may be commenced after the expiration of the time limited and within six months after the termination of the first action unless the termination resulted from voluntary discontinuance or from dismissal for failure or neglect to prosecute.

(4) This section does not alter the law on tolling of the statute of limitations nor does it apply to causes of action which have accrued before this Act becomes effective.

Contracts for Improvements to Real Property

Appendix B contains a listing of these statutes of limitation for use in determining the specific retention period for your records.

Most states have enacted a specific statute of limitations covering improvements to real property—land or buildings. These statutes of limitations generally specify that any court actions related to an improvement to real property must be brought within two or three years from the time of the breach of contract or injury but within a number of years—from four to 20 years depending on the state—from the "substantial completion of the improvement." These provisions cover contracts with architects, contractors, builders, builder vendors, engineers, inspectors, and land surveyors. If the breach of contract or injury occurs at a date later than the one specified, it is forever barred. Keep, therefore, all records supporting your activities for the time period specified in the statute of limitations for the state where you made the improvement.

A typical statute of limitations for improvements to real property reads as follows:

Texas Civil Practice and Remedies Code § 15.008 and § 16.009.

§ 16.008. Architects and engineers furnishing design, planning, or inspection of construction of improvements.

(a) A person must bring suit for damages for a claim listed in Subsection (b) against a registered or licensed architect or engineer in this state, who designs, plans, or inspects the construction of an improvement to real property or equipment attached to real property, not later than 10 years after the substantial completion of the improvement or the beginning of operation of the equipment in an action arising out of a defective or unsafe condition of the real property, the improvement, or the equipment.

(b) This section applies to suit for:
> (1) injury, damage, or loss to real or personal property;
> (2) personal injury;
> (3) wrongful death;
> (4) contribution; or
> (5) indemnity.

(c) If the claimant presents a written claim for damages, contribution, or indemnity to the architect or engineer within the 10-year limitations period, the period is extended for two years from the day the claim is presented.

§ 16.009. Persons furnishing construction or repair of improvements.

(a) A claimant must bring suit for damages for a claim listed in Subsection (b) against a person who constructs or repairs an improvement to real property not later than 10 years after the substantial completion of the improvement in an action arising out of a defective or unsafe condition of the real property or a deficiency in the construction or repair of the improvement.

(b) This section applies to suit for:
> (1) injury, damage, or loss to real or personal property;
> (2) personal injury;
> (3) wrongful death;

(4) contribution; or
(5) indemnity.
(c) If the claimant presents a written claim for damages, contribution, or
indemnity to the person performing or furnishing the construction or repair
work during the 10-year limitations period, the period is extended for two
years from the date the claim is presented.
(d) If the damage, injury, or death occurs during the 10th year of the
limitations period, the claimant may bring suit not later than two years after
the day the cause of action accrues.
(e) This section does not bar an action:
(1) on a written warranty, guaranty, or other contract that expressly provides
for a longer effective period;
(2) against a person in actual possession or control of the real property at the
time that the damage, injury, or death occurs; or
(3) based on willful misconduct or fraudulent
concealment in connection with the performance of the construction or repair.
(f) This section does not extend or affect a period prescribed for bringing an
action under any other law of this state.

These same provision apply to contracts as well as personal injury or
property damage.

Other Written Contracts

See Appendix B for the statutes of limitations periods for the states in which you do business.

All other written contracts, not falling among the exceptions above, can
clearly be destroyed after the statute of limitations period, if not sooner.
Because a lawsuit can be brought in a number of different locations, you
must be guided by the rules for the state where the property or performance
in question is located, the state where either party has offices, or the state
where the breach occurred.

See Chapter 8 for details.

While the records need not be kept any longer than the statute of
limitations period, they may, in fact, be destroyed at an earlier date. Review
the factors carefully to determine whether a shorter period is appropriate.

Contract documentation (including change orders) should be kept from
the date of termination of the contract plus the designated retention period,
typically while the contract is active plus six years (ACT+6) or active plus
ten years (ACT+10).

The specific records supporting the implementation of the contract such
as reports, work products, drawings, and shipments, which represent final
products or deliverables under the contract, need only be kept for the statute
of limitations period, typically six or ten years.

CLIENT RECORDS

See Appendix B for a listing of the various statutes of limitations covering professional liability.

Legal, accounting, consulting, advertising firms, and others maintain
records of client projects and activities. Rarely, if ever, does a legal
requirement exist for these records unless they are held in a custodial or
fiduciary capacity. For activities such as medical or legal, the statute of
limitations for professional liability should be considered when determining
the legal retention period. The statute of limitations for professional liability
ranges from two to ten years after the last contact with the client, depending
on the state. Records can then be safely destroyed within this two to ten year
period, although some firms will keep them longer for future reference.

MANUFACTURING RECORDS

The kinds of products manufactured generally establishes the legal retention requirements for manufacturing records. Products such as drugs, nuclear material, automobiles, automobile tires, and hazardous chemicals are regulated by agencies which specify retention periods. Because this book is geared toward general business and cannot provide specific guidance for all industries, you are encouraged to contact your state or federal regulatory agencies for the unique requirements for your industry.

See Appendix B for the specific statute of limitations for personal injury in the states where you do business.

All states recognize the concept of product liability. You are responsible for injury resulting from products manufactured or distributed by your organization. The statute of limitations generally begins at the time an individual was injured by your product and runs two to three years.

Currently eleven states have laws similar to the following product liability statute which run from the time the product was first sold:

Arizona Revised Statutes

§ 12-551. Product liability.

A product liability action as defined in § 12-681 shall be commenced and prosecuted within the period prescribed in § 12-542, except that no product liability action may be commenced and prosecuted if the cause of action accrues more than twelve years after the product was first sold for use or consumption, unless the cause of action is based upon the negligence of the manufacturer or seller or a breach of an express warranty provided by the manufacturer or seller.

States with statutes of limitation on product liability starting from the time the product was first sold: Alabama, Arizona, Florida, Illinois, Kansas, Nebraska, New Hampshire, North Carolina, Oregon, Rhode Island, and Washington

Those states with this type of product liability statute of limitations limit the exposure to lawsuits against the manufacturer for the period of time stated—"after the product is first sold for use or consumption." Those states not adopting this provision permit a lawsuit to be initiated within two to three years of the date of injury. This extends liability for an indefinitely long period of time— twenty, thirty, or a hundred years after the product was originally brought to the marketplace.

A manufacturer is not fully protected, however, by the Arizona-type statute when the injuries occur in states which do not have similar product liability statutes of limitations. The United States Congress is reviewing product liability to develop a uniform statute of limitations, limit risk for product manufacturers, and reduce liability claims.

In today's environment, product manufacturers cannot safely destroy records related to product development, testing, design, and manufacturing until the product ceases to be used. These records are excellent candidates for microfilm because they must be kept for very long periods of time, perhaps indefinitely.

See Chapter 8 for details

The manufacturer can expect its records to be subpoenaed in product litigation because only it has the product records necessary to determine liability. Carefully review the strategies for statutes of limitation because some courts may expect the manufacturer to preserve records for the public welfare and may not accept destruction of records after any time. Most manufacturers keep these types of records for very long periods of time.

See Chapter 8 and the
contract section in this
chapter.

Similar considerations apply to improvements to real property. While most states have limited liability for contractors, architects, surveyors, and others, many still allow law suits to be initiated any time an injury occurs. If the improvements are in states with statutes of limitations starting from the time of substantial completion, then you can safety destroy records after that time. If the improvements are in other states, then you have to retain records for longer periods.

ACCOUNTING RECORDS

See Chapter 9 for the
requirement related to tax
records.

Legal requirements are generally not placed on accounting records except when they support tax returns. Statutes and regulations do not address accounts receivable, accounts payable, banking or other records normally maintained by a business, except for payroll records as they relate to possible discrimination or tax purposes.

RECORDS MANAGEMENT DOCUMENTATION

Documentation supporting the records management program should be preserved to demonstrate that records are created, maintained and destroyed as part of a regular business program without intent to defraud and deceive. Some of the documentation usually maintained includes the following:

- Documentation supporting the development of the general records management program, including specifically the records retention program,

- Written procedures including the procedures in effect each year (rather than just the current procedures),

- Written approval for the records management program,

- Documentation of the destruction of records under a records retention program, and

- Audit reports indicating compliance with the program.

No specific legal requirements exist controlling how you document your records management program. Many court decisions, however, indicate that this documentation is important to show a court or regulatory agency that you have established a reasonable program and implemented procedures to comply with that program.

As with any other records for which there are no specific retention periods, you must retain the documents supporting the recordkeeping program for a "reasonable period of time" —long enough to demonstrate a pattern of activity and regular compliance.

Some organizations keep this documentation for about ten years while others keep it for longer or shorter periods of time based upon their estimate of what constitutes a reasonable retention period. The decision should reflect the nature of your organization, the likelihood of litigation or government audit, and the volume of records involved.

POLICIES AND PROCEDURES

Documentation of other policies and procedures should also be maintained for approximately ten years to demonstrate that regular procedures were followed, similar to the records management documentation.

SPECIAL INDUSTRIES

There are unique requirements set by federal and state agencies for some industries. You should contact the relevant regulatory agencies to determine which special requirements apply to your organization.

CONCLUSION   **CHAPTER 11**

☐ Records documenting the organization of corporations and partnerships are governed by state laws which rarely specify records retention periods.

☐ Record retention periods for written contracts are generally determined from the statutes of limitations which affect the four categories of contracts: government contracts, sales contracts under the Uniform Commercial Code, contracts related to improvements to real property, and all other written contracts.

☐ No legal requirements exist for client records kept by law, accounting, consulting, or advertising firms, but the statutes of limitation for professional liability for medical and legal organizations should be considered.

☐ Record retention requirements for manufacturers generally depend upon the products manufactured. Under product liability statutes of limitations in some states, manufacturers can be sued for injury caused by their products for only a specified period after the product was first sold. In the other states, the manufacturer can be sued for two to three years after the date of injury, regardless of how long the product has been in the marketplace.

☐ Preserve the records supporting your policies and procedures, including your records management program, for a reasonable period of time, such as ten years, in order to demonstrate that records were created, maintained, and destroyed in the regular course of business under an approved records management program and without intent to defraud or deceive.

☐ Most industries have unique recordkeeping requirements governed by federal or state agencies. You should contact the relevant regulatory agencies to determine what additional requirements apply to your organization.

Chapter 12 Records Retention Periods for Selected Common Business Records

You are now ready to identify the records retention requirements for your organization. The information presented in this chapter is based on the extensive analysis presented earlier in this book and the applicable legal requirements.

See Chapter 14 for details about customizing the program for your organization.

The information presented here will be sufficient for many organizations to determine their minimum, maximum, and typical retention periods for records. Depending on the nature of your business, the states in which you do business, and the amount of risk you are willing to take, one of the three stated retention periods will probably be appropriate for your organization. Part D of this book provides additional help in customizing your records retention periods to your organization's needs.

To simplify the presentation of Figure 12.1, the Legal Group File used as a basis for the various retention requirements has been placed in Appendix G. You may wish to review that analysis when making your retention decisions.

DESCRIPTION OF FIGURE 12.1

Function

The listing in Figure 12.1 is organized by functions. A function is an activity of an organization rather than a particular department. Many individuals within your organization, for example, handle accounts payable records, although your accounting department is ultimately responsible for them.

Records assigned to the same functional group generally have the same or similar retention periods. This similarity occurs because either the law relates to a particular functional activity rather than specific records or your organization needs most of the records in the functional area for the same period of time.

You should assign someone or some group within the organization as the "Office of Record" to take responsibility for maintaining the "official" set of records for each function defined for the records retention period. In some cases, someone in your organization will already be responsible for certain records; in other cases, you must designate who will be responsible. Records, other than the official set, may be destroyed after the users no longer need them for daily activities.

Records

The records are listed in alphabetical order by function. You should review the list to determine the records maintained by your organization. In some cases, you will maintain similar records but may refer to them by different names.

See Chapter 22 for an explanation of legal groups and Appendix G for the Legal Group File used to produce this figure.

Legal Group

This code indicates the legal group assigned to the record to identify the applicable legal requirement. The legal group is a summary of the legal requirements taken from all those laws which relate to the same records or functional activity.

Legal group code "NONE" was assigned to records not covered by any legal requirements. The retention period for these records will be determined solely by the user period discussed below.

Legal Period

If a legal requirement has been identified, then the minimum and maximum retention period is shown. As a general rule, the minimum requirements are those of the federal government and represent specific retention periods which you must follow; the maximum requirements are often those of specific states that correspond to legal consideration such as statutes of limitations. You may select a legal retention period less than the maximum based on the strategies explained in this book.

User Period

This column shows the typical periods during which records are needed by record users for operational purposes—to do their jobs. The user periods will vary significantly for each organization. A one- to three-year user period was assigned, since three years is always "reasonable," unless experience and logic indicated some other typical user period. You may wish to take these user periods or develop other ones which better meet the needs of your organization.

Typical Period

This column shows typical records retention periods for each type of record. If a legal requirement has been identified for a particular record, the retention period shown is for at least the minimum legal requirement, sometimes the maximum requirement, and, when appropriate, sometimes a typical legal period reflecting a reasonable legal period for approximately 80 percent of the states. When no legal retention requirements or considerations were identified, or the typical user period was longer than the legal period, the user period was assigned.

See Appendix B for the statutes of limitation and Appendix D for the tax requirements in the states.

Your organization may take some risks by selecting the minimum legal requirements, depending on the states in which you do business. The minimum retention requirements shown should meet the requirements of the United States federal government but not those for some of the states.

Similarly, the maximum legal retention requirements meet the specific retention requirements for the United States federal government and *all* 50 states; but they may not meet the longest legal considerations—such as statutes of limitations—that are not recordkeeping requirements but which some feel should be followed, anyway. If your organization only does business in certain states, the maximum legal retention period may be too long and create unnecessary burdens.

The "typical" legal retention period corresponds to the requirements found in most states, when records retention requirements exist, and excludes those state requirements which are clearly exceptional. You take some risk by adopting the typical retention period, but the risks are minimal, provided you destroy records according to the guidelines presented in Part D. For most organizations, the typical records retention periods will be sufficiently conservative to alleviate your concerns and the concerns of others.

ABBREVIATIONS USED IN FIGURE 12.1

ACT: Active; while the matter is active. For example, while the contract is active or you own the property.

ATX: ACT+TAX; active plus tax return filing date.

CY: Current year; all records created in the same year are treated as though they were created on December 31 of that year.

IND: Indefinite; the retention for certain records cannot be determined in advance so those records must be reviewed periodically to determine whether or not they can be destroyed.

SUP: Superseded; keep the records until they are replaced by more current ones.

TAX: Tax return filing date; all records created to document information in a tax return, including the tax return, are treated as though they were created on the day the tax return was filed.

+: Plus; some retention periods consist of two or more components. For example, capital asset records should be kept while they are active plus six years (ACT + 06).

All records retention periods are in "years" unless months (M) or days (D) are specified.

For convenience and to eliminate mistakes, *all records retention periods should start on the last day of the year in which the records were created (CY)*, unless otherwise indicated.

Figure 12.1 Records Retention Periods for Common Business Records

Function Record	Legal Group	Legal Period Min.	Legal Period Max.	User Period	Typical Period

Accounting

Accounts Payable

accounts payable	ACC000	TAX+03	TAX+06	03	CY+04
accounts payable invoices	ACC000	TAX+03	TAX+06	03	CY+04
accounts payable ledgers	ACC000	TAX+03	TAX+06	03	CY+04
amortization records	ACC000	TAX+03	TAX+06	03	CY+04
bills	ACC000	TAX+03	TAX+06	03	CY+04
cash disbursements	ACC000	TAX+03	TAX+06	03	CY+04
commission statements	ACC000	TAX+03	TAX+06	03	CY+04
cost accounting records	ACC000	TAX+03	TAX+06	03	CY+04
cost sheets	ACC000	TAX+03	TAX+06	03	CY+04
cost statements	ACC000	TAX+03	TAX+06	03	CY+04
credit card charge slips	ACC000	TAX+03	TAX+06	03	CY+04
credit card statements	ACC000	TAX+03	TAX+06	03	CY+04
debit advices	ACC000	TAX+03	TAX+06	03	CY+04
donations	ACC000	TAX+03	TAX+06	03	CY+04
expense reports	ACC000	TAX+03	TAX+06	03	CY+04
invoices	ACC000	TAX+03	TAX+06	03	CY+04
petty cash records	ACC000	TAX+03	TAX+06	03	CY+04
property taxes	ACC000	TAX+03	TAX+06	03	CY+04
purchase requisitions	ACC000	TAX+03	TAX+06	03	CY+04
royalty payments	ACC000	TAX+03	TAX+06	03	CY+04
travel expenses	ACC000	TAX+03	TAX+06	03	CY+04
unemployment insurance payments	ACC000	TAX+03	TAX+06	03	CY+04
vouchers	ACC000	TAX+03	TAX+06	03	CY+04
workers compensation insurance payments	ACC000	TAX+03	TAX+06	03	CY+04

Accounts Receivable

accounts receivable	ACC000	TAX+03	TAX+06	03	CY+04
accounts receivable ledgers	ACC000	TAX+03	TAX+06	03	CY+04
cash books	ACC000	TAX+03	TAX+06	03	CY+04
cash journals	ACC000	TAX+03	TAX+06	03	CY+04
cash receipts	ACC000	TAX+03	TAX+06	03	CY+04
cash sales slips	ACC000	TAX+03	TAX+06	03	CY+04
collection notices	NONE	–	–	ACT	ACT
collection records	NONE	–	–	ACT	ACT
credit advices	ACC000	TAX+03	TAX+06	03	CY+04
receipts	ACC000	TAX+03	TAX+06	03	CY+04
sales receipts	ACC000	TAX+03	TAX+06	03	CY+04
uncollected accounts	ACC500	TAX+03	TAX+06	03	CY+04

Capital Property

acquisitions	ACC100	ATX+03	ATX+06	ACT	ACY+04
capital asset records	ACC100	ATX+03	ATX+06	ACT	ACY+04
depreciation schedules	ACC100	ATX+03	ATX+06	01	ACY+04
fixed assets	ACC100	ATX+03	ATX+06	ACT	ACY+04
material transfer files	ACC100	ATX+03	ATX+06	03	ACY+04
mortgage payments	ACC000	TAX+03	TAX+06	03	CY+04
plant ledgers	ACC100	ATX+03	ATX+06	03	ACY+04
property detail records	ACC100	ATX+03	ATX+06	03	ACY+04
property inventory	ACC100	ATX+03	ATX+06	ACT	ACY+04
property, sold	ACC000	TAX+03	TAX+06	03	CY+04

Figure 12.1 Records Retention Periods for Common Business Records (continued)

Function Record	Legal Group	Legal Period Min.	Legal Period Max.	User Period	Typical Period
General					
account ledgers	ACC000	TAX+03	TAX+06	03	CY+04
accounting procedures	POL200	00	IND	ACT	ACT+10
balance sheets	ACC000	TAX+03	TAX+06	03	CY+04
books of accounts	ACC000	TAX+03	TAX+06	03	CY+04
credit applications	NONE	–	–	01	01
general ledger, annual	ACC000	TAX+03	TAX+06	03	CY+04
general ledger, monthly	NONE	–	–	01	01
journal entries	ACC000	TAX+03	TAX+06	03	CY+04
journals	ACC000	TAX+03	TAX+06	03	CY+04
ledgers	ACC000	TAX+03	TAX+06	03	CY+04
ledgers, subsidiary	ACC000	TAX+03	TAX+06	03	CY+04
registers	ACC000	TAX+03	TAX+06	03	CY+04
trial balances	ACC000	TAX+03	TAX+06	03	CY+04
Payroll					
garnishment accounting	ACC000	TAX+03	TAX+06	03	CY+04
garnishment orders	LEG200	00	ACT	ACT	ACT
payroll checks	ACC300	TAX+04	TAX+06	03	CY+04
payroll history	ACC300	TAX+04	TAX+06	03	CY+04
payroll records	ACC300	TAX+04	TAX+06	03	CY+04
payroll registers	ACC000	TAX+03	TAX+06	03	CY+04

Administration

Function Record	Legal Group	Legal Period Min.	Legal Period Max.	User Period	Typical Period
General					
authorizations, table of	POL200	00	IND	ACT	ACT+10
calendar books	NONE	–	–	01	01
chronological files	NONE	–	–	01	01
correspondence (see specific listing)	NONE	–	–	01	01
directives	POL100	00	IND	ACT	ACT+10
feasibility studies	NONE	–	–	03	ACT
organization charts	NONE	–	–	ACT	ACT
policies	POL100	00	IND	ACT	ACT+10
policy statements	POL100	00	IND	ACT	ACT+10
procedure manuals	POL200	00	IND	ACT	ACT+10
reading files	NONE	–	–	01	01
table of authorizations	POL200	00	IND	ACT	ACT+10
telephone calls	NONE	–	–	30D	30D
Property / Facilities					
building permits	LEG200	00	ACT	ACT	ACT
deeds	CON000	ACT+03	ACT+20	ACT	ACT+06
lease abstracts	NONE	–	–	ACT	ACT
lease acquisitions	NONE	–	–	ACT	ACT
maintenance records	NONE	–	–	ACT	ACT
motor vehicle maintenance	NONE	–	–	ACT	ACT
motor vehicle records	NONE	–	–	ACT	ACT
office improvements	NONE	–	–	ACT	ACT
office layout	NONE	–	–	ACT	ACT
property summaries	ACC100	ATX+03	ATX+06	ACT	ACY+04
property title	CON000	ACT+03	ACT+20	ACT	ACT+06
real estate records	NONE	–	–	ACT	ACT
repair records	NONE	–	–	ACT	ACT
water rights	CON000	ACT+03	ACT+20	ACT	ACT+06
zoning permits	LEG200	00	ACT	ACT	ACT

Figure 12.1 Records Retention Periods for Common Business Records (continued)

Function Record	Legal Group	Legal Period Min.	 Max.	User Period	Typical Period
Records Management					
computer tape indexes	NONE	–	–	ACT	ACT
record destruction documentation	POL200	00	IND	03	10
records inventory	NONE	–	–	01	01
records management procedures	POL200	00	IND	ACT	ACT+10
Security					
badge lists	NONE	–	–	ACT	ACT
employee clearance listings	NONE	–	–	ACT	ACT
visitor registration	NONE	–	–	01	01

Business Organization

Function Record	Legal Group	Legal Period Min.	 Max.	User Period	Typical Period
Partnership					
partnership agreements	CON000	ACT+03	ACT+20	ACT	ACT+06
Corporation					
S.E.C. filing	BUS120	03	IND	01	10
annual reports	BUS120	03	IND	IND	IND
articles of incorporation	BUS100	03	IND	IND	IND
board of directors meeting minutes	BUS120	03	IND	IND	IND
board of directors meeting notices	BUS120	03	IND	01	10
bonds, surety	CON000	ACT+03	ACT+20	ACT	ACT+06
bylaws	BUS100	03	IND	ACT	IND
capital stock certificates	BUS110	03	IND	ACT	ACT+03
capital stock ledgers	BUS110	03	IND	03	ACT+03
capital stock records	BUS110	03	IND	03	ACT+03
capital stock sales	BUS110	03	IND	03	ACT+03
capital stock transfers	BUS110	03	IND	03	ACT+03
certificates of incorporation	BUS100	03	IND	IND	IND
corporate reorganizations	BUS120	03	IND	03	10
dividend records	BUS120	03	IND	03	10
fidelity bonds	CON000	ACT+03	ACT+20	ACT	ACT+06
incorporation records	BUS000	03	IND	IND	IND
minute books	BUS120	03	IND	IND	IND
proxies, signed	BUS120	03	IND	01	10
quarterly reports	NONE	–	–	01	01
shareholder meeting minutes	BUS120	03	IND	10	10
shareholder meeting notices	BUS120	03	IND	01	10
shareholder proxies	BUS120	03	IND	01	10
stock ledgers	BUS110	03	IND	ACT	ACT+03
stockholders meetings	BUS120	03	IND	10	10
stockholders proxies	BUS120	03	IND	01	10
stockholders, listing of	BUS110	03	IND	ACT	ACT+03
voting records	BUS120	03	IND	01	10
General					
business permits	LEG200	00	ACT	ACT	ACT
charters	BUS000	00	IND	ACT	IND
licenses	LEG200	00	ACT	ACT	ACT
mergers	CON000	ACT+03	ACT+20	ACT	ACT+06

Figure 12.1 Records Retention Periods for Common Business Records (continued)

Function Record	Legal Group	Legal Period Min.	Legal Period Max.	User Period	Typical Period
Finance					
Banking					
bank deposits	ACC000	TAX+03	TAX+06	03	CY+04
bank reconciliations	ACC000	TAX+03	TAX+06	01	CY+04
bank statements	ACC000	TAX+03	TAX+06	03	CY+04
check registers	ACC000	TAX+03	TAX+06	03	CY+04
check stubs	ACC000	TAX+03	TAX+06	03	CY+04
checks, canceled	ACC000	TAX+03	TAX+06	03	CY+04
deposit slips	ACC000	TAX+03	TAX+06	03	CY+04
wire transfers	ACC000	TAX+03	TAX+06	03	CY+04
General					
audit reports, external	NONE	–	–	03	03
audit reports, internal	NONE	–	–	01	01
budget work papers	NONE	–	–	01	01
budgets - 1 year	NONE	–	–	CY+01	CY+01
budgets - 5 year	NONE	–	–	CY+05	CY+05
financial plan	NONE	–	–	ACT	ACT
financial reports - annual	BUS120	03	IND	03	10
financial reports - monthly	NONE	–	–	01	01
financial statements	BUS120	03	IND	03	10
financial statements, certified	BUS120	03	IND	03	10
forecasts - 1 year	NONE	–	–	CY+01	CY+01
forecasts - 5 year	NONE	–	–	CY+05	CY+05
profit and loss statements	BUS120	03	IND	03	10
profit reports	NONE	–	–	03	01
Investments / Insurance					
bond investments	ACC100	ATX+03	ATX+06	ACT	ACY+04
futures investments	ACC100	ATX+03	ATX+06	ACT	ACY+04
insurance policies, active	CON000	ACT+03	ACT+20	ACT	ACT+06
insurance policies, canceled	CON010	03	20	03	06
inventory, property	ACC100	ATX+03	ATX+06	ACT	ACY+04
investments	ACC100	ATX+03	ATX+06	ACT	ACY+04
letters of credit	CON000	ACT+03	ACT+20	ACT	ACT+06
mortgage records	CON000	ACT+03	ACT+20	ACT	ACT+06
notes, canceled	CON010	03	20	03	06
notes, outstanding	CON000	ACT+03	ACT+20	ACT	ACT+06
notes, paid	CON010	03	20	03	06
options contracts	CON000	ACT+03	ACT+20	ACT	ACT+06
options and futures	ACC100	ATX+03	ATX+06	ACT	ACY+04
securities sales	ACC000	TAX+03	TAX+06	03	CY+04
stock investments	ACC100	ATX+03	ATX+06	ACT	ACY+04
General					
client files	PRO000	02	10	ACT	ACT+06
project files	NONE	–	–	ACT	ACT+03
reference files	NONE	–	–	ACT	ACT

Figure 12.1 Records Retention Periods for Common Business Records (continued)

Function Record	Legal Group	Legal Period Min.	Max.	User Period	Typical Period

Legal

Contract Administration

agreements	CON000	ACT+03	ACT+20	ACT	ACT+06
buy / sell agreements	CON000	ACT+03	ACT+20	ACT	ACT+06
contracts, general					
contract compliance	CON010	03	20	03	06
contract documentation	CON000	ACT+03	ACT+20	ACT+03	ACT+06
contracts, changes to	CON000	ACT+03	ACT+20	ACT	ACT+06
employment contracts	CON000	ACT+03	ACT+20	ACT	ACT+06
contracts, government					
contract compliance	CON510	ACT+03	ACT+03	03	ACT+03
contract documentation	CON500	ACT+03	ACT+03	ACT	ACT+03
cost accounting	CON520	04	04	03	04
pay administration	CON530	02	02	03	03
procurement	CON520	04	04	03	04
production	CON520	04	04	03	04
salary administration	CON530	02	02	03	03
contracts, property improvement					
contract compliance	CON310	04	20	03	10
contract documentation	CON300	ACT+04	ACT+20	ACT	ACT+10
contracts, sale					
contract compliance	CON110	03	06	03	04
contract documentation	CON100	ACT+03	ACT+06	ACT	ACT+04
easements	CON000	ACT+03	ACT+20	ACT	ACT+06
leases	CON000	ACT+03	ACT+20	ACT	ACT+06
mortgages	CON000	ACT+03	ACT+20	ACT	ACT+06
patent agreements	CON000	ACT+03	ACT+20	ACT	ACT+06
promissory notes	CON000	ACT+03	ACT+20	ACT	ACT+06
title documentation	CON000	ACT+03	ACT+20	ACT	ACT+06
warranties, product	CON000	ACT+03	ACT+20	ACT	ACT+06

General

legal opinions	LEG000	00	IND	ACT	ACT+03
patent applications	NONE	–	–	ACT	ACT
patents	CON000	ACT+03	ACT+20	ACT	ACT+06
trademark records	CON000	ACT+03	ACT+20	ACT	ACT+06

Legal / Tax Compliance

employment tax filings	ACC000	TAX+03	TAX+06	03	CY+04
excise tax filings	ACC000	TAX+03	TAX+06	03	CY+04
income tax filings	ACC000	TAX+03	TAX+06	03	CY+04
sales tax filings	ACC000	TAX+03	TAX+06	03	CY+04
tax returns	ACC000	TAX+03	TAX+06	03	CY+04
tax returns, employment	ACC000	TAX+03	TAX+06	03	CY+04
tax returns, excise	ACC000	TAX+03	TAX+06	03	CY+04
tax returns, income	ACC000	TAX+03	TAX+06	03	CY+04
tax returns, motor fuel	ACC000	TAX+03	TAX+06	03	CY+04
tax returns, property	ACC000	TAX+03	TAX+06	03	CY+04
tax returns, sales	ACC000	TAX+03	TAX+06	03	CY+04
tax returns, unemployment	ACC000	TAX+03	TAX+06	03	CY+04
tax returns, use	ACC000	TAX+03	TAX+06	03	CY+04

Figure 12.1 Records Retention Periods for Common Business Records (continued)

Function Record	Legal Group	Legal Period Min.	Max.	User Period	Typical Period
Litigation / Claims					
affidavits	LIT000	00	ACT	ACT	ACT
claims, affirmative action	LIT000	00	ACT	ACT	ACT
complaints	LIT000	00	ACT	ACT	ACT
court case files	LIT000	00	ACT	ACT	ACT
court records	LIT000	00	ACT	ACT	ACT
depositions	LIT000	00	ACT	ACT	ACT
disputes	LIT000	00	ACT	ACT	ACT
exhibits	LIT000	00	ACT	ACT	ACT
grievances	LIT000	00	ACT	ACT	ACT
litigation files	LIT000	00	ACT	ACT	ACT

Personnel

Benefits					
actuarial records	EMP100	03	06	ACT	ACT+06
disability records	EMP120	03	IND	03	IND
education assistance files	EMP100	03	06	03	06
employee benefits	EMP100	03	06	03	06
employee relocation records	EMP100	03	06	03	06
employee stock purchase agreements	CON000	ACT+03	ACT+20	ACT	ACT+06
incentive plans	EMP110	ACT+01	ACT+06	ACT	ACT+06
pension plan vesting files	EMP120	03	IND	IND	IND
pension plans	EMP110	ACT+01	ACT+06	ACT	ACT+06
profit sharing plans	EMP110	ACT+01	ACT+06	ACT	ACT+06
retirement benefits	EMP120	03	IND	IND	IND
retirement plans	EMP110	ACT+01	ACT+06	ACT	ACT+06
service records	EMP120	03	IND	IND	IND
sick leave benefits accrued	EMP100	03	06	ACT	06
thrift plan reports	EMP100	03	06	03	06
years of services	EMP120	03	IND	IND	IND
Equal Employment Opportunity					
affirmative action plan	NONE	–	–	ACT	ACT
form EEO-2	LEG000	00	IND	01	03
racial / ethnic identification report (Form EEO-1)	LEG000	00	IND	01	03
General					
attendance records	EMP000	01	03	01	03
collective bargaining agreement	CON000	ACT+03	ACT+20	ACT	ACT+06
driving exams	TRA100	ACT+03	ACT+03	ACT	ACT+03
employee manuals	POL200	00	IND	ACT	ACT+10
job descriptions	POL200	00	IND	ACT	ACT+10
labor union contracts	CON000	ACT+03	ACT+20	ACT	ACT+06
labor union meetings	EMP000	01	03	01	03
performance standards	POL200	00	IND	ACT	ACT+10
Health and Safety					
accident reports	EMP700	CY+05	CY+05	03	CY+05
audiometric tests	EMP510	02	02	03	03
damage reports	EMP700	CY+05	CY+05	03	CY+05
elevator certification	LEG200	00	ACT	ACT	ACT
emergency action plans	EMP710	ACT	ACT	ACT	ACT
employee exposure records	ENV100	30	30	03	30
employee medical complaints	EMP700	CY+05	CY+05	03	CY+05

Figure 12.1 Records Retention Periods for Common Business Records (continued)

Function Record	Legal Group	Legal Period Min.	Max.	User Period	Typical Period
Personnel (cont.)					
Health and Safety (cont.)					
employee medical records	EMP500	ACT+30	ACT+30	ACT	ACT+30
environmental monitoring records	EMP700	CY+05	CY+05	03	CY+05
environmental testing methodology	EMP700	CY+05	CY+05	03	CY+05
environmental testing reports	EMP700	CY+05	CY+05	03	CY+05
environmental testing worksheets	EMP700	CY+05	CY+05	03	CY+05
fire extinguisher records	EMP711	01	01	01	01
fire prevention programs	EMP710	ACT	ACT	ACT	ACT
hazard communications records	ENV100	30	30	03	30
hazardous exposure records	ENV100	30	30	03	30
hazardous substance identity records	ENV100	30	30	03	30
health and safety bulletins	EMP700	CY+05	CY+05	03	CY+05
health insurance claims	NONE	–	–	ACT	ACT
injury reports	EMP700	CY+05	CY+05	03	CY+05
log, accident (OSHA Form 200)	EMP700	CY+05	CY+05	03	CY+05
log, injury (OSHA Form 200)	EMP700	CY+05	CY+05	03	CY+05
material safety data sheets	ENV100	30	30	03	30
medical records	EMP500	ACT+30	ACT+30	ACT	ACT+30
medical surveillance	ENV100	30	30	03	30
noise exposure measurements	EMP510	02	02	03	02
radiation exposure records	EMP500	ACT+30	ACT+30	03	ACT+30
safety records	EMP700	CY+05	CY+05	03	CY+05
supplementary records (OSHA Form 101)	EMP700	CY+05	CY+05	01	CY+05
toxic substance exposure records	ENV100	30	30	03	30
Personnel Actions					
applications, hired	EMP900	01	01	01	01
applications, rejected	EMP900	01	01	01	01
apprenticeship records	EMP910	02	02	01	02
demotion records	EMP900	01	01	01	01
education records	EMP900	01	01	01	01
employee evaluations	EMP300	01	03	03	03
employment history, current	EMP310	01	03	ACT	IND
employment history, previous	EMP900	01	01	03	03
employment summary records	EMP310	01	03	ACT	IND
hiring records	EMP900	01	01	01	01
job annoucements	EMP900	01	01	01	01
layoff records	EMP300	01	03	03	03
personnel actions	EMP300	01	03	03	03
personnel files, active	EMP120	03	IND	ACT	IND
personnel files, terminated	EMP300	01	03	03	03
promotion records	EMP300	01	03	03	03
tenure records	EMP900	01	01	ACT	ACT
termination records	EMP900	01	01	03	03
testing records	EMP900	01	01	01	01
training records	EMP900	01	01	ACT	ACT
transfer records	EMP900	01	01	01	01
work appraisals	EMP900	01	01	03	03

Figure 12.1 Records Retention Periods for Common Business Records (continued)

Function Record	Legal Group	Legal Period Min.	Max.	User Period	Typical Period
Personnel (cont.)					
Salary Administration					
bonuses	EMP900	01	01	01	01
cost of living records	EMP900	01	01	01	01
earnings records	EMP000	02	03	03	03
form W-2	ACC000	TAX+03	TAX+06	01	CY+04
form W-4	ACC000	TAX+03	TAX+06	01	CY+04
pay rates	EMP000	02	03	ACT	ACT+03
payroll deductions	ACC000	TAX+03	TAX+06	03	CY+04
salary surveys	EMP000	02	03	ACT	ACT
time cards	ACC000	TAX+03	TAX+06	03	CY+04
time sheets	ACC000	TAX+03	TAX+06	03	CY+04
wage rate tables	EMP000	02	03	03	03
Product Development					
blueprints	NONE	–	–	ACT	ACT
design records	MAN000	1	IND	ACT	IND
engineering records	NONE	–	–	ACT	ACT
laboratory reports	MAN000	1	IND	ACT	IND
product design specifications	MAN000	1	IND	ACT	IND
product testing	MAN000	1	IND	ACT	IND
production tool design records	NONE	–	–	ACT	ACT
research records	MAN000	1	IND	ACT	IND
testing reports	MAN000	1	IND	ACT	IND
Production					
inspection records	MAN000	1	IND	03	IND
product inventory	ACC100	ATX+03	ATX+06	03	ACY+04
production costs	NONE	–	–	01	01
production reports	NONE	–	–	01	01
production specifications	NONE	–	–	ACT	ACT
quality control reports	MAN000	1	IND	01	IND
warehouse inventory records	ACC100	ATX+03	ATX+06	03	ACY+04
work orders	NONE	–	–	ACT	ACT
work status reports	NONE	–	–	01	01
Public Relations					
advertising	ADV000	CY+01	CY+01	ACT	ACY+01
artwork	NONE	–	–	ACT	03
customer complaints	LIT000	00	ACT	01	ACT
government docket files	NONE	–	–	ACT	ACT
legislation, pending	NONE	–	–	ACT	ACT
mailing lists	NONE	–	–	ACT	ACT
market research data	NONE	–	–	ACT	ACT
media packets	NONE	–	–	IND	IND
news releases	NONE	–	–	CY+02	CY+02
newsletters, internal	NONE	–	–	IND	IND
newspaper clippings	NONE	–	–	ACT	ACT
publicity photographs	NONE	–	–	IND	IND
publicity records	NONE	–	–	IND	IND
slide presentations	NONE	–	–	03	03
speeches	NONE	–	–	03	03

Figure 12.1 Records Retention Periods for Common Business Records (continued)

Function Record	Legal Group	Legal Period Min.	Legal Period Max.	User Period	Typical Period
Purchasing					
bids, accepted	CON000	ACT+03	ACT+20	ACT	ACT+06
bids, rejected	NONE	–	–	01	01
catalogs	NONE	–	–	ACT	ACT
price lists	NONE	–	–	ACT	ACT
purchase orders	ACC000	TAX+03	TAX+06	03	CY+04
quotations	NONE	–	–	01	01
receiving documents	NONE	–	–	01	01
vendor literature	NONE	–	–	ACT	ACT
Sales					
back order records	NONE	–	–	01	01
customer credit files	NONE	–	–	ACT	ACT
customer lists	NONE	–	–	ACT	ACT
market surveys	NONE	–	–	ACT	ACT
marketing plans	NONE	–	–	ACT	ACT
orders	NONE	–	–	03	03
orders, acknowledgment	NONE	–	–	01	01
price lists	NONE	–	–	ACT	ACT
price proposals / quotations	NONE	–	–	ACT+01	ACT+01
proposals	NONE	–	–	ACT+01	ACT+01
sales activity records	NONE	–	–	01	01
sales records	NONE	–	–	01	01
sales reports	NONE	–	–	01	01
sales slips	ACC000	TAX+03	TAX+06	01	CY+04
service requests	NONE	–	–	01	01
Shipping / Transportation					
bills of lading	CON010	03	20	03	06
export declarations	FOR000	02	02	01	02
freight records	CON010	03	20	03	06
packing lists	CON010	03	20	03	06
shipping instructions	NONE	–	–	01	01
shipping manifests	CON010	03	20	03	06
shipping tickets	CON010	03	20	03	06
waybills	CON010	03	20	03	06

PART D — DEVELOPING A LEGALLY ACCEPTABLE RECORDS RETENTION PROGRAM

Chapter 13   Components of a Legally Acceptable Records Retention Program

You should establish appropriate procedures to protect your organization before embarking on a program to destroy records. In hundreds of state and federal court decisions handed down over the years, the courts have imposed fines, penalties, and sanctions for the inappropriate destruction of records.

While no state or federal law specifies how you must develop and operate a records retention program, the accumulated knowledge gained from court decisions does indicate which procedures are legally acceptable.

This chapter outlines the criteria by which a records retention program becomes legally acceptable. Chapter 14 incorporates these components into program procedures to help you meet the needs of your organization.

PROGRAM DEVELOPMENT

Component 1. Systematically develop the records retention program

A records retention program is systematically developed if done in the regular course of business and you evaluate the records, document how the program was created, and have the program properly approved. Systematic development ensures that the program addresses all retention requirements. It also establishes the fact that the retention program has been well conceived and executed over a period of time, rather than developed to deliberately destroy unfavorable documentary evidence prior to litigation, government investigation or audit.

A records retention program is not systematically developed if the decision to destroy records is based upon whim or impulse and you do not have a records retention schedule to guide their destruction.

PROGRAM SCOPE

Component 2. Address all your records in the records retention schedules, including reproductions

See Chapter 17 for the admissibility of microfilm and duplicate copies of records in evidence.

Records retention schedules which address only the original or "record" copy in paper form are inadequate to fully protect an organization. The law clearly indicates that reproductions of records have the same legal significance as the original and may be used in place of the original for all purposes including evidence.

Many records retention programs do not address the issue of "information copies" or "personal copies" maintained in the organization. Copies can be subpoenaed and used against the organization during litigation, government investigation or audit, even though the original records were properly destroyed under the records retention schedule. Personal copies of records may be particularly important during government investigations into price-fixing or anti-trust. Copies as well as the originals of records should, therefore, be covered by the records retention program.

RECORD MEDIA

Component 3. Address all media in the records retention schedules, including microfilm and machine-readable computer records

Most records retention schedules only provide for paper records. Some schedules specify when the records should be microfilmed and the original paper destroyed.

See Chapter 18 for the requirements of the Internal Revenue Service for maintaining computer records in machine-readable format even when the data has been printed onto paper.

You should provide for the destruction of microfilm records, computer records and other media in the records retention schedule. Rarely, if ever, should you retain microfilm copies of business records "forever." Make similar provisions to destroy machine-readable computer records, especially back-up records when they are no longer needed.

WRITTEN APPROVALS

Component 4. Obtain written approvals for the records retention schedules and the program procedures

The entire records retention program must be approved in writing by your chief executive officer, legal counsel, and tax advisor. Department requirements can also be approved in writing by their managers. These approvals demonstrate that the records retention program was systematically developed in the regular course of business, instead of in anticipation of litigation or government investigation. Copies of these approvals should be kept indefinitely.

Written approvals by key people in your organization also protect you. When records are actually destroyed under the records retention schedule, the approvals indicate that you acted on behalf of your organization, rather than out of self interest. Otherwise, you might be held personally liable for destroying the wrong records or destroying them at the wrong time.

RECORDS DESTRUCTION

Component 5. Systematically destroy records when permitted by the records retention program

Once you have an approved program, records should be systematically destroyed in accordance with the records retention program and in the regular course of business. Most organizations destroy records on a regular basis, generally every month or year. Never destroy records in a haphazard or selective manner, even when their destruction is permitted under the retention schedule, because it creates the impression that the records retention program is not properly administered.

PROGRAM MANAGEMENT

Component 6. Control and manage the operation of the records retention program

A records retention program does not function on its own. You must manage the program to ensure that it is up-to-date, your staff is properly trained, and destruction proceeds in an orderly manner. You should also be very familiar with its background and operation in order to testify in court, if necessary, about the program.

PROGRAM SUSPENSION

Component 7. Stop destroying records, even when permitted by the records retention programs, when litigation, government investigation or audit is pending or imminent

The destruction of records must stop immediately when the organization receives a notice of pending or imminent litigation, government investigation or audit, even when destruction is permitted under the records retention program. Otherwise, the company could be liable for obstruction of justice or contempt of court.

Any staff member receiving information regarding potential litigation, government investigation or audit should immediately inform your legal counsel or chief executive officer. Notices should be sent to managers, records custodians and other appropriate staff. Immediately stop the destruction of *all* records, since it is often unclear at first which records are involved. As more information becomes available to your legal counsel or tax advisor, permission may be granted to continue destroying records, not relevant to the litigation or investigation, under the records retention program.

PROGRAM DOCUMENTATION

Component 8. Maintain documentation supporting the development and implementation of the records retention program, including records retention schedules, procedures, changes in procedures, approvals, legal research, and listings of records destroyed

You must document the records retention program to demonstrate its systematic operation. The records supporting development of the program, original signed retention schedules, and listings of records destroyed, are critically important evidence showing that the records in question were destroyed in the regular course of business. You may be required to appear in court some day with the supporting documents and testify about the development and operation of the program.

The record of legal research performed indicates that you used your "best efforts" to find and comply with the retention requirements. Because some legal requirements are difficult to locate or interpret, an organization can easily and inadvertently fail to locate them. A court or government agency may be be less likely to impose harsh consequences on an organization when presented documented proof that it tried to comply with the law. While "ignorance of the law" is no defense for failure to comply with the law, a documented record of your efforts to locate statutes or regulations may spare you from harsh penalties.

CONCLUSION   **CHAPTER 13**

☐ Systematically develop the records retention program.

☐ Address all records in the records retention schedules, including reproductions.

☐ Address all media in the records retention schedules, including microfilm and machine-readable computer records.

☐ Obtain written approvals for the records retention schedules and program procedures.

☐ Systematically destroy records when permitted by the records retention program.

☐ Control the operation of the records retention program.

☐ Stop destroying records, even when permitted by the records retention programs, when litigation, government investigation or audit is pending or imminent.

☐ Maintain documentation supporting the development and implementation of the records retention program, including records retention schedules, procedures, changes in procedures, approvals, legal research, and listings of records destroyed.

Chapter 14 Advanced Records Retention Program Procedures

See also Records Retention Procedures, **Information Requirements Clearinghouse, Denver, Colorado. An order form is provided at the back of this book for your convenience.**

You now know the legally acceptable records retention requirements for most records. Some additional work will be necessary to customize the program to your business activities and to meet the unique needs of individuals within the organization. This chapter presents the major steps for developing and implementing a legally acceptable records retention program that meets the needs of your organization.

SCOPE AND PURPOSE

Determine the scope and purpose of your records retention program before you start. Because records are defined to include paper, microfilm, computer and other forms of commonly maintained records, you should approach your company's needs from a broad perspective. Most laws identify the requirements for recordkeeping without specifying their form.

See Chapter 3 for detail related to benefits of a records management program.

The program will provide more efficient access to valuable records and yield significant savings by reducing space and equipment requirements in addition to providing litigation protection and ensuring legal compliance.

PROGRAM RESPONSIBILITIES

You should begin by contacting those who generate and use records to determine their needs, what legal requirements apply, and how the program can best meet its legal obligations. Some organizations may designate a records manager and form a committee composed of people from major departments to coordinate the effort across the organization. Other, especially smaller organizations, should designate an administrative manager, preferably with records experience, to direct this effort.

POLICIES AND PROCEDURES

You should develop a policy statement that recognizes the scope and purpose of the project, designates the person responsible, and authorizes its implementation. Specific procedures implementing the program and a detailed records retention schedule will emerge as the program develops.

The statement of policy and approved procedures show that management supports the program.

RECORDS INVENTORY

You should perform a records inventory for all departments within the organization to ensure that the program covers all major records. The inventory can be as simple as a list of records maintained by each group (for smaller organizations) or a more formal and detailed inventory of each records series (for larger organizations). The degree of detail required depends upon the size of the organization and the amount of staff time available.

See Chapter 12 for a listing of records found in a typical organization.

A listing of records is often as valuable a tool as a formal inventory. Secretaries in each filing area can prepare this list in the format you specify.

USER INTERVIEWS

You maintain records first to meet the needs of record users and then to comply with the law. Meetings with record users should be scheduled to assess their needs and to determine how the recordkeeping program can best serve them.

See our listing in Chapter 12.

Your staff will have their own views of record requirements and will express their needs according to their experience and knowledge. These divergent and often contradictory views should be considered early in the process so that key individuals cooperate with the retention program and do not reject the retention periods during the final review stage or refuse to destroy records once the retention period expires.

LEGAL RESEARCH

Chapter 20 through 22 (Part F) provide the appropriate methodology for locating and organizing the legal research for a records retention program.

You can find many of the recordkeeping requirements imposed by government in this book. Special requirements for your industry or special business activities may call for more extensive research in your local law library.

DATA ANALYSIS

Review the records inventory, user interviews, and legal research to determine what retention periods should be incorporated into the program. Use a spread sheet to display the names of the records, operational retention periods requested by records users, and legal requirements.

Organize the records by individual record titles or by groups (series) based upon function. A functional grouping is particularly easy to implement and use because all or most records within a group are handled in the same or similar manner.

THE RECORDS RETENTION PERIOD

The next step is to assign a value to each record series or functional group. The values should represent the legal, fiscal, research, operational, and historical worth of the records. Some records will be assigned values in all categories, while others may be useful only in specific areas.

This book suggests records retention guidelines based only upon the legal and operational values for records—this is sufficient for most businesses. You may consider other values as you customize the program. Government entities, for example, tend to give historical value substantial weight.

The total retention period is the longest (not the sum) of any of the record values within the group. In some cases, the final retention period may include an indeterminate retention period (such as ACT, active) plus a determinate amount of time (such as three years).

You can determine the retention period for accounts receivable records, for example, by following these steps. Ask your accountants how long they need the records for their purposes—not for tax purpose. They will probably tell you that the records are normally needed for one to two years. If they do not collect the money or resolve discrepancies by that time, they probably never will. You can then determine your tax requirements after reviewing Chapter 9 and Appendix D for the states where you do business. Then assign a retention period, such as current year plus four years (CY+4), in order to meet tax requirements. Assuming these records do not have a research or historical value, the total retention period could be calculated as follows:

User / Operational Value:	2
Legal Value:	CY+4
Research Value:	0
Historical Value:	0
Longest Period:	CY+4

If you later decide that a legal retention period of CY+7 is more acceptable for the Legal Value, simply insert the new figure. You can readily determine why a particular retention period was selected by keeping track of each value.

PROGRAM APPROVALS

Once you have developed a retention schedule, distribute copies to key people within the organization for their review and comment. Include tax advisors, legal counsel, department and division heads, records management staff, and upper level management in the distribution. Revise the program to respond to the comments received.

The retention schedule should then be formally approved in writing by the tax advisor, legal counsel, department or division heads, and the highest ranking company official available (preferably the chief executive officer). The president or managing partner, tax advisor, and legal counsel in small organizations can approve the retention program on behalf of the entire organization.

The approval process is important to indicate company-wide approval of the program and to provide the required clout for implementation. It also indicates that records were destroyed pursuant to a systematic policy rather than at the whim of an individual.

PUBLISHING THE RETENTION REQUIREMENTS

Prepare the records retention schedule in a simplified form and distribute it throughout the organization. Individuals cannot comply with a program they do not know about. Review the program periodically and update it to ensure that the information is current, and meets organizational needs and legal requirements.

DESTROYING RECORDS

You can safely destroy records when the period of time specified in the records retention schedule has concluded. Most organizations destroy all records, for which the retention period has expired, at the same time. Every January, for example, review the records to determine which can be destroyed under the retention program.

Prepare a "Notice of Destruction Form" listing the records to be destroyed. Formal approval for destruction is not needed, however, provided that the original records retention program was approved by the appropriate authority and the procedures for suspension of destruction are followed. Maintain a list of the destroyed records.

SUSPENDING DESTRUCTION

See Chapter 13 for details related to records destruction and litigation.

Relevant records cannot be destroyed when litigation, government investigation or audit is pending or imminent. Either segregate records on hold from the files or mark them in some obvious manner indicating that they are subject to litigation or a government investigation or audit. They should not be destroyed until the "hold" is formally terminated, even if destruction would otherwise be allowed by the records retention program. Always check with tax, legal, and other sectors of the organization before destroying records to determine if the "holds" have been removed from the records.

PROGRAM AUDITS

Periodically review the records retention schedule and destruction procedures to ensure they are being followed. If the retention schedule calls for the destruction of records and you have not destroyed some or all of them without a compelling reason, courts may view this as "selective retention." And, if selected records are destroyed as part of a retention program or destroyed outside the program, the courts may view this as "selective destruction." Either selective retention or selective destruction can subject the organization to substantial fines, penalties, and the loss of rights.

You can determine what changes are necessary in the retention program through periodic internal audits. Schedule additional staff training when appropriate or adopt some coercive methods to ensure compliance with the program. Some organizations restrict the purchase of new filing equipment until all appropriate records have been destroyed or transferred to the warehouse for long-term storage.

DOCUMENTATION

Documentation of the records retention program should be maintained in the following areas:

- Program development, including legal research,

- Program approval,

- Final records retention schedules including revisions, and

- Record of destruction.

There are no specific legal rules telling you how to document the actual destruction of records or how long you should keep the records of destruction. The goal is to demonstrate that you follow a records retention program and that records are regularly destroyed under the program with no intent to deceive or defraud.

A "reasonable" amount of documentation should, therefore, be kept for a reasonable period of time. Many organizations believe that these records should be retained about ten years to create the appropriate history and appearance of propriety. Others advocate longer or shorter periods based upon their view of what constitutes a "reasonable" period.

CONCLUSION   **CHAPTER 14**

☐ The procedures for developing and implementing a records retention program include customizing records retention programs to special industries and meeting the unique needs of individuals within each organization.

☐ The records retention program should specify the scope and purpose of the program, persons responsible for implementing the program, and procedures to be followed throughout the organization.

☐ Establish records retention periods by reviewing the records created by your organization, interviewing users, and doing the legal research.

☐ Distribute your proposed records retention program for approval throughout the organization, including your tax advisor, legal counsel, department or division heads, records management staff, and other appropriate upper level management.

☐ Widely distribute the records retention schedule throughout your organization and train the staff in its use.

☐ Stop the destruction of relevant records when litigation, government investigation or audit is pending or imminent.

☐ Periodically audit the program to ensure that records are being appropriately destroyed and modify the program as necessary.

☐ Retain a reasonable amount of documentation covering program development, program approvals, retention schedules and revisions, and records of destruction for a reasonable time, such as ten years, to demonstrate that records are regularly destroyed under the program with no intent to deceive or defraud.

Chapter 15   Special Issues About the Destruction of Records

See Chapter 17 for details related to the laws on destruction of records after microfilming.

The law generally permits you to destroy records under a records retention program or to destroy them after microfilming. Statutes, regulations, and case decisions, however, advise the public to perform these acts in the "regular course of business," under an approved program, and prior to litigation, government investigation or audit. Through consistency and practice, the law hopes to promote accuracy, reliability, and trustworthiness.

It is sometimes necessary, however, to implement exceptional or "one-time" programs to meet special needs. As part of a new records retention program, for example, an organization must develop a plan to deal with old records not previously covered by a records retention program. Old records may document transactions and projects no longer relevant to the organization. Or, they may be files of defunct companies, miscellaneous files belonging to employees no longer with the organization, or records acquired during mergers or acquisitions which have never been accessed from the time of receipt. Almost every organization has bundles of unwanted, valueless records heaped in warehouses, storage rooms or offices.

It is both difficult and costly, especially for smaller organizations, to conduct a full records inventory and develop a comprehensive records retention program for inactive records. The law recognizes circumstances when a one-time project to destroy valueless records, or to microfilm the valuable ones, fits within the "regular course of business."

RECORD DESTRUCTION IN THE REGULAR COURSE OF BUSINESS

See Chapter 17 for additional detail related to the Uniform Photographic Copies of Business and Public Records as Evidence Act.

The concept of "regular course of business" is well established in federal and state law. The "Uniform Photographic Copies of Business and Public Records as Evidence Act" permits the admissibility of microfilm or other duplicate records in any judicial or administrative proceeding and permits the destruction of the original paper records after microfilming. The law refers to the "regular course of business" as follows:-

- If the original records were made in the regular course of business and

- The original records are recorded or reproduced in the regular course of business by a method which accurately reproduces the originals, then

- The original records can be destroyed in the regular course of business.

See Chapter 16 for additional detail related to the Uniform Rules of Evidence.

Similarly, the Uniform Rules of Evidence permits the introduction of records as evidence in a judicial proceeding if the records are "kept in the course of a regularly conducted business activity," among other specified criteria.

These two laws plus numerous judicial opinions form the cornerstone of the legal view that records are readily admissible in evidence if produced in the "regular course of business." When the courts are certain that records are produced consistently, according to standardized procedures, and as an everyday pursuit of the organization, they feel more confident that these records are accurate, reliable, and trustworthy. Records created only one time or perhaps in anticipation of litigation may be viewed as self-serving, and, perhaps, less reliable.

Courts have reviewed the issue of destruction of records in hundreds of court cases. They have consistently concluded that records may be destroyed in the regular course of business under an approved records retention program prior to litigation.

DESTROYING RECORDS AS PART OF A ONE-TIME DESTRUCTION PROGRAM

It is sometimes necessary to conduct a one-time destruction program to eliminate quantities of old, valueless records not covered by the current retention program. While the destruction of records in the regular course of business under an approved records retention schedule would be viewed favorably by the courts, a one-time destruction program may be suspect.

A one-time destruction or microfilm project can be structured, however, to be in the "regular course of business." If done correctly, the procedures followed can instill the same type of confidence in judges as those programs operated in the "regular course of business"—in fact, the procedures may yield the same result as records destroyed in the "regular course of business."

See Chapter 16 for details related to identification and authentication under the Uniform Rules of Evidence.

The Uniform Rules of Evidence requires that all records be authenticated and identified prior to their admission into evidence. The records will be admitted provided that they can be authenticated by evidence describing the process or system used to create them and that the process or system produces an accurate result.

By developing a trustworthy process or system for destroying records on a one-time basis, you will probably also meet the courts' requirements for records destruction. These procedures should be written, staff trained in implementing the procedures, and an audit conducted to ensure that the procedures are followed.

Determine the Scope of the Project

Select the fewest number of records possible for one-time destruction and have the remainder destroyed under the regular records retention program. Some excellent candidates for one-time destruction are records of defunct organizations, miscellaneous records for individuals no longer with the organization, unused records from acquisitions or mergers, and other valueless records which have not been used for many years.

Review the Content of the Records Under Consideration

Conduct a random survey of the selected records to determine their content and scope. The review also helps to determine the last time the records were used and their value to the organization. A complete inventory generally cannot be justified for this type of project.

Classify the Records Into Specific Groups

After the review is complete, classify the records into specific groups or records series. For example, candidates for destruction can be classified as "records of all defunct organizations which ceased to exist prior to 1975" or "miscellaneous records older than ten years for employees no longer with the organization."

Compare the Records Selected for One-time Destruction With the Current Records Retention Schedule

The records selected for a one-time destruction program should not include records which must be retained under the current retention schedule. For example, even old records covered by current audits or litigation must be maintained and old contracts should be maintained while still current.

Document the Plans for the One-time Destruction Project and Obtain Appropriate Approvals

Prepare a description of each group of records to be destroyed and describe the scope of the one-time destruction program. Records still subject to a retention period should be clearly identified and retained. Once the one-time destruction plan has been completed, get approval from the appropriate people such as your legal counsel, tax advisor, department managers, and a high-ranking administrative officer.

Destroy the Selected Group of Records

Destroy the selected records at the time designated in the one-time destruction plan as consistently as possible. The courts are very concerned when records are selectively destroyed or selectively withheld from destruction. One-time "search and destroy missions" are frowned upon, especially when it is later determined that you destroyed records subpoenaed in litigation. This can create the impression that the organization is trying to hide something. Since a one-time destruction program by definition is selective, and therefore more suspect than a regular records retention program, the one-time destruction program should be carefully developed and implemented to alleviate concerns.

Records can be selectively withheld from destruction when they are maintained for litigation, government investigation or audit, maintained to meet on-going requirements of the current records retention schedule, or maintained because of their historical value. The record of the one-time destruction program should clearly identify the criteria used for selectively withholding records from destruction.

Document the Destruction of Records

Thoroughly document the scope of the records destroyed and the date they were destroyed. As mentioned above, old records usually have no operational value to the organization and rarely have legal value. It is therefore inappropriate to devote a lot of time or resources to inventorying, organizing, or appraising them.

Because the one-time destruction program will be based upon a random survey of these records, it is recognized that some valuable records may be inadvertently destroyed in the process. Some of these valuable records may also include records with on-going legal retention requirements. The procedures outlined above, however, should result in a sufficient degree of accuracy to meet the needs of the organization and create the impression that the organization attempted to act reasonably to comply with the law. Documentation is critical to demonstrating your intent.

DESTROYING RECORDS AFTER MICROFILMING

See Chapter 17 for details related to the destruction of records after microfilming.

While records can clearly be destroyed after they have been microfilmed in the regular course of business, some question remains as to whether they can be destroyed after microfilming if the microfilm was not prepared in the regular course of business. The Uniform Rules of Evidence clearly permits this practice since it does not require microfilm to be prepared in the regular course of business.

A one-time microfilm program, however, may be viewed as in the regular course of business if it is properly planned and documented. Follow the procedures outlined above for the destruction of records. Clearly identify, randomly review, and obtain specific approval for the destruction of records appropriate for the one-time microfilm program. The microfilm plan should be documented along with the procedures followed.

Because microfilming, as opposed to destruction of records, can take several weeks or months to complete, a one-time microfilm project does, in fact, appear similar to an on-going microfilm program. The major difference is that a one-time microfilm project is not an annual affair. Additionally, the records are preserved on microfilm, rather than destroyed.

DEFENDING THE DESTRUCTION OF RECORDS IN COURT OR BEFORE AN ADMINISTRATIVE AGENCY

See Chapter 11 for detail for retaining documentation related to a records management program.

When records have been destroyed under an existing records retention program, the organization may have to produce evidence in court or before a government agency demonstrating the existence of the records retention program and that records were destroyed under the program in the regular course of business. The documentation supporting the records management program can be introduced in evidence.

CONCLUSION

CHAPTER 15

☐ The law generally permits you to destroy records under a records retention program or to destroy them after microfilming.

☐ The law tends to view those activities conducted in the regular course of business as trustworthy.

☐ The destruction of records in the regular course of business under an approved records retention schedule will generally be deemed trustworthy by the courts and regulatory agencies.

☐ The destruction of records as part of a one-time destruction program may be viewed as trustworthy by the courts and regulatory agencies provided that a limited number of records are destroyed, strict procedures are followed, and you can demonstrate that the program has been conducted without intent to defraud or deceive.

☐ The destruction of records after a one-time microfilm project may also be deemed trustworthy by the court or regulatory agency provided that appropriate procedures are followed to ensure the trustworthiness of the microfilm and to demonstrate that there was no intent to defraud or deceive.

☐ You may be required by the court or regulatory agency to defend the destruction of records within your organization by presenting documentation of their destruction and evidence about the procedures followed.

PART E   RECORD MEDIA REQUIREMENTS

Chapter 16   Requirements for Original Records

See also Legal Rquirements for Microfilm, Computer and Optical Disk Records, **Information Requirements Clearinghouse, Denver, Colorado. An order form is provided at the back of this book for your convenience.**

An "admission" is a confession or acknowledgment of facts relevant to the case of an adversary.

See Chapter 17 through 19, respectively, for the requirements for microfilm and duplicate records, computer records, and optical disk or digitized images.

The law in the United States is based upon British Common Law, except that Louisiana state law is based upon Civil or Roman Law.

Records are the principal form of evidence used in court and administrative proceedings. The proper creation and maintenance of records ensures that your organization can prove compliance with the law, show regular patterns of activities, and support your case in litigation. Without appropriate records, your organization can be fined or penalized, lose rights, or experience adverse judicial or administrative decisions.

Records are generally introduced in evidence under one of two circumstances. First, the records may be introduced in support of your case or point of view. The records must be created and maintained according to certain requirements to be admissible. Second, records may be subpoenaed from you by an adverse party and used against you. Usually, all records created by the opposing party are admissible because, in the eyes of the law, they are "admissions" or "information against interest" of the creating party.

This chapter reviews the general principles of law found in the United States as they apply to the admissibility of original records in evidence or submission of original records to regulatory agencies.

BRITISH COMMON LAW

Some people mistakenly think that records have always been admissible as evidence. This is incorrect. In fact, the courts have traditionally excluded records from evidence. In modern times, however, courts have admitted records that qualify for admissibility under a recognized exception.

Our system of law is based primarily on British Common Law. Through the Middle Ages, live testimony from witnesses or tangible evidence (for example, the stolen object) served as the principal evidence in British courts. At that time, records in any form were generally not admissible. Courts viewed live testimony as the most dependable evidence because the witnesses swore an oath to tell the truth and felt compelled to tell the truth when confronted with the solemnity of the court proceedings. The other party also had a fair opportunity to question or "cross examine" the witness in order to uncover the truth in the matter.

Until the fifteenth or sixteenth century, the exclusion of records as evidence in courts did not pose a major problem because few people could write and records rarely served as a vehicle for documenting transactions. As more people became literate and the industrial revolution opened new commercial markets, records quickly became a primary method for preserving information. It was no longer possible nor desirable to deal solely in cash transactions or to keep accounts by memory.

Records such as contracts and land deeds proved to be an effective method for preserving information and establishing relationships. Records also served a mobile population as a long-lasting "memory" of transactions, especially when some of the parties moved (perhaps to the colonies), died, or simply could not be found. This changing environment caused the courts to revise their attitudes toward records as evidence.

HEARSAY

Courts were initially reluctant to accept records because the judges felt that live testimony made under oath in court was trustworthy and both parties could effectively cross examine or challenge the other's witnesses. Records, on the other hand, were not prepared under oath and could not be cross examined in order to challenge their content—paper cannot answer questions. Of course, the people preparing the records could be cross examined, but often they were unavailable or could not remember the details of the transactions.

Some argued, on behalf of allowing records as evidence, that records were often more reliable than live testimony because they documented transactions close to the time the event occurred. Live testimony, on the other hand, was often given several months or years after the event and was subject to distortion or fabrication. Since records were often produced every day in order to document business transactions, they had to be accurate.

The primary reason for excluding records as evidence was that courts viewed records as "hearsay." "Hearsay" may be defined as follows:

Uniform Rules of Evidence, 28 United States Code Appendix. See Appendix H for other applicable sections plus a listing of states which have adopted this law. The law has been adopted by the United States federal government and 30 states.

ARTICLE VIII. HEARSAY

Rule 801. Definitions . . .

(c) *Hearsay.* "Hearsay" is a statement other than one made by the declarant while testifying at the trial or hearing, offered in evidence to prove the truth of the matter asserted.

Rule 802. Hearsay Rule

Hearsay is not admissible except as provided by law or by these rules.

In essence, records are considered "statements" from a source other than a "live" witness, offered to prove that the matter described in the record actually occurred. Records would normally be excluded under the Common Law "Hearsay Rule" unless the courts provided an exception. As the use of records to preserve information increased, the courts were forced to develop exceptions so that society could continue to function in an orderly manner.

PUBLIC RECORDS EXCEPTIONS TO THE HEARSAY RULE

The first exception to the Hearsay Rule permitted the introduction of public records in place of direct testimony by public officials. Public records were generally maintained to show land ownership and other property rights. Public policy and common sense dictated that the courts recognize these records because they established land ownership far better than live testimony and preserved information for long periods of time. The original parties or public recorder were often unavailable to testify or deceased.

Under the "Public Records Exception to the Hearsay Rule," a public official introduced the original recorded document. Modern law permits the public official to produce a duplicate, instead of bringing the original record to court.

BUSINESS RECORDS EXCEPTIONS TO THE HEARSAY RULE

Courts soon recognized the importance of admitting business records in evidence because the records often accurately documented business transactions. Although the safeguards provided by oaths and cross examination of witnesses are not available with records, the courts added safeguards to ensure their "trustworthiness". Parties desiring to admit records in evidence must generally show compliance with these requirements, and judges reserve the right to exclude records from evidence which do not prove to be trustworthy. These requirements are designed to exclude self-serving, inaccurate, or fraudulent records from evidence and to enhance the trustworthiness of the "testimony" provided by the records.

STATUTES AND RULES OF EVIDENCE

Every state and the federal government has some version of the common law "Business Records Exception to the Hearsay Rule." Most states have adopted the Uniform Rules of Evidence based upon the 1974 version of the Federal Rules of Evidence.

Uniform laws are developed by the National Conference of Commissioners on Uniform State Laws in response to the need for consistency and uniformity. When the wording of a uniform law is approved by the Commissioners, it is offered to the federal government and state legislatures for consideration. The law becomes effective and controls activities only in the states approving it. If a law is approved by Congress, it controls only the activities of the federal government and those individuals subject to federal jurisdiction (e.g., working on a federal contract).

See Appendix H for the full text of the Uniform Rules of Evidence and a list of those jurisdictions which have adopted the rules.

The Uniform Rules of Evidence states this exception as follows:

Rule 803. Hearsay Exceptions: Availability of Declarant Immaterial.

The following are not excluded by the hearsay rule, even though the declarant is available as a witness:

(6) *Records of Regularly Conducted Business Activity.* A memorandum report, record, or data compilation, in any form, of acts, events, conditions, opinions, or diagnosis, made at or near the time by, or from information transmitted by,

a person with knowledge, if kept in the course of a regularly conducted business activity, and if it was the regular practice of that business activity to make the memorandum, report, record, or data compilation, all as shown by the testimony of the custodian or other qualified witness, unless the source of information or the method or circumstances of preparation indicate lack of trustworthiness. The term "business" as used in this paragraph includes business, institution, association, profession, occupation, and calling of every kind, whether or not conducted for profit.

Records will be admitted in evidence under the Uniform Rules of Evidence and other state laws containing the Business Records Exception to the Hearsay Rule only if the requirements of the exceptions have been met. Otherwise, the judge may exclude the records from evidence or, in some case, admit the records but diminish the weight of evidence attributed to them.

REQUIREMENTS FOR CREATING ORIGINAL RECORDS

Rule 803(6) states the requirements that must be met for records to be admissible. The requirements form the basis for good records creation practices and should be followed in all records management programs:

- *Records must be made at or near the time of the event.* Records made at or near the time of the event to which they relate are considered more reliable because the details are fresh in the mind of the person creating them and there is generally no reason to fabricate the information. After a period of time, people tend to forget, confuse, or fabricate details of the event.

- *Records must be made by or from a person with knowledge of the event.* Records are made "by a person with knowledge" if that person actually participated in the event or transaction. Records are made "from a person with knowledge" if the person creating the record received the information from someone who participated in the event or transaction. Obviously, records made by people with no knowledge of what transpired or based upon rumors are not reliable.

- *Records must be kept in the regular course of business.* This requirement reflects the courts' belief that records kept in the regular course of business will generally be accurate because the business requires accurate records to function properly. Records created on a one-time or haphazard basis do not achieve the same level of confidence.

- *Records are regularly created by that type of business activity.* This provision is usually not included in the Common Law version of the Business Records Exception to the Hearsay Rule. It would exclude certain records such as self-serving records or records created in anticipation of litigation. Records regularly created by a particular type of business or industry will be admitted in evidence if the other requirements are met.

- *The custodian of the records or other qualified witness must testify that the records submitted to the court meet the requirements for admissibility.* All evidence, even live testimony, must be properly introduced and authenticated to be admissible in court. To admit records, the custodian of the records or some other knowledgeable person must testify in court as to how the records were created. Often, the custodian does not have personal knowledge as to how the records were created. A written procedures manual plus evidence that these procedures have been followed may, therefore, be critical to authenticating and identifying records.

Even when the above criteria have been met, the court may elect to exclude certain records or diminish their weight if it finds the information or the method of creation for these records lacking in trustworthiness.

ENSURING THE TRUSTWORTHINESS OF RECORDS

The purpose of the Business Records Exception to the Hearsay Rule is to ensure that records introduced in evidence are trustworthy since, in many instances, no sworn testimony is available to corroborate the details of the event or transaction. Because the outcome of cases may often be based upon the admissibility of certain records, these exceptions have been closely reviewed by courts.

Records created under the following scenarios are usually presumed to be trustworthy.

- *Records prepared in the regular course of business.* The on-going, continuous preparation of records to meet legitimate business needs or legal requirements, generates records considered to be very trustworthy.

- *Records having an independent business purpose.* If the records are prepared in the regular course of business to meet legitimate business needs, the courts will view the records as trustworthy.

- *Records required by law.* Records prepared to meet specific legal requirements are consider trustworthy, especially since the courts and regulatory agencies levy severe fines and penalties for fraud.

- *Records prepared with no motive to misrepresent or change them. When* records are prepared to meet legitimate business needs, rather than to protect an individual or the organization, there is generally no motive to prepare fraudulent records. On the other hand, when you prepare records to document certain activities in anticipation of litigation or other concerns, these may be viewed as self-serving and unreliable.

- *Records prepared before litigation is foreseen.* Records made specifically for litigation are viewed as self-serving and may not be admissible.

- *Records prepared by an independent third party.* Records prepared by public officials, religious organizations, and private attorneys or accountants on behalf of others are considered more reliable than records created by parties to the litigation. This particular view of trustworthiness, however, has led to certain undesirable results. Some groups, for example, have submitted fraudulent or inaccurate documents to public agencies, subpoenaed those records in later litigation, and attempted to have them admitted as trustworthy records because they were obtained from a public agency. Courts are now more sensitive to this ploy.

- *Records corroborated by independent evidence.* The trustworthiness of records is enhanced if live testimony corroborates the information contained in the records. Most jurisdictions, however, have special rules about live testimony or "parole evidence" in support of written contracts. The sanctity of written contracts is so well protected in our legal system that additional evidence about their content is often excluded under a "Parole Evidence Rule." Under a Parole Evidence Rule, the written contract constitutes the complete agreement between the parties and can not be interpreted through external evidence. This view reflects society's reliance on written contracts and ensures that interpretation is based upon the words as written and approved by both parties.

- *Records containing factual information rather than opinions.* Records such as general ledgers, customer orders, and canceled checks represent factual information prepared in the regular course of business. On the other hand, internal memos or general correspondence often contain opinions and self-serving information.

- *Records prepared by an experienced person.* Records prepared by an experienced person should generally be more accurate than those prepared by trainees or inexperienced persons.

ABSENCE OF RELEVANT INFORMATION

Rule 803(6) addresses the conditions under which original records will be admitted in evidence. In some cases, the absence or lack of certain information can show that an event did not occur.

Rule 803(7) permits your organization to submit proof that certain information did not exist in your records system:

Uniform Rules of Evidence § 803(7). See Appendix H for the full text of the Uniform Rules of Evidence related to records.

Rule 803. Hearsay Exceptions: Availability of Declarant Immaterial.

The following are not excluded by the hearsay rule, even though the declarant is available as a witness:

(7) *Absence of entry in records kept in accordance with the provisions of paragraph (6).* Evidence that a matter is not included in the memoranda, reports, records, or other data compilations, in any form, kept in accordance with the provisions of paragraph (6), to prove the nonoccurrence or nonexistence of the matter, if the matter was of a kind of which a memorandum, report, record, or data compilation was regularly made and preserved, unless the sources of information or other circumstances indicate lack of trustworthiness.

You must demonstrate that you met the requirements of paragraph (6) and did not find the records or information related to a particular matter. You can then introduce information that the event or transaction did not take place because if it had, you would have maintained a record.

The ability to show that a transaction did not take place can be critical to your case. For example, you may be involved in litigation where a vendor claims that because you failed to deliver a part ordered by his company, he incurred substantial losses. If a search of your sales records shows you never received the sales order (as evidenced by the lack of an entry indicating the order), you may not be held liable for your opponent's losses.

The courts fully recognize that the absence of a record in your system could indicate either that the event or transaction did not occur or that you could not find the record because of poor recordkeeping practices. You will probably be closely scrutinized under paragraph (6) to ensure that your recordkeeping system is trustworthy and that information is missing or nonexistent only because it never existed in the first place.

AUTHENTICATION AND IDENTIFICATION

All records must be identified and authenticated prior to admissibility in court. The Uniform Rules of Evidence states this requirement as follows:

Uniform Rules of Evidence § 901. See Appendix H for the full text of the Uniform Rules of Evidence related to records.

ARTICLE IX. AUTHENTICATION AND IDENTIFICATION

Rule 901. Requirements of Authentication or Identification

(a) *General provision.* The requirement of authentication or identification as a condition precedent to admissibility is satisfied by evidence sufficient to support a finding that the matter in question is what its proponent claims.

(b) *Illustrations.* By way of illustration only, and not by way of limitation, the following are examples of authentication or identification conforming with the requirements of this rule: . . .
(9) *Process or system.* Evidence describing a process or system used to produce a result and showing that the process or system produces an accurate result.

When witnesses are called to testify, the attorney first asks their name, address and, perhaps, occupation to establish they are who they claim to be. This established, the witnesses are then asked questions about their knowledge of the subject; for example, "Were you at the corner of 12th Street and Vine on Monday at 12:00 noon and what did you see?"

Because records cannot provide this identification or authentication themselves, the court will expect you, your records custodian, or the authors of the records to supply it.

Assuming, however, that you or the records custodian do not know how the records were created, how can you identify and authenticate them for purposes of evidence? This issue is extremely important, especially in large organizations, because records may be produced by hundreds of individuals over many years, some of whom will no longer be available to testify. In other cases, you may not know who was the author of the records.

The key to successful identification and authentication of records is an established records management program. Rule 901(b)(9) identifies a method by which an individual with no knowledge as to how the records were created can introduce them in evidence. The rule permits you or your records custodian to present evidence describing the process or system used to create records and that the process or system produced an accurate result.

A records management program is certainly a process or system capable of producing an accurate result. You will be asked to show that your records management program did in fact provide the procedures for creating and maintaining records and that the records in question are in fact accurate because they were created and maintained under this program.

Generally, three components are required to show that the records management program produced trustworthy records:

- Written procedures,

- Training, and

- Audits.

Written procedures demonstrate to the court that your organization carefully developed its records management program and specified the practices to be followed. For purposes of evidence, you must maintain a copy of the actual procedures in effect at the time the records were created, not just the current procedures.

The training component shows the court that your staff was fully aware of the recordkeeping requirements and thus were likely to follow them.

Finally, the audit component verifies that the records management procedures were actually followed by your staff. Audits are particularly trustworthy when performed by a group other than the one responsible for preparing the records.

The three components, written procedures, training, and audit, are important not only for written records, but become critical in the case of microfilm or duplicate records, computer records, and digitized records. By demonstrating that your organization has established procedures for creating, maintaining, and destroying records, you can overcome your inability to produce the authors of the records as witnesses. Without a records management program, the courts may bar the introduction of important records as evidence supporting your claims.

SCOPE OF ORIGINAL RECORDS

Rules 803(6) and 803(7) apply to any "memorandum, report, record or data compilation, in any form" which meet the stated requirements. The definition, then, encompasses computer output, microfilm, computer records, audio or video recordings, photographs, and digitized records.

Uniform Rules of Evidence § 1001. See also Appendix H for the full text of the Uniform Rules of Evidence provisions related to records.

ARTICLE X—CONTENTS OF WRITINGS, RECORDINGS, AND PHOTOGRAPHS

Rule 1001. Definitions.

For purposes of this article the following definitions are applicable:

(1) Writings and recordings. "Writings" and "recordings" consist of letters, words, sounds or numbers, or their equivalent, set down by handwriting, typewriting, printing, photostating, photographing, magnetic impulse, mechanical or electronic recording, or other form of data compilation.
(2) Photographs. "Photographs" include still photographs, X- ray films, video tapes, and motion pictures.
(3) Original. An "original" of a writing or recording is the writing or recording itself or any counterpart intended to have the same affect by a person executing or issuing it. An "original" of a photograph includes the negative or any print therefrom. If data are stored in a computer or similar device, any printout or other output readable by sight, shown to reflect the data accurately, is an "original."

Even though jurisdictions accept most duplicate records in evidence, you may still be required to demonstrate their trustworthiness and authenticity. The trustworthiness of duplicates is no better or worse than for original records. Trustworthiness is not based on the media but rather the the procedures followed in producing the record.

Finally, the law recognizes that summaries of certain voluminous records are easier to review than original records:

Uniform Rules of Evidence § 1006. See also Appendix H for the full text of the Uniform Rules of Evidence provisions related to records.

Rule 1006. Summaries.

The contents of voluminous writings, recordings, or photographs which cannot conveniently be examined in court may be presented in the form of a chart, summary, or calculation. The originals or duplicates, shall be made available for examination or copying, or both, by other parties at a reasonable time and place. The court may order that they be produced in court.

Even though summary records may have been prepared specifically for a judicial proceeding and would otherwise not be viewed as trustworthy, they will often be admitted provided that the records from which the summaries were derived are available for review by the court or other parties.

RECORDS SUBMITTED TO REGULATORY AGENCIES

Regulatory agencies prefer records to live testimony because records can be reviewed at any convenient time and are generally more trustworthy. Agencies also prefer the information to be standardized on forms which present the facts in convenient formats.

Records created for submission to or inspection by a regulatory agency will not be subjected to the high level of trustworthiness required by courts. They must still be accurate and reliable, but the methods of preparation are rarely specified.

Some regulatory agencies also have quasi-judicial authority. In this capacity, they can conduct hearings or administrative proceedings to determine whether you complied with the agency's regulations. The rules of evidence used in these hearings will also be less strict than those used in court.

You are generally permitted to appeal any decision of a regulatory agency or administrative tribunal to the court system. Once there, the court rules of evidence will apply. By following the court requirements for records, you can safely submit your records to regulatory agencies, introduce them in administrative hearings, and ensure their admissibility in court.

CONCLUSION   **CHAPTER 16**

☐ Records represent an important form of evidence in court or regulatory proceedings.

☐ You may introduce records to support your case or point of view or they may be subpoenaed from you by an adverse party and used against you.

☐ Records are viewed as "hearsay" and have traditionally not been admitted into evidence.

☐ Modern rules of evidence, such as the Uniform Rules of Evidence, recognize the importance of records and permit their introduction at trial or hearings if certain specified conditions are met.

☐ Under the Uniform Rules of Evidence, records will be admitted into evidence if they are made at or near the time of the event, by or from a person with knowledge, in the regular course of business, as a regular practice of the business, and a custodian of the records or other qualified witness can demonstrate to the court's satisfaction that these requirements are met.

☐ Records will be admitted into evidence only if the judge determines that they are trustworthy and can be relied upon with confidence.

☐ Records can be identified and authenticated by a records custodian with no direct knowledge about them provided that they were created as part of a records management program.

☐ When identifying and authenticating records under a records management program, you will be required to document the procedures, training, and audits to prove the trustworthiness of the records.

☐ The Uniform Rules of Evidence permits the introduction of records in any form, including microfilm and computer records.

☐ Summaries of records can also be introduced in evidence if it would be difficult for the court to examine the original records, even if the summaries were prepared as a result of the court proceedings.

☐ Records meeting the requirements for admissibility in evidence will also be acceptable to regulatory agencies or in administrative proceedings.

Chapter 17   Requirements for Microfilm and Duplicates

See also Legal Rquirements for Microfilm, Computer and Optical Disk Records, **Information Requirements Clearinghouse, Denver, Colorado. An order form is provided at the back of this book for your convenience.**

The term "microfilm" includes all forms of microfilm (roll film, microfiche, film jackets, etc.) used to reproduce original documents, as well as duplicate copies of microfilm. Computer output microfilm (COM) is an original computer record and is controlled by the laws related to computer records; but it is often treated like microfilm in some laws.

See Appendix I for the microfilm laws applicable to the states not adopting the uniform laws affecting microfilm and Appendix C for the specific requirement of the Internal Revenue Service.

Although attention has focused on the legality of microfilm in the last few years, it represents only a specialized form of duplicate records. In fact, paper duplicates often create more cost and space problems. Large quantities of these duplicates are produced every day. Since these paper duplicates are sometimes indistinguishable from originals, organizations now use these duplicates interchangeably with originals.

The law concerning duplicate records is much different than for original records. Most government agencies accept microfilm in place of the original but impose additional standards on its production. Some businesses require copies of contracts to contain original signatures, instead of producing copies from one properly signed original. In addition, organizations place emphasis on the "record" copy (generally, the original) for records retention purposes and often ignore the problems resulting from the failure to destroy duplicates.

This chapter reviews the major laws which apply to microfilm and duplicate records in the United States. The law is fairly uniform on the federal level and among most states. In other states, the wording of the laws differ dramatically, but the legal principles are basically the same. You should research the particular laws concerning microfilm and duplicates for those states in which you do business.

THE PROBLEM WITH DUPLICATES

The law of microfilm and duplicates has evolved slowly from the British Common Law. Some factors that have affected the acceptance of duplicates include the following:

- *The law in most areas has traditionally been conservative and slow to evolve.* While this ensures the stability of the legal process, it also slows the process of accepting new approaches. While the rate of change in the law is much faster today, it still evolves slowly.

- *Records in general (including originals) were initially considered less trustworthy than live testimony at trial.* Today, business records are generally considered very reliable and save substantial time in proving business transactions.

See Chapter 16 for the business records exception to the hearsay rule which allows records, in general, to be admitted in evidence.

Records traditionally were considered to be "hearsay." Today records are still classified as "hearsay" but are admissible in court under exceptions and safeguards provided under the rules of evidence.

- *Original records have traditionally been considered more reliable than duplicates because duplicates were first made by copying the original by hand.* Today, microfilm and office copiers reproduce images very reliably—dot for dot. A duplicate copy, however, can still be modified from the original.

- *The law evolved for hundreds of years based upon a familiarity with paper only.* Microfilm was a new and different technology. Today, microfilm and office copiers are widely used, even by judges.

- *The authenticity of duplicates (whether the record is in fact what it seems to be) traditionally has been questioned.* It is still true today that handwriting analysis from duplicates, for example, is much more difficult and imprecise; although most aspects of handwriting analysis can still be accomplished from duplicates.

As a result of these concerns, the requirements developed to accommodate microfilm and duplicates over the years have often been strict and burdensome. Higher standards have been required for microfilm and duplicates than for paper originals.

BEST EVIDENCE RULE

As the British Common Law developed in the United States and business records became an accepted form of evidence in court, the "Best Evidence Rule" evolved to provide alternatives when original records were not available. Simply stated, the Best Evidence Rule permits the introduction of a duplicate as evidence only if the absence of the original is satisfactorily explained. Some of the satisfactory explanations include:

- The original has been lost or destroyed without fraud (i.e. the original was not destroyed to conceal harmful information in anticipation of trial),

- The original is in the possession of a third party and could not be obtained,

- The original is in the possession of an adversary who failed to produce the records upon request, or

- The record is a public record and the original record cannot reasonably be brought to court.

In any of these circumstances, a duplicate record, if satisfactorily identified, can be introduced in place of the original.

STATUTES AND RULES OF EVIDENCE

See Appendix H for uniform laws that affect records. The United States government has adopted both laws; 30 states have adopted the UPA and the Uniform Rules of Evidence. As a practical matter, therefore, these two laws represent the major principles which govern the treatment of microfilm and duplicate records in the United States.

The basic concepts of the Best Evidence Rule have been expanded by Congress and state legislatures through the enactment of statutes. The two most significant statutes related to microfilm and duplicate records are the "Uniform Photographic Copies of Business and Public Records as Evidence Act (UPA)," developed in 1949, and the "Uniform Rules of Evidence," developed in 1974.

The federal government and those states which adopted the UPA or the Uniform Rules of Evidence have generally maintained their original language with only minor variations. Those states which have not enacted the UPA or Uniform Rules of Evidence have adopted either their own statutes or some form of the Best Evidence Rule. Generally, these other laws impose similar requirements on the preparation and use of duplicates and rarely permit original records to be destroyed after microfilming as permitted by the UPA. Applicable state laws should be researched to determine their specific requirements.

Uniform Photographic Copies of Business and Public Records as Evidence Act (UPA)

The UPA, as adopted by the federal government reads as follows:

United States Code, 28 USC 1732. See also Appendix H for the Uniform Photographic Copies of Business and Public Records as Evidence Act and a listing of the states that have adopted this law.

Section 1732. Record made in regular course of business; photographic copies.

If any business, institution, member of a profession or calling, or any department or agency of government, in the regular course of business or activity has kept or recorded any memorandum, writing, entry, print, representation or combination thereof, of any act, transaction, occurrence, or event, and in the regular course of business has caused any or all of the same to be recorded, copied, or reproduced by any photographic, photostatic, microfilm, micro-card, miniature photographic, or other process which accurately reproduces or forms a durable medium for so reproducing the original, the original may be destroyed in the regular course of business unless its preservation is required by law. Such reproduction, when satisfactorily identified, is as admissible in evidence as the original itself in any judicial or administrative proceeding whether the original is in existence or not and an enlargement or facsimile of such reproduction is likewise admissible in evidence if the original reproduction is in existence and available for inspection under direction of court. The introduction of a reproduced record, enlargement, or facsimile does not preclude admission of the original. This subsection shall not be construed to exclude from evidence any document or copy thereof which is otherwise admissible under the rules of evidence.

This is the principal statute permitting the use of microfilm and duplicates in the regular course of business and in judicial or administrative proceedings. Some key points of this statute are:

- *The UPA only applies to microfilm or other duplicates prepared in the regular course of business.* If the reproduction program is challenged, the organization must prove that microfilming or duplication took place on a regular, consistent basis over a period of time. This requirement might therefore preclude microfilming of records just before a trial. One-time microfilm projects—for example, a project to film records dated before 1980—are conducted in the regular course of business if properly planned and documented.

- *Only one of two requirements must be met for microfilm or duplicate records: (1) the duplicates must accurately reproduce the original **OR** (2) the duplicates must form a durable medium for reproducing the original.* This is a particularly important section of the UPA and one that is frequently misinterpreted and misunderstood, especially by government agencies.

The rules of logic applied to the word "or" require us to interpret it to mean that only one of the two requirements stated must be fulfilled. As a result, the reproduction process must either accurately reproduce the original or the reproduction process must form a durable medium for reproducing the original. There is no requirement that the reproduction process perform *both* functions. If the reproduction process, therefore, accurately reproduces the original on a medium which is not permanent or archival, the requirement of the UPA has been met. It might reasonably be assumed, however, that the medium must last as long as the information is needed.

- *The UPA permits the original record to be destroyed in the regular course of business ("unless its preservation is required by law").* According to the UPA, therefore, no government agency subject to the UPA can prevent an organization from microfilming records and destroying the originals, unless the law (statute or regulation) specifically requires the original records to be kept. A government agency has no authority to act contrary to a statute like the UPA. Verbal or unpublished interpretations which conflict with the UPA may not be binding on those affected.

See Chapter 2 for details regarding your responsibility when maintaining records in a custodial or fiduciary capacity.

Some states have added a second clause prohibiting the destruction of originals even after microfilming if they are held in a custodial or fiduciary capacity. The same requirement would still hold even for those states that have not adopted this phrase based upon general principles of law. In short, you may not destroy records that do not belong to you, without the owner's permission, even though the records have been microfilmed.

- *Under the UPA, duplicates can be used in place of originals as evidence in administrative and judicial proceedings.*

- *The UPA also permits the use of duplicates of a duplicate (second generation microfilm) as evidence.*

The UPA establishes the guidelines for the use of microfilm and the destruction of the original records. As a practical matter, the procedures for preparing reasonably good quality microfilm also meet the requirements of the UPA.

Uniform Rules of Evidence

The definitions and requirements in the Uniform Rules of Evidence apply to duplicates as follows:

Uniform Rules of Evidence § 1001, § 1002, and § 1003. See also Appendix H for the full text of the law related to records and a listing of states that have adopted the law.

ARTICLE X—CONTENTS OF WRITINGS, RECORDINGS, AND PHOTOGRAPHS

Rule 1001. Definitions.

For purposes of this article the following definitions are applicable: . . .

(4) Duplicate. A "duplicate" is a counterpart produced by the same impression as the original, or from the same matrix, or by means of photography, including enlargements and miniatures, or by mechanical or electronic re-recording, or by chemical reproduction, or by other equivalent techniques which accurately reproduces the original.

Rule 1002. Requirement of Original

To prove the content of a writing, recording, or photograph, the original writing, recording, or photograph is required, except as otherwise provided in these rules or by [rules adopted by the Supreme Court of this State or by] statute.

Rule 1003. Admissibility of Duplicates

A duplicate is admissible to the same extent as an original unless (1) a genuine question is raised as to the authenticity or the continuing effectiveness of the original or (2) in the circumstances it would be unfair to admit the duplicate in lieu of the original.

The Uniform Rules of Evidence also enables microfilm to be admitted in evidence under most circumstances. A duplicate can be admitted in evidence under the rules unless there is a problem with the duplicate or original. The language of the rules indicate that the nature of the problem would have to be substantial to prevent the introduction of duplicates in evidence. Rule 1003 does not require that the duplicate be made in the regular course of business or that the duplicate meet any standards other than accurately reproducing the original. This may therefore be the principal method for introducing those records in evidence which were produced as a result of a one-time microfilming project or were produced specifically for trial—not in the regular course of business.

The Uniform Rules of Evidence does not grant explicit permission to destroy original records after microfilming. The rules were designed primarily to control the submission of records as evidence in court, rather than the use of microfilm or duplicate record technologies in daily activities. The authors, therefore, may not have deemed it necessary to include specific permission to destroy records after they were reproduced.

Even though specific permission to destroy original records is not granted in the Uniform Rules of Evidence, the original records can in fact be destroyed, provided that the reproduction accurately reproduces the originals. Rule 1003 specifically indicates that duplicate records can be admitted in place of originals. Since you will have two sets of records (the originals and the duplicates) containing the same information and equally acceptable as evidence in court, you do not need to maintain both. As a practical matter, after inspecting the microfilm or duplicate records, you can destroy the originals unless another law specifically requires you to retain them.

Finally, Rule 1003 identifies two circumstances when duplicate records may not be admissible in place of originals. If a genuine question is raised as to the authenticity of an original, you would certainly expect the same question to be raised about the duplicate. Creation of a duplicate record does not eliminate the requirement that all records (in fact, all evidence) be authenticated and identified prior to submission to the court.

Duplicates cannot be admitted in place of originals under Rule 1003 if it would be unfair to admit them in place of originals. One can only surmise the circumstances when it would be unfair to admit duplicates. No known cases have interpreted this second condition (or the first one, for that matter). Handwriting analysis, for example, can still be performed from a duplicate copy although not to the degree of certainty that one can expect from the original. If original records have been destroyed in the regular course of business with good intent, it would never be unfair to introduce duplicates because the originals no longer exist.

One-Time Microfilm Projects

See Chapter 15 for procedures to be followed for the destruction of records as part of a one-time microfilm project.

An organization may consider microfilming old, but valuable records on a one-time basis. Old records occupy a great deal of space yet must be kept for long periods of time. Under the Uniform Photographic Copies of Business and Public Records as Evidence Act, microfilming must be done in the regular course of business if the original records are to be destroyed. The Uniform Rules of Evidence do not require microfilming to be done in the regular course of business.

A one-time microfilm project can be viewed as being in the regular course of business if it is properly planned and documented. Those records appropriate for a one-time microfilm project should be clearly identified, randomly reviewed, and specifically approved for microfilming. The microfilm plan should be documented along with the procedures followed. If these conditions are met, a one-time microfilming project can be viewed as being conducted in the regular course of business.

COMPARISON OF LAWS

The UPA clearly provides the strongest support for the use of duplicates and the destruction of originals, while the Uniform Rules of Evidence serves to expand the admissibility of microfilm and duplicate records in evidence. The following comparison is made between the UPA and the Uniform Rules of Evidence:

- The UPA permits destruction of original records after duplicates have been prepared which meet the stated requirements. The Uniform Rules of Evidence does not address the destruction of originals.

- The UPA applies to both judicial and administrative proceedings. The Uniform Rules of Evidence was designed for judicial proceedings and applies to administrative proceedings only when specifically adopted by the agency.

- The UPA requires that microfilm or duplicates be produced in the regular course of business. The Uniform Rules of Evidence permits microfilm or duplicates to be produced at any time.

- The UPA specifies that the duplicates must adequately reproduce the originals or form a durable medium for reproducing originals. The Uniform Rules of Evidence also requires duplicates to accurately reproduce the originals.

The UPA and the Uniform Rules of Evidence, together, provide comprehensive support for an organization that microfilm or duplicates records. Some gaps in protection exist in those states that have not adopted both laws.

WHEN MICROFILM OR DUPLICATES ARE NOT SUFFICIENT

Although the law permits the use of microfilm and duplicate in place of originals, an original record may still be required or preferred in some of the following cases:

- *The duplicates are poor quality reproductions.* Poor quality reproductions can be difficult if not impossible to read and most judges and regulatory agencies will request the original records.

  To protect your organization, duplicates, especially microfilm, should be carefully inspected to ensure readability and completeness. If the original records are of a poor quality, you can either attempt to enhance their quality or microfilm targets before the poor quality originals to indicate "best copy available."

  If your microfilm or other duplicate cannot be read, however, the court or regulatory agency may treat you as though the records did not exist in the first place. Some tax deductions may be disallowed because you were unable to substantiate them through readable records. In a judicial proceeding, you may not be able to support your claims without readable records. The importance of good quality control, therefore, cannot be stressed enough.

- *Duplicate records cannot be analyzed for handwriting as readily as the originals.* Handwriting experts have indicated that while their analysis can proceed from duplicate copies, it can only proceed to about a 70 percent degree of certainty. An analyst working from a duplicate cannot determine the weight of the impression made by the writer—often a critical factor in deciding the authenticity of the handwriting.

  In a criminal case, the standard of proof for conviction is "beyond a reasonable doubt"—a 90 percent certainty of guilt. If handwriting analysis of a forged check, for example, is a critical piece of evidence for conviction, the handwriting analysis cannot achieve 90 percent certainty of guilt because analysis of handwriting from a microfilm copy can only determine authenticity to a 70 percent degree of confidence. Banks and other organizations that regularly microfilm and destroy records may therefore be unable to convict forgers.

On the other hand, in a civil case, a party will win if they are right by a "preponderance of the evidence"—a 51 percent certainty that they are right. In the case of handwriting analysis, the 51 percent certainty that a party is right can be achieved with a microfilm of a record because handwriting analysis can reach a 70 percent certainty. Banks and other organizations who rely on microfilm should be able to recover amounts owed from forgeries in civil suits.

- *Microfilm and other reproduction techniques do not adequately reproduce photographs, pictures, and other information having a tonal quality.* Microfilm, in particular, uses a high-contrast film which records material as either black or white, without any gray tones. Valuable information in the original may, therefore, be lost in the duplicates.

- *The physical character of original records generally cannot be transmitted to the duplicates.* Physical character includes paper texture, age of paper, paper color, and paper size. This information can be valuable for criminal investigations and historical preservation. While microfilm and other duplicate technologies preserve the information, they cannot preserve the original character of the documents.

FEDERAL REGULATIONS FOR MICROFILM AND DUPLICATES

Microfilm Requirements of the Internal Revenue Service

Internal Revenue Service, Revenue Procedure 81-46. See Appendix C for the full text of the IRS microfilm requirements.

The Internal Revenue Service has issued regulations governing the preparation of microfilm for tax purposes. Prior approval for microfilm is not required but taxpayers will be held responsible for meeting the standards specified. If records are microfilmed and the originals destroyed, the IRS may disallow deductions or other tax benefits if the microfilm records are not adequate.

The basic provisions of Revenue Procedure 81-46 are as follows:

- Taxpayers must follow these requirements if they microfilm from source documents or produce computer output microfilm (COM) from computers,

- Taxpayers must obtain written approval for the microfilm program from the board of directors (corporations), general partners (partnership), or owner (sole proprietorship),

- The microfilm system must be complete and used regularly within the business,

- Taxpayers must establish procedures and document them so that the microfilm procedures can be audited,

- Taxpayers must provide internal procedures for inspection and quality control,

- Taxpayers must identify and preserve the microfilm for the period of time necessary for tax purposes,

- Taxpayers must document the production of the microfilm,

- Taxpayers must produce microfilm that is legible (individual letters can be read) and readable (groups of letters can be read),

- Taxpayers must produce an index to the microfilm to enable the retrieval of particular information,

- Taxpayers must produce microfilm which meets industry standards, and

- Taxpayers must make available a reader printer for use by the Internal Revenue Service when it examines microfilm on site.

Microfilm Requirements for Federal Contracts

The federal government has specific requirements for the use of microfilm in place of original contracts and the subsequent destruction of records after microfilming. If you have a contract, grant, lease or other agreement with the federal government, review these requirements carefully before microfilming these records.

- Contractor may use any microfilm format,

- Contractor must microfilm all relevant notes, worksheets, and other papers necessary to reconstruct and understand the original records,

- Contractor must review all microfilm before destroying the original records to ensure legibility and reproducibility,

- Contractor may not destroy the original documents after microfilming unless the retention period has expired, the contracting officer agrees to a lesser retention period, all claims under the contract are settled, or 18 months has passed since final payment,

- Contractor must maintain an effective indexing system,

- Contractor must provide strict security measures to prevent the loss of the microfilm and to safeguard classified information,

- Contractor must store the microfilm in a fireproof vault and protect the microfilm during the records retention period,

While industry standards do exist for manufacturers of microfilm equipment and supplies, no mandatory standards exist for users. You should produce legible and readable microfilm using recognized procedures.

See Appendix F for the full text of the records retention and microfilm requirements for federal contracts.

This very restrictive provision may effectively prohibit the use of microfilm for federal contracts in some cases.

- Contractor must provide adequate microfilm readers and produce paper prints close to the original size, and

- Contractor must produce legible and readable microfilm and paper prints.

STATE REQUIREMENTS FOR TAX RECORDS MAINTAINED ON MICROFILM

The states generally defer to the Internal Revenue Service for microfilm requirements for their tax records. The states often develop their own requirements, however, for sales tax records, because sales taxes are totally within the control of the individual states. A typical microfilm regulation for sales tax records is as follows:

California State Board of Equalization, California Administrative Code, § 1698.

Sales and Use Tax Regulations

§ 1698. Records . . .

(b) *Microfilm Records.* Microfilm reproductions of general books of account, such as cash books, journals, voucher registers, ledgers, etc., are not acceptable in lieu of original records. However, microfilm reproductions of supporting records of details, such as sales invoices, purchase invoices, credit memoranda, etc., may be maintained providing the following conditions are met:

(1) Appropriate facilities are provided for preservation of the films for periods required.

(2) Microfilm rolls are indexed, cross referenced, labeled to show beginning and ending numbers or beginning and ending alphabetical listing of documents included, and are systematically filed.

(3) The taxpayer agrees to provide transcriptions of any information contained on microfilm which may be required for purposes of verification of tax liability.

(4) Proper facilities are provided for the ready inspection and location of the particular records, including modern projectors for viewing and copying the records.

A posting reference must be on each invoice. Credit memoranda must carry a reference to the document evidencing the original transaction. Documents necessary to support claimed exemptions from tax liability, such as bills of lading and purchase orders, must be maintained in an order by which they readily can be related to the transactions for which exemption is sought . . .

State requirements for microfilming tax records generally correspond to good microfilm practices. You should review the specific requirements for the states in which you do business.

AUTHENTICATION AND IDENTIFICATION

See Chapter 16 for details regarding authentication and identification.

The requirements for identification and authentication also apply to microfilm (and all other records in evidence, for that matter). Many people film a "Certification of Authenticity" at the beginning and end of a role of microfilm to indicate the content of the roll, the date the film was prepared, the name of the preparer, and a statement that the microfilm accurately reproduces the original records. While this kind of authentication is not specifically required by law for private records (although it may be required for public records), a certificate of authenticity is easy to prepare and microfilm and can substantially reduce the time and effort required to identify and authenticate records in court.

As a practical matter, photocopies must also be identified and authenticated. Most courts seem to waive that requirement for photocopies because they "look like original records." When challenged, however, you must provide the same identification and authentication for photocopies as you would for microfilm or any other record.

THE MYTH ABOUT MICROFILM AND DUPLICATES

The law related to the acceptance of microfilm by courts and regulatory agencies has evolved slowly over the last 50 years. Acceptance has been hampered by poor equipment, procedures and image quality. The law often specifies quality standards in order to force users to produce readable and legible duplicate records.

When microfilm or other duplicate records are produced on good equipment following appropriate procedures, the output is generally readable and legible. Even without specific knowledge of the microfilm laws and regulations, you should be able to produce microfilm meeting the requirements of courts and government agencies throughout the United States, merely by following good practices.

The acceptance of these technologies has also been slowed because of the mistaken belief that original records are more reliable than duplicates. As a practical matter, original records can easily be forged or modified. A three-page contract, for example, held together by a flimsy staple, can be altered by removing the staple, replacing page two, and restapling it through the original holes. Documents are not trustworthy just because they are originals.

But, you can also alter microfilm and duplicate copies. Information from the original document can be erased and replaced with new information and the change is not detectable on the photocopy. The microfilm itself, however, cannot be altered without a trace because of the nature of the technology.

The trustworthiness of the information really depends upon following trustworthy procedures, and does not depend upon the media.

A system is made trustworthy by following written procedures, providing adequate training, and following up with audits. These components of a program should exist for microfilm, computer, and paper record systems. By identifying the proper procedures, ensuring that your staff knows them, and verifying that the procedures are followed, you can be certain that the information created and maintained is trustworthy, admissible in evidence, and acceptable to government agencies.

Microfilm and duplicate records have the same legal status as original records for most purposes of the federal government and those states where the Uniform Photographic Copies of Business and Public Records as Evidence Act (UPA) and the Uniform Rules of Evidence have both been adopted. The legal status of microfilm and duplicates is weaker, however, in jurisdictions where only one or neither of these laws have been adopted.

CONCLUSION   **CHAPTER 17**

☐ Most courts and regulatory agencies accept microfilm and duplicate copies in place of originals but impose additional standards on the production of microfilm, in particular.

☐ The law related to microfilm and duplicates has evolved gradually from the British Common Law because law traditionally evolves slowly, records were considered less trustworthy than live testimony, original records were considered more reliable than duplicates, and the ability to authenticate duplicates has been questioned.

☐ Duplicate records were originally admitted into evidence under British Common Law only when the original records were unavailable.

☐ The Uniform Photographic Copies of Business and Public Records as Evidence Act permits the use of microfilm and other duplication technologies and the destruction of the original records after reproduction provided the duplicates accurately reproduce the originals.

☐ The Uniform Rules of Evidence permits duplicate records to be admitted in evidence in place of originals provided the duplicates accurately reproduce the originals. After records have been microfilmed or reproduced under the Uniform Rules of Evidence, the original records can be safely destroyed.

☐ The Uniform Photographic Copies of Business and Public Records as Evidence Act and the Uniform Rules of Evidence are different laws which address different aspects of the production of microfilm and duplicate copies.

☐ The Internal Revenue Service has developed regulations specifically addressing the creation and use of microfilm records for tax purposes.

☐ The trustworthiness of records does not relate to whether they are original or duplicate records, but rather to the procedures followed in creating and maintaining the records which ensure that they are trustworthy.

Chapter 18   Requirements for Computer Records

See also Legal Rquirements for Microfilm, Computer and Optical Disk Records, **Information Requirements Clearinghouse, Denver, Colorado. An order form is provided at the back of this book for your convenience.**

Organizations use the speed and accuracy of computers to manage great quantities of information. Although accounting functions represented the primary application of the computer in the 1970's, additional applications such as word processing, project management, data base management, electronic mail, and telecommunications have become significant.

The widespread use and availability of computers in the last twenty years have forced the legal system to develop new principles of law to handle this technology. Laws affecting paper records and microfilm provide the cornerstone for the legal attitudes toward computer records. Computers, however, present some unique problems which have influenced the associated body of law:

- Information stored in memory, magnetic media, or optical media cannot be read directly. The information must first be displayed on a terminal or printed on paper or microfilm.

- Computer information is often entered directly into the computer without the creation of an original paper document or data entry worksheet.

- While the content of the information may remain the same, the form of storage, display, and output requires a transformation of the information into a different form.

- Questions remain as to which records are originals and which are duplicates for legal purposes.

- Special procedures are necessary to ensure that data entry, processing, and production function properly and yield accurate information.

Current legal attitudes toward computer records are reflected in both statutes and case law. This chapter summarizes the existing federal requirements for computer records. Readers should review state laws to determine whether or not additional requirements exist.

UNIFORM RULES OF EVIDENCE

See Chapter 16 for a
detailed discussion of the
general requirements for
the admissibility of records
in evidence under the
Uniform Rules of Evidence.

The Uniform Rules of Evidence provides the basis for admitting all types of records, including computer records, into evidence. The rules specifically refer to computer records in Rule 803(6) by using the term "data compilation." The definitions in Rule 1001(1) for "writing and recordings" also address computer records by using the terms "magnetic impulse, mechanical or electronic recording, or other form of data compilation."

Visible Records

The Uniform Rules of Evidence contains only one specific requirement for computer records. This requirement identifies the form in which the computer record will be admitted in evidence:

Uniform Rules of Evidence,
Rule 1001(3). See also
Appendix H for the full
text of the law related to
records and a listing of the
states that have adopted
the law.

ARTICLE X. CONTENTS OF WRITINGS, RECORDINGS AND PHOTOGRAPHS.

Rule 1001. Definitions.

For purposes of this article the following definitions are applicable: . . .

(3) *Original.* . . . If data are stored in a computer or similar device, any printout or other output readable by sight, shown to reflect the data accurately, is an "original."

Jurisdictions adopting the Uniform Rules of Evidence have taken the position that only the visible form of the computer record can be admitted into evidence. Clearly, magnetic media including disk, tape, and memory cannot be read directly and do not possess the enduring qualities of a paper printout or other visible record. The law does not place any time limit on when the visible record is produced and does not specifically establish the status of the magnetic media.

Computer output microfilm (COM), although technically microfilm, is considered an original computer record under this definition. While some may claim that COM is not visible because the image must be enlarged, this technicality can be overcome by characterizing COM as a visible image which is enlarged for easier reading.

Authentication and Identification

See Chapter 16 for an
analysis of the
requirements in the
Uniform Rules of Evidence
for authentication and
identification of records.

The authentication and identification of computer systems is critical to determining the trustworthiness of the computerized information. Only through a process of written procedures, training, and audit can your organization be certain that records produced by computers will be admitted in evidence.

Computer information can be added to, deleted, or modified, generally, without a trace. Certain questions can be expected about the integrity of this information. You will then be responsible for clearly demonstrating that the computer information is trustworthy and can be relied upon as evidence.

As part of your documentation of the computer system, you need to maintain information about the operation of the computer hardware, the versions of computer software used, the dates each version of the computer software was used, auditing performed to verify the validity of data, and other records to indicate that your computer system operated properly and no deceptive practices are followed.

Summary Computer Records

See Chapter 16 for additional discussion.

Rule 1006 enables an organization to enter summary computer records in evidence rather than presenting all the detailed raw data. This rule is provided for the convenience of both the litigants and the court to reduce the quantity of information considered during the judicial proceedings. If questions arise about the accuracy or the propriety of the summary information, the judge or opposing party may require the production of the original detailed records.

STATE RULES OF EVIDENCE

Most states, other than those which have adopted the Uniform Rules of Evidence, do not have specific rules of evidence or other laws admitting computer records into evidence. These states depend upon the principles of the Best Evidence Rule which allow computer records to be admitted in evidence in those situations where they constitute the best evidence for the matter to be proven.

California adopted one of the few specific statutes establishing criteria for admitting computer records into evidence:

California Evidence Code, § 1500.5.

§ 1500.5. Printed representation of computer information or computer program used by or stored on computer or computer readable storage media; admissibility of evidence; presumption; burden of proof.

Notwithstanding the provisions of Section 1500, a printed representation of computer information or a computer program which is being used by or stored on a computer or computer readable storage media shall be admissible to prove the existence and content of the computer information or computer program.

Computer recorded information or computer programs, or copies of computer recorded information or computer programs, shall not be rendered inadmissible by the best evidence rule. Printed representations of computer information and computer programs will be presumed to be accurate representations of the computer information or computer programs that they purport to represent. This presumption, however, will be a presumption affecting the burden of producing evidence only. If any party to a judicial proceeding introduces evidence that such a printed representation is inaccurate or unreliable, the party introducing it into evidence will have the burden of proving, by a preponderance of evidence, that the printed representation is the best available evidence of the existence and content of the computer information or computer programs that it purports to represent.

ENSURING THE TRUSTWORTHINESS OF COMPUTER RECORDS

Computer records must meet a higher standard of trustworthiness than ordinary paper records, especially since data can so readily be altered:

- *Reliability of Equipment.* Because equipment which is not functioning properly can alter the content of computerized information, the organization may be required to present evidence that the equipment operated reliably the day the computer record was prepared. A log of computer operations indicating the absence of any malfunction is generally adequate.

- *Integrity of Data Entry.* Computer errors often result from mistakes made during the entry of data. Trustworthiness is enhanced by verifying or proofreading the data following entry into the system.

- *Methods Used to Prevent Loss of Data.* The reliability of computer records is enhanced if an accurate audit trail traces the steps followed in processing the data and the methods used to prevent loss of data.

- *Reliability of Computer Programs.* Errors in computer records can result from errors in the computer programs. You may be required to present evidence about the development and testing of the programs. Programs are often examined by an expert witness to determine their accuracy or reliability.

  You may also be required to present the specific version of the computer program used to process the data on the date the information entered into evidence was created. A different version of the program may be considered, if it is the only one available, but the absence of the exact version of the program may raise some serious questions about the trustworthiness of the computer records.

- *Time and Method for Preparing Printouts.* Computer printouts prepared in the regular course of business are considered more trustworthy than similar computer printouts prepared for trial. As a practical matter, however, if the organization can show an adequate audit trail leading to the creation of the data and merely a time lag before printing, no adverse consequences should result.

COMPUTER RECORDS REQUIREMENTS OF THE INTERNAL REVENUE SERVICE

Internal Revenue Service, Revenue Procedure 91-59. See Appendix C for the full text of this regulation.

In 1991 the Internal Revenue Service adopted Revenue Procedure 91-59 which substantially modified its requirements related to computer records maintained for tax purposes. Because many computer records contain tax-related information, this regulation probably affects your organization.

- *All computer records must be retained by the taxpayer in a retrievable, machine-sensible form.* Previous rules did not require taxpayers to maintain the tax information in computer-readable format for review by the Internal Revenue Service. Instead, the IRS required only visible tax records and audit trails to ensure that information was correctly processed.

Under the new regulation, the Internal Revenue Service can request your computer tapes or disks for analysis and review. The computer-readable information must therefore be fully documented and maintained in a retrievable and usable form. Even when a service bureau or time-sharing service is used, the taxpayer is still responsible for maintaining the information as indicated.

- *Documentation must be provided describing the computerized accounting system including record formats, flowcharts, label descriptions, software program listings, software program changes maintained in chronological order, and detailed charts of accounts.* Audit trails should be provided to ensure that the steps leading from detailed to summary information can be examined by the IRS.

The IRS specifically requires that major changes in the computer system be documented and preserved in chronological order. This means that each major version of the software programs must be retained for review by the IRS. No guidelines are provided, however, as to how to differentiate between a major and a minor change in software.

See Chapter 9 for detailed analysis of records retention requirements for tax records.

- *The computer records should be retained "so long as the contents may become material in the administration of any Internal Revenue law."* The Internal Revenue Service suggests that the retention period should match the limitation of assessment for federal tax purposes (generally three to six years except for special circumstances such as fixed assets, insurance loss reserve, and voluntary extension of the audit period).

- *Accounting records should also be retained in visible form, either on paper or microfilm.* Although the requirement for creating a visible or hardcopy record in the original regulation has been preserved, the Internal Revenue Service stresses that the maintenance of a visible record does not replace the requirement for the retention of machine-sensible records. Microfilm may be retained in place of paper records.

- *All computer records maintained for tax purposes should be clearly labeled and maintained in a secure environment, with backup files stored off-site.* This requirement actually conforms to good computer practices for records storage and the protection of vital records.

- *Computer records must be maintained in a retrievable form for the entire time they are needed for tax purposes.* Even if the taxpayer converts to a new computer system, the computer records must be converted to that new format or maintained in a format that can be readily retrieved.

This requirement is probably the most difficult and costly one to implement. Whenever an organization converts to a new computer system, the old computer tapes and disks may have to be converted to the new format. Under the previous regulation, taxpayers could simply produce visible output from the records and not worry about the various computer tapes or disks maintained in the storage area. Under the new regulation, all computer-readable material relevant for tax purposes must be maintained in a readily retrievable format. This creates a tremendous burden for some companies because audits are frequently extended more than ten years while computerized accounting systems change substantially almost every three years.

The problem becomes complicated in the case of acquisitions and mergers. Until the audit period expires, the surviving organization may be responsible for the computer records maintained by the former organizations. Since these computer records are often incompatible with the system used by the surviving organization and rarely are adequately documented, the survivor probably has no choice but to convert the tax records to one standard format.

- *Computer records should be inspected periodically to ensure the integrity of the information.* If information is lost or damaged, the taxpayer is responsible for notifying the Internal Revenue Service immediately.

The computer records must be carefully protected by the taxpayer. Under previous regulations, the taxpayer was only responsible for producing a record in visible form and could ignore aging computer tapes. The new regulation requires the taxpayer to ensure that all computer records are protected and available. Standard computer practices should, therefore, include periodic inspection, rewinding of tapes, and storage in environmentally-protected areas.

- *Database management systems may be used for maintaining tax records, but additional documentation is needed.* In particular, the taxpayer must maintain a sequential file of all transactions entered into the database along with the appropriate documentation for the sequential file and the database management system.

While many organizations maintain a dynamic database for tax purposes, the Internal Revenue Service requires an audit trail for all transactions and modifications made to the database. For some organizations, however, this is no burden because the required sequential file and audit trails are a part of a good database management system.

- *Electronic Data Interchange (EDI) records may be kept in electronic form.* No paper or other visible printout is required unless these reports or records are made in the regular course of business.

The following suggestions should be implemented to ensure that your organization will not be assessed additional tax or be subject to criminal penalties for failing to properly maintain computer records.

- *Conduct a tax audit of your existing computer system based upon the new Internal Revenue Service regulation.* While computer systems containing tax information should be audited regularly to ensure their compliance with tax laws, the new regulation highlights the importance of such an audit. During the review, an auditor should focus on system documentation, storage procedures for computer records, and the compatibility of older computer records with the current computer system.

- *Inventory existing magnetic tapes and disk files to determine their readability by the current computer system.* Many older computer files were created with old versions of a computer system. Some of these records may have been prepared by outside service bureaus, time-sharing companies, or companies which have since been acquired by or merged into your organization.

  Internal Revenue Service Revenue Ruling 91-59 requires that all computer records still subject to review by the Internal Revenue Service must be available and readable in machine-sensible format. Computer tapes and disks produced by other computer systems may now be totally incompatible and unreadable by your current system.

  According to this regulation, these computer tapes and disks must be converted into a retrievable format at the request of the Internal Revenue Service. This new format can conform to your existing computer system or it may conform to some other computer system. If the latter option is selected, the user is responsible for ensuring that the other computer or service bureau is capable of converting the information to a format usable on request by the Internal Revenue Service.

- *When developing new computer systems, include the Internal Revenue Service requirements in the design.* For the most part, the requirements of the Internal Revenue Service conform to good computer practices. Documentation should be provided for all computer systems, not just because the IRS says so, but because you need this information to run the business. The requirements of the Internal Revenue Service Revenue Procedure 91-59, should be followed.

COMPUTER RECORDS REQUIREMENTS OF THE STATE REVENUE DEPARTMENTS

The departments of revenue in most states follow the requirements of the Internal Revenue Service regulations for income tax purposes because state income tax returns are generally based on the federal income tax returns with some adjustments. As a result, they have little choice but to follow the federal requirements for recordkeeping in the area of computer records.

The state departments of revenue, however, often develop additional recordkeeping regulations applicable to sales tax records, since sales tax falls totally within the control of the state. While many of these sales tax requirements parallel those of the IRS, most states have not revised their computer record requirements to correspond with IRS Revenue Procedure 86-19 introduced in 1986. The typical state tax requirements for computer records, therefore, often remain similar to the previous IRS regulation:

Colorado Department of Revenue, Regulation 26-116(c). This regulation contains the major recordkeeping provisions previously found in IRS Revenue Procedure 64-12, previously adopted in 1964 and completely replaced by Revenue Procedure 91-59 in 1991.

Regulation 26-116. Records

(c) *Records prepared by automated data processing systems.* An ADP tax accounting system must be capable of producing visible and legible records for verification of taxpayers' tax liability.

(1) *Recorded or reconstructible data.* ADP records must provide an opportunity to trace any transaction back to the original source or forward to a final point total. If detail printouts are not made of transactions at the time they are processed, the systems must have the ability to reconstruct these transactions.

(2) *General and Subsidiary Books of Account.* A general ledger, with source references, will be written out to coincide with financial reports for tax reporting periods. In cases where subsidiary ledgers are used to support the general ledger accounts, the subsidiary ledgers should also be written out periodically.

(3) *Supporting Documents and Audit Trail.* The audit trail should be designed so that the details underlying the summary accounting data may be identified and made available to the Department upon request. The system should be so designed that supporting documents, such as sales invoices, purchase invoices, credit memoranda, etc., are readily available.

(4) *Program Documentation.* A description of the ADP portion of the accounting system should be available. The statements and illustrations as to the scope of operations should be sufficiently detailed to indicate, (A) the application being performed, (B) the procedures employed in each application (which, for example, might be supported by flow charts, block diagrams, or other satisfactory description of the input or output procedures), and (C) the controls used to insure accurate and reliable processing. Important changes, together with their effective dates, should be noted in order to preserve an accurate chronological record . . .

The typical state tax law specifies audit trails, maintenance of detailed records, program documentation, and other features commonly found in a good computer accounting system.

CONCLUSION

CHAPTER 18

- ☐ The legal requirements for original and microfilm records serve as the basis for the legal attitudes toward computer records.

- ☐ The Uniform Rules of Evidence specifically permits the introduction of computer records in evidence if the output is readable by sight and the requirements for original records have been met.

- ☐ The trustworthiness of computer records will be scrutinized much more carefully than for original records because of issues related to equipment, computer software, data entry integrity, potential for loss or manipulation of information.

☐ Records must be maintained of the various versions of computer software programs operating within the computer system at various times.

☐ The Internal Revenue Service has adopted regulations which specifically govern the creation and use of computer records for tax purposes. These regulations require computer records to be maintained in a retrievable, machine-sensible form, with documentation and audit trails, capable of preparing visible records including computer output and microfilm, and with protection and periodic inspection.

☐ The requirements for computer records under the Internal Revenue Service regulations can best be implemented through an internal tax audit, an examination of the readability of magnetic information, and adherence to IRS requirements.

☐ State revenue departments generally regulate computer records only for sales taxes and often include provisions found in outdated IRS requirements.

Chapter 19   Requirements for Scanned Records and Electronic Imaging Systems

See also Legal Rquirements for Microfilm, Computer and Optical Disk Records, **Information Requirements Clearinghouse, Denver, Colorado. An order form is provided at the back of this book for your convenience.**

This chapter considers technologies used to store *image* information. When the same technologies are used to store computer *data*, the requirements of Chapter 18 apply.

Vendors have recently announced the availability of a new generation of "electronic imaging systems (EIS)" which record images of documents on optical disks and other high density storage devices. These systems are capable of scanning documents, converting the images into electronic form, storing the images, and rapidly retrieving them. Experienced observers expect this technology to gain wide acceptance in the marketplace as a alternative to traditional microfilm or paper-based systems. Vendors and potential users alike, however, have expressed concern about the legality of records maintained with this technology, including specifically the admissibility of these records in evidence and their acceptance by government agencies. The courts have not yet dealt with records maintained in digitized form and may not even comment for several years, if history is any guide.

What should you do in the interim? Should you wait until a body of law evolves similar to microfilm and computer records? Or postpone buying a system until new legislation is enacted, or the technology has passed judicial review in a number of test cases? Should you wait several years to take advantage of the improved speed of retrieval and information sharing offered by this new technology?

The acceptance of this new technology depends upon the comfort level of the judges and administrators. It took several hundreds of years for the courts to accept paper records in evidence, approximately 40 years to accept microfilm, approximately 10 years to accept computer records. It will take a few more years for courts to accept electronics imaging systems and digitized records—based on comfort level, not the law.

Those using electronic imaging systems should carefully establish and follow procedures designed to ensure the trustworthiness of the image information and provide a detailed audit trail. You can capitalize on the benefits of this new technology if the system is properly designed and implemented to meet the anticipated legal requirements of tomorrow.

ADMISSIBILITY IN EVIDENCE

While traditional microfilm and computer laws do not specifically mention optical disk storage, these laws can serve as the basis for the admissibility of records maintained with this technology because it has characteristics of duplicate records such as microfilm and yet utilizes computers.

Uniform Photographic Copies of Business and Public Records as Evidence Act (UPA)

See Chapter 17 for details regarding the Uniform Photographic Copies of Business and Public Records as Evidence Act. See also Appendix H for the full text of this law.

While the Uniform Photographic Copies of Business and Public Records as Evidence Act (UPA) deals primarily with the problems of microfilm or copier reproduction, it can be applied without change to the electronic imaging technology and storage of digitized records.

To qualify as a reproduction under this law, it must be produced "by any photographic, photostatic, microfilm, micro-card, miniature photographic, or *any other process which accurately reproduces or forms a durable medium for so reproducing the original . . .*" The law recognizes the use of *any technology* which "accurately reproduces . . . the original."

Electronic imaging systems basically convert the original document into a series of electronic "dots" (comparable to "bits" in a computer). These electronic "dots" are compressed and then stored on an optical disk or other high density storage media. The image information can be read from the optical disk and either displayed on a high resolution terminal or printed on paper. This paper image "accurately reproduces . . . the original" and would be considered a duplicate copy under the UPA. The optical disks themselves, or other high-density storage devices, and the associated technology merely serve as the vehicle for storing the image until it is requested, and would not have any status in the law.

The UPA explicitly permits you to destroy the original documents, provided that the duplicates are produced in the regular course of business. This is particularly important with an electronic imaging system because one of the reasons for employing the technology is to reduce the costs of storing paper.

Uniform Rules of Evidence

See Chapter 17 for the analysis of the Uniform Rules of Evidence as it applies to microfilm and duplicate copies. See also Appendix H for the full text of this law.

The Uniform Rules of Evidence also addresses duplicate records such as microfilm and computer records. Rule 1001(4) specifies that a duplicate is any record produced "from the same matrix" as the original (i.e., dot-for-dot transformation from the original to the duplicate) or by "other equivalent techniques which accurately reproduce the original." Since electronic imaging systems meet the stated criteria, these duplicate records would be admissible in evidence under Rule 1003, just like microfilm records. The printed output from the electronic imaging system would clearly be acceptable as a duplicate record under the Uniform Rules of Evidence. The optical disks or other storage devices might academically be considered duplicate records but could not themselves be introduced in evidence.

The Uniform Rules of Evidence would also accept the records prepared by an electronic imaging system as computer records. Rule 1001(1) states that a "writing or recording" consists of information produced by "electronic recording, or other form of data compilation."

Under the definition of original records in Rule 1001(3), the original record of "data stored in the computer" (such as the image stored in an electronic imaging system) would be defined as "any printout or other output readable by sight, shown to reflect the data accurately." A paper printout or microfiche produced by a computer output microfilm device, or a display of the image on a screen, would meet the requirements of the rule. Again, the actual storage media would not be admissible.

Because of the unique and dual nature of visible records produced by this technology, the Uniform Rules of Evidence leads to a bizarre and contradictory conclusion. Under Rule 1001(4) related to duplicates, the optical disk is considered a duplicate copy. Under Rule 1001(3) as it applies to computer records, the visible output is an original, even though it was produced from the "duplicate," optical disk.

Although, some courts may find it unpalatable to conclude that an "original" can be produced from a "duplicate" under the law, they would be required to accept visible records produced from the system which accurately reflects those images. Perhaps the Uniform Rules of Evidence could be revised to read "If data are stored in the computer or similar device, any printout or other output readable by sight, shown to reflect the data accurately, will be *treated* as an original."

Authentication and Identification

See Chapter 16 for details related to authentication and identification of all records admitted in evidence.

Under the Uniform Rules of Evidence and the UPA, duplicate or computer records must be satisfactorily identified and authenticated before they are admissible in evidence. In the case of electronic imaging systems, the identification and authentication information cannot effectively be stored with each individual image. However, it is possible to scan and digitize a certificate of authenticity, similar to microfilm, and store that information in sequence with the scanned images. When the images are viewed on the optical disk in sequential order, the certification would appear in its proper place.

The records could also be identified and authenticated by showing that the process or system produces an accurate result. Strict procedures must be followed with this technology to alleviate concerns presented in the next section. There is, in particular, the potential for forging or altering signatures. By providing written procedures, training, and audits, you can ensure that proper procedures are followed and that the integrity of the information is preserved.

State Requirements Related to Electronic Imaging Systems

See Appendix H for a listing of states adopting the Uniform Photographic Copies of Business and Public Records as Evidence Act or the Uniform Rules of Evidence.

Forty four states have either adopted the Uniform Photographic Copies of Business and Public Records as Evidence Act or the Uniform Rules of Evidence. Either law would be available to permit the admissibility of records produced by electronic imaging systems.

Only one state has modified its existing microfilm law to specifically permit records to be "transferred to other material using photographic, video or other electronic processes":

Vernon's Annotated
Missouri Statutes § 109.120
and § 109.130.

TITLE 8. PUBLIC RECORDS.

CHAPTER 109. TRANSCRIBING AND REBINDING.

§ 109.120. Records reproduced by photostatic process . . .

1. The head of any business, industry, profession, occupation or calling, or the head of any state, county or municipal department, commission, bureau or board may cause any and all records kept by such official, department, commission, bureau, board or business to be photographed, microphotographed, photostated or transferred to other material using photographic, video, or electronic processes and the judges and justices of the several courts of record within this state may cause all closed case files more than five years old to be photographed, microphotographed, photostated or transferred to other material using photographic, video, or electronic processes. Such reproducing material shall be of durable material and the device used to reproduce the records shall be such as to accurately reproduce and perpetuate the original records in all details . . .

§ 109.130. Reproduced records deemed original . . .

Such reproduction of the original records shall be deemed to be an original record for all purposes provided that the reproduction is equal in resolution to microfilm produced under those standards set forth in subsection 4 of section 109.241 and shall be admissible in evidence in all courts or regulatory agencies. A facsimile, exemplification, or certified copy thereof shall, for all purposes recited in sections 109.120 and 109.140, be deemed to be a transcript, exemplification or certified copy of the original.

Only a few jurisdictions on either the federal or state level have developed new language to specifically authorize the use of electronic imaging technology or optical disk records.

CONCERNS ABOUT THIS TECHNOLOGY

To determine the impact of existing laws on this new technology, you should anticipate the problems which might create legal obstacles to its use. These are the same issues which must be dealt with in designing an electronic imaging system, even after the legality of the technology has been established.

- *The image stored on an optical disk may not be an exact reproduction of the original.* Most scanners detect a maximum of 200 to 300 dots per inch (DPI) across a page. While the resolution is adequate to fully reproduce the image, it means that some dots from the original do not appear in the duplicate. While this may seem to be a major obstacle, other technologies such as microfilm or other duplication methods also fail to reproduce *every* dot contained in the original, but generally reproduce enough so that the image appears complete and readable. In fact, the quality of a digitized image may sometimes exceed the quality of a microfilm image.

  Although the dot-for-dot transformation from the original document to an image on an optical disk may suffice for legal acceptance, most systems do not store the image in terms of a series of "electronic dots." Instead, after scanning, the image is compressed ten or more times using a technique called "run length encoding (RLE)." Besides reducing storage requirements, RLE also enables the image to be transmitted to terminals or remote locations much faster. The RLE version of the image can, however, be reconverted back into the dot version by applying the appropriate decompression algorithm.

Although the stored version of the image will have been electronically compressed and cease to have the same attributes as the original image, the information and visual qualities of the displayed image are not altered. Because the law looks to the visual image, rather than the stored image, this concern may not be relevant.

- *Information contained in an image (such as a signature or text) can be removed or modified without a trace.* Once the image is stored in computer memory (either after scanning or retrieval from the optical disk), sections of the image may be electronically modified by deleting information, inserting new information, or transferring information from other documents. The resulting final image can then be stored and the index pointers directed to the new image. While the original image might still exist on the non- erasable optical disk, the index would reference only the revised image. With erasable optical disks, the previous image can be removed without a trace.

  While some believe the ability to alter the image may be the "kiss of death" for this technology, you should consider the analogy with computer records. Computer information can be added to, deleted, or modified on magnetic disk and the new version stored without any trace that changes have taken place. Yet, courts and regulatory agencies have already established the legal acceptance of computer records in judicial or administrative proceedings.

  The pivotal issue is not the erasability of the media or potential for modification of the image, but the trustworthiness of the procedures which created the records. Courts and regulatory agencies will require written procedures, training, and audits confirming what has occurred to the information in the system.

- *Electronic images cannot be certified in terms of authenticity like microfilm records.* Actually, certifications can be scanned and stored on the optical disk before and after each batch of scanned images. This procedure, however, might waste a substantial amount of storage space on the optical disk.

  The certificate of authenticity, however, is not generally a requirement of the law. Computer records, for example, cannot readily be certified and yet they are admissible in court and before regulatory agencies if properly identified and authenticated. Records produced using electronic imaging systems can be introduced to the courts or regulatory agencies by showing that the process or system produces an accurate result.

- *The electronic image can be enhanced after scanning and before storage on the optical disk.* Image enhancement creates the biggest concern in terms of the legal acceptance of this technology. Image enhancement enables the system to actually improve the image by sharpening line edges, removing stains or colored background, removing specks from the background, and filling in broken letters. The purpose of image enhancement is to make the electronic image more readable, even if the original record was difficult to read.

The concerns related to image enhancement have prompted some systems designers to suggest that the original images be micro-filmed or an unaltered version of the original image be scanned and stored on optical disk prior to image enhancement. While both proce-dures may facilitate the acceptance of electronic images, they re-quire substantial additional time and expense on the part of the user to create duplicate for legal purposes. These procedures are probably not necessary in the first place.

The argument can be made that the image enhancement algorithms merely improve the image rather than change the information. Since the information contained in a record ultimately is more im-portant than its appearance, the courts or regulatory agencies may not object too strenuously. An audit trail must be maintained indicat-ing the types of image enhancement algorithms used and, perhaps, the percentage of change that resulted when the algorithm was ap-plied. The key, again, will be the "trustworthiness" of the procedures employed to generate the electronic image.

- *Optical disk is not considered an archival storage medium.* Some have expressed concern that the law requires information to be maintained on an archival media such as microfilm. In reality, the issue related to archival quality or longevity of the information has no relationship to its legal acceptance. The information must merely last as long as required by law or just long enough to be admitted in evidence. If a visible record can be made, no one really cares that the media will last for a hundred years.

  The "Uniform Photographic Copies of Business and Public Records As Evidence Act" and the Uniform Rules of Evidence do not require microfilm to be archival but merely require that the technology "ac-curately reproduces . . . the original." Magnetic media are not archi-val and visible records produced from computer data are accepted in both courts and administrative proceedings. Even if the optical disk begins to deteriorate prematurely, the information can be trans-ferred electronically with no loss of quality (as compared to micro-film which loses 10 to 20 percent of its quality when duplicated).

IMPACT OF TAX REGULATIONS

See Chapter 17 for details related to IRS Revenue Ruling 81-46 affecting microfilm and Chapter 18 for details related to IRS Revenue Procedure 91-59 affecting data processing. Also see Appendix C for the full text of these IRS regulations.

While the Internal Revenue Service has not specifically indicated whether or not this technology will be treated under Revenue Ruling 81-46 (Microfilm) or Revenue Procedure 91-59 (Data Processing), you might anticipate that both requirements should be followed, when appropriate, for this technology.

For microfilm, you must be certain that an accurate, visible image can be produced from the optical disk on request and that documented procedures are carefully followed to indicate the process used to convert the source documents to the digitized format. For data processing, you must also maintain documentation about the computer system and maintain the computer information in a format that can be retrieved at the request of the Internal Revenue Service.

This latter requirement may prove to be a hardship for those companies acquiring the optical disk technology only to find that the manufacturer of their equipment has gone out of business or that their technology has become incompatible with the industry standard. Whenever you convert to a new system, make sure you have a method for converting the old electronic images into a new machine-readable format for IRS audit.

CONCLUSION **CHAPTER 19**

☐ The new electronic imaging systems are available to maintain records as digitized images in a high-density storage media such as optical disks.

☐ The admissibility in evidence or acceptability to regulatory agencies of this new technology can be determined from existing laws.

☐ The Uniform Photographic Copies of Business and Public Records as Evidence Act permits the admissibility in evidence of visible output from electronic imaging systems. The visible record could be in the form of a paper printout or computer output microfilm and would be classified as a duplicate of the original input records.

☐ The Uniform Rules of Evidence permits the admissibility in evidence of visible output from electronic imaging systems. The visible output record would either be classified as a duplicate under the definition of duplicates or as an original under the definition of computer records. The optical disk or other storage media could not be admitted into evidence as a record.

☐ The requirements related to authentication and identification of records produced by this technology will be closely scrutinized by the court. You should carefully document your procedures, training, and audits and all other aspects of the operation and implementation of this system.

☐ While existing laws may be sufficient to permit the introduction of records produced by electronic imaging systems in evidence, at least one state has modified its statute to permit this technology.

☐ Concerns about this technology include the accuracy of the reproduction, potential for modification of information, difficulty with certification, image modification through enhancement techniques, and lack of archival quality. These concerns can be overcome by adopting proper procedures for using the technology.

☐ Systems developed with this technology should meet the requirements of the Internal Revenue Service for both microfilm and computer records.

PART F   LEGAL RESEARCH AND ANALYSIS

Chapter 20   Introduction to Legal Research

Ignorance of the law is no excuse. But the inability to find the law after a reasonable effort just might be.

"Statutes" are laws enacted by the United States Congress or state legislatures. "Regulations" are laws prepared by federal or state regulatory agencies under authority granted to them by Congress or the state legislatures.

The "inability to find the law as an excuse" has never been recognized as an axiom of law but does reflect the frustration felt by researchers attempting to identify the legal requirements for their records. Clearly, we are expected to comply with statutes and regulations. Penalties for non-compliance could include fines and imprisonment.

Our system for publishing and indexing the law is not designed for researching records requirements. The research process is also made more difficult because it must often be done by people without legal training.

INABILITY TO FIND LEGAL REQUIREMENTS FOR RECORDS

Even the best researcher will not find *all* the legal requirements contained in statutes and regulations. You can usually find many of the more obvious ones by using research methods—such as indexes, computer-assisted research, and visual scanning—but do not expect to find them all. Research tools have not been designed for comprehensive research in this special area.

The law is not clear as to the potential consequences if you do not find particular statutes or regulations even after exhaustive research. Normally, "ignorance of the law is no excuse" for non-compliance with a legal requirement. Fundamental fairness and public policy dictate that it would be blatantly unfair, however, to punish you for not finding some laws after a reasonable research effort, especially since some laws are so difficult to find. You should be cautioned, however, that this doctrine of "inability to find the law as an excuse" has never been upheld by the courts.

To protect your organization, keep records of the research performed, indicating the methods used, the citations examined, and the requirements found. The information could then be presented in an administrative or judicial hearing to explain the conduct of the organization and, perhaps, avoid any adverse consequences arising from the failure to comply with legal requirements.

WORKING WITH YOUR LEGAL COUNSEL

A few large organizations have in-house legal counsel to perform the legal research for the records system; most small ones do not and must rely on outside legal counsel. Regardless of who performs the research, work closely with your legal counsel to ensure that the research is complete, well documented, and performed with minimal expenditure of time and money. Legal counsel can be extremely helpful to you in guiding the research, determining the relevance of the statutes and regulations, and interpreting various requirements.

See Chapter 22 for tips on how to organize your legal research.

If you do the legal research yourself, seek the assistance of legal counsel *before* the results of your legal research are implemented as part of the records program. Provide your legal counsel with a complete list of statutes and regulations found during the search and copies of the actual text of those requirements. Legal counsel can then review these in a comprehensive and effective manner.

LEGAL RESEARCH TOOLS

Many large organizations have law libraries that contain many of the materials necessary to perform legal research. Most major public libraries have the basic federal and state laws. In some cases, you may have to go to a law library.

Become familiar with the legal resources available in your community. Ask your librarian for assistance in finding the material you need and reference books describing legal research.

CONCLUSION   **CHAPTER 20**

☐ Ignorance of the law is no excuse, but the inability to find a law after reasonable effort just might be.

☐ Our system for publishing and indexing the law is not designed for researching recordkeeping requirements.

☐ Even the best researcher will not find all relevant legal recordkeeping requirements.

☐ Legal counsel should review the recordkeeping requirements for your organization before they are implemented in order to ensure their accuracy and completeness.

☐ Most legal research materials are available in your local public library or law library.

Chapter 21   Sources of Legal Requirements

This book provides most of the legal requirements for your records. You may also contact the publisher using the form in the back of this book for more information about the reference loose-leaf service *Legal Requirements for Business Records.*

You must comply with the federal requirements for records as well as the requirements for each state in which your organization does business. This chapter presents the basic approaches to researching these requirements.

FEDERAL LEGAL REQUIREMENTS FOR RECORDS

Government and private publications containing federal legal requirements are available in most law libraries because federal law has a nationwide impact. Most records requirements are found in published regulations, although a few appear in statutes. Several sources are suggested below.

Federal Statutes

The United States Code (USC) is Printed by the U. S. Government Printing Office and is the official compilation of statutes enacted by Congress. The United States Code is re-published every six years; new or revised statutes are published in supplements during the interim period. As a result, the United State Code and supplements are rarely used by researchers.

United States Code Annotated, West Publishing Company, St. Paul, Minnesota. *United States Code Service, Lawyers Edition*, Lawyer Cooperative Publishing Company, Rochester, New York.

Most researchers for federal requirements use one of two private services: United States Code Annotated or United States Code Service, Lawyers Edition. Both of these reference services have advantages over the United States Code including: (1) each title is published in one or more separate volumes; (2) the entire set is kept up-to-date by annual cumulative pocket supplements; (3) pamphlets are issued during the year updating the pocket supplements; (4) more detailed indexing is provided in both the bound volumes and supplements; and (5) each section contains annotations to court decisions which are cited and interpreted.

The indexes for the United States Code Annotated and the United States Code Service contain references to the following terms useful for researching recordkeeping requirements: "Records," "Reporting," and "Limitations of Actions."

On the other hand, federal statutes rarely state specific records requirements. They usually authorize a federal agency to develop rules and regulations and specify that records must be kept accordingly. You must search for these regulations separately. In addition, federal statutes usually specify only those recordkeeping requirements required to be followed by federal agencies.

Federal Regulations

A regulatory agency is a governmental authority, but not a court or legislative body, which exercises authority over private parties through either adjudication or rule making. After Congress delegates authority to a regulatory agency, the agency implements the intent of Congress through rules and regulations.

Titles for the Code of Federal Regulations are revised as follows:
Title 1-16: January 1
Title 17-27: April 1
Title 28- 41: July 1
Title 42-50: October 1.

Current federal rules and regulations can be found in two publications: the Code of Federal Regulations (CFR) and the Federal Register (FR). The Code of Federal Regulations is revised quarterly to reflect changes in regulations (additions, deletions, or modifications) which have occurred during the previous 12 months. The CFR is arranged in order of the citations assigned to each agency. For example, regulations issued by the Nuclear Regulatory Commission currently in force may be located in "Title 10 - Energy" of the CFR and are current through the last revision date.

The Federal Register publishes each business day new and proposed rules and regulations, plus notices and other matters. Adopted rules and regulations first appear in the Federal Register and are then reprinted in the next CFR edition. You must therefore research the current CFR and then check the daily Federal Register volumes for newer laws containing recordkeeping requirements.

The Code of Federal Regulations and the Federal Register, together, serve as the primary source of information for locating federal regulatory requirements for records. The indexes for both services, however, are poor and difficult to use. The CFR index has approximately 1600 references to "Reporting and Recordkeeping" requirements. Many references point to a "Part" of the CFR, requiring the researcher to search page-by-page for the particular records-related requirements. More than half of the records requirements contained in the CFR cannot be found through the index.

The index for the Federal Register is even more difficult to use since it is organized by government agency. Descriptive index terms such as "Records" or "Reporting" are never used. You must therefore scan the text of a rule or regulation for its recordkeeping requirements.

Once the basic research using the CFR and the Federal Register has been completed, you must check the *List of CFR Sections Affected*. This is a monthly pamphlet which indicates the changes made since the last edition of the CFR volume.

Request for Information from Federal Agencies

You can request information about records requirements directly from the agencies involved. Some agencies will respond quickly and completely, while others will not be very helpful. First determine which agencies and departments may be responsible for promulgating rules and regulations affecting your organization. Then contact those agencies again which failed to respond or responded incompletely.

Your organization should not request a special "private ruling" from an agency to clarify or establish legal requirements for records. A private ruling is often harmful to an organization and rarely helpful. Most regulatory agencies are very restrictive in private rulings and tend to be more conservative in their approach than necessary. Nothing prevents an organization from interpreting and relying upon the law just as it is written. Once a private ruling is made, however, it may bind you but not other organizations. If you contact a regulatory agency, ask only that they tell you " which legal requirements affect the records of your organization."

A few regulatory agencies publish opinions and rulings in other sources. For example, the Internal Revenue Service publishes Revenue Rulings and Revenue Procedures on a weekly basis—the IRS requirements for microfilm and computer records were found there. You should also check these sources.

STATE LEGAL REQUIREMENTS FOR RECORDS

State legal requirements for records are more difficult to find than federal requirements. Sometimes state statutes and regulations are similar to the federal requirements. In other cases, the state requirements are totally different and cover records not addressed by federal requirements.

See Chapter 2 for determining in which states you are "doing business."

An organization should review the law for every state in which it "does business." As a minimum, state statutes and regulations should be researched for every state in which the organization has employees, an office or facility, or does a substantial volume of business. Legal research for state requirements may, therefore, be substantially more difficult and time consuming than federal research. While there are several ways to conduct federal research, only two are available for state research: (1) direct research from published statutes and regulations, and (2) requests for information from government agencies. The data bases of the computer-assisted legal research services include only some state statutes and no state regulations.

State Statutes

Statutes for your state are probably available in local public libraries. However, state statutes for other states may only exist in law libraries. Some smaller law libraries may maintain statutes only for the home state or for states in the surrounding geographical area.

The amount of records-related requirements found in state statutes varies dramatically from state to state. In some states, rules and regulations prepared by state regulatory agencies are approved by state legislatures and published as statutes. In other states, these regulations are published separately.

The quality of the indexes to the state statutes also varies substantially between states. You should check under a variety of indexing terms including "Records," "Recordkeeping," and "Reporting" in order to find the information you need.

State Regulations

About forty states publish their regulations through state printing offices or private contractors. The other ten states do not publish regulations at all, so you must request the regulations directly from the agencies.

You may purchase these regulations and subscribe to updates for those states in which you do business. If your organization is involved in business nationwide, however, the cost of these rules and regulations could exceed $25,000 (one time purchase) and $10,000 annually for updates.

The Library of Congress, Legal Reading Room (Washington, DC) is probably the only place in the country where published state regulations for a few states can be found in one location.

The quality of the indexes for state regulations also vary dramatically. Occasionally, indexing terms such as "Records and Reporting" are provided to assist the researcher. More often, however, indexes fail to include references to recordkeeping or reporting requirements. You must then scan the subject matter to locate the relevant information.

Requests for Information from State Agencies

You can ask appropriate state agencies for their records requirements. This may be the only way to get regulations for any state, especially for those states that do not publish their regulations. The responses are usually adequate if the proper agencies are contacted.

Keep a record of all agencies contacted and the responses received in order to show that your organization made a good faith attempt to comply with the state's requirements. Ask the agency to respond even if no requirements exist. The record of research and procedures followed could be very important if you mistakenly overlooked a major legal requirement and had to explain the oversight to a government agency.

OTHER RESEARCH SERVICES

Three other sources of information should be considered to simplify the research task.

Legal Requirements for Business Records

Legal Requirements for Business Records, **Information Requirements Clearinghouse, Denver, Colorado, 2500 pages. Annual update service also available. An inquiry form is provided at the end of this book for your convenience.**

Legal Requirements for Business Records is a three-volume loose-leaf service dedicated to reporting the legal requirements published by state and federal governments affecting recordkeeping. The publication contains the full text of the actual legal records requirements, the source citation, a series of comprehensive indexes, and informative articles to help you quickly and confidently locate the legal requirements affecting your organization. *Federal Requirements* contains the recordkeeping requirements found in federal statutes and regulations for all regulated industries and activities. *State Requirements* contains the basic state requirements needed by most organizations in the areas of taxes, employment, statutes of limitation, business organization and records media.

Legal Requirements for Business Records served as the source for information contained in this book.

Full Text Data Bases

LEXIS is owned by Mead Data Central, Dayton, Ohio. WESTLAW is owned by West Publishing Company, St. Paul, Minnesota.

LEXIS and WESTLAW are on-line, full text legal information retrieval systems which provide access to federal statutes and regulations plus some state statutes. Few state regulations are available through these services.

Both systems enable you to access the full text of the law through your own search inquiries. For example, the inquiry "RECORD OR DOCUMENT OR REPORT W/10 KEEP OR STORE OR RETRIEVE OR MAINTAIN! OR RETAIN" will identify legal requirements in the database, such as: "records shall be maintained for three years" or "documents may be maintained in microfilm form."

Because these databases contain the full text of the entire statute or regulation, rather than just recordkeeping provisions, you will often retrieve laws not relevant to your purposes. You will also have difficulty locating laws that contain inconsistent or unusual terminology that was not anticipated in the search. They are also very expensive for extensive searches.

Guide to Records Retention Requirements

Contact Superintendent of Documents, U.S. Government Printing Office, Washington D.C. 20402

The National Archives and Records Administration, through the Office of the Federal Register, publishes the *Guide to Record Retention Requirements* with annual supplements. The *Guide* contains abstracts of many of the legal requirements for records found in the federal statutes and regulations, including retention periods. Information is organized by federal government agency.

While the abstracts may be useful to identify some basic records retention information, they generally do not provide you with the information needed to accurately determine records retention requirements. First, the information is not complete even for federal requirements and by design contains no state requirements. Second, the index is not complete, so you will have difficulty locating all the requirements for your industry. Third, you will still have to go to the library and read the full text of the requirements to determine their applicability to your records.

CONCLUSION   **CHAPTER 21**

☐   Most federal recordkeeping requirements are published by federal regulatory agencies in the *Code of Federal Regulations* and the *Federal Register*; few legal requirements are published in statutes.

☐   The federal regulations used by your organization should be periodically checked against the *List of CFR Sections Affected* to determine whether those requirements have been modified or deleted.

☐   Federal regulatory agencies can be contacted to obtain any legal requirements in their possession affecting your records, but they should not be asked to provided private rulings or other opinions about your records program.

☐   You are required to comply with the legal requirements for every state in which you "do business."

☐   Your state statutes are probably available in the local public library, but statutes for other states may only be available in a law library.

☐   Many state recordkeeping requirements are found in statutes; some state requirements are found in regulations.

☐   Regulations for your state may be available in your local law library. Regulations for other states are usually not available anywhere in your state.

☐   You must contact state regulatory agencies directly for their recordkeeping requirements, especially for the ten states that do not publish any regulations.

☐   *Legal Requirements for Business Records* is a publication, including an update service, containing the full text of state and federal recordkeeping requirements plus research indexes and informative articles.

☐   LEXIS and WESTLAW provide on-line databases containing the entire federal statutes and regulations plus some state statutes which enable you to search for the recordkeeping provisions based upon occurrences of specific words in the text.

Chapter 22   Organizing the Legal Research

You will encounter a large number of different legal requirements on both the federal and state levels when developing a records program and need to carefully organize and index this information before using it.

This chapter addresses some of the techniques successfully used in actual records programs for organizing the legal research. It is recommended that you prepare a legal research notebook containing the full text of the law utilized, a legal research index, and a legal group file.

WHY ORGANIZE LEGAL RESEARCH

Legal research should be organized for the following reasons:

- *Future reference.* Organize the legal research so that information can be found quickly, is readily accessible for use in developing the records program, and answers questions regarding the actual legal requirements.

- *Accuracy.* By organizing the research and preparing indexes, you may uncover some additional relevant legal requirements.

- *Simplifying the legal requirements.* There are a large number of difficult, overlapping, and sometimes contradictory laws to be considered in developing a records retention program. An index assists you to organize the information and simplifies the process of interpretation. While the full text of the law should be available for consideration and review, a simplified index enables you to focus on those essential legal requirements for the records program.

- *Future updating.* The index usually contains the citations for each legal requirement. The citations can be researched periodically to check changes in the law. This process is much easier than reading the full text and analyzing the legal requirements again each time you update the research.

Expediting review and approval. Your legal counsel must review the research. The research index and legal group file makes it possible for legal counsel to quickly review the various citations and legal requirements, and determine the accuracy of the retention schedule. Whenever a question arises, the full text of the legal requirement is available for review.

ORGANIZING ORIGINAL RESEARCH

See Chapter 21 for details regarding legal research.

Whenever you identify a legal requirement, reproduce the relevant pages and highlight the specific paragraphs applicable to your records. Also reproduce the cover page of the publication to indicate the source of the law. Finally, reproduce additional indexes, titles, or subsections to indicate the structure of the legal requirement and, perhaps, its applicability to your organization.

Organize the reproduced sections of the law according to citation, by jurisdiction (federal or state), and statute or regulation. Legal counsel often needs to review the full text of the law as well as the indexes to determine if the research is complete.

THE LEGAL RESEARCH INDEX

Once the research is complete, analyze the information and prepare an index summarizing the critical data similar to Figure 22.1. While the form of the index will vary, the index should typically include the following:

- Jurisdiction (state or federal)

- Citation

Develop a simple reference number to organize items in your legal research index. Some federal citations to specific paragraphs of a text are over 30 characters long.

- Reference number

- Issuing agency (for regulations)

- Function or subject (generally two or three line hierarchical subject classifications)

- Records affected

- Legal group code (discussed later in this chapter)

- Retention period (use multiple entries for multiple retention periods)

The most difficult part of creating an index is establishing the subject or function classifications. Use simple categories, with only a limited number of options. The objective of the index is to bring similar laws together under a single category, rather than organize the universe of law (like the Dewey decimal system).

Some organizations successfully organize the laws by function (e.g., tax, employment, etc.) rather than by subject. The functional index simplifies the process of extracting the legal requirements, grouping them, and then applying them to specific records within your organization.

Figure 22.1 Sample Legal Research Index

Jur.	Citation	Reference Code	Subject	Legal Group	Retention Period	Type of Records / Agency
CA	LC 1174	CA 140-0020-00	EMPLOYMENT WAGE AND HOUR	EMP300	2	payroll
CO	CRS 8- 4-102	CO 108-0010-00	EMPLOYMENT WAGE AND HOUR	EMP300	3	payroll
CO	CRS 8-46-102	CO 108-0030-00	EMPLOYMENT WAGE AND HOUR	EMP300	MAINT	payroll
CO	Order No. 19	CO 210-0010-00	EMPLOYMENT WAGE AND HOUR	EMP300	2	payroll Labor and Employment, Department of
CT	CGSA 31- 31	CT 131-0010-00	EMPLOYMENT WAGE AND HOUR	EMP300	3	payroll
CT	CGSA 31- 66	CT 131-0020-00	EMPLOYMENT WAGE AND HOUR	EMP300	3	payroll
CT	Reg. 31-60-12	CT 210-0010-00	EMPLOYMENT WAGE AND HOUR	EMP300	3	payroll Labor Department: Wages, Division of
DC	DCC 36-211	DC 136-0005-00	EMPLOYMENT WAGE AND HOUR	EMP300	3	payroll
DE	19 DCA 907	DE 119-0010-00	EMPLOYMENT WAGE AND HOUR	EMP300	3	payroll
DE	19 DCA 1108	DE 119-0020-00	EMPLOYMENT WAGE AND HOUR	EMP300	3	payroll
GA	OCGA 34-4-4	GA 134-0010-00	EMPLOYMENT WAGE AND HOUR	EMP300	MAINT	payroll
GU	GCG 46008	GU 150-0010-00	EMPLOYMENT WAGE AND HOUR	EMP300	MAINT	payroll
HI	21 HRS 387-6	HI 121-0030-00	EMPLOYMENT WAGE AND HOUR	EMP300	MAINT	payroll
IA	5 ICA 86.10	IA 105-0010-00	EMPLOYMENT WAGE AND HOUR	EMP300	MAINT	payroll

Make fine distinctions within classifications only when experience and knowledge indicate that certain legal requirements uniquely apply to specific records within your organization. For example, a state public utilities commission might have a specific requirement for customer records. Since this might be the only legal requirement that covers customer records, you might provide a special subject classification for this topic.

A computer database management system works best. The sorting capability of the computer enables you to organize information by subject, citation, record type, or any other method. For example, during the annual review of the legal requirements, the index can be sorted by citation so that each can be carefully reviewed for its continued applicability. Or, sort the database by agency so that their specific requirements can be examined.

THE LEGAL GROUP FILE

Sort the legal research index by function (or subject) to bring together the legal requirements applicable to the same types of records, regardless of jurisdiction or source.

See Chapter 9 for details related to tax requirements. Appendix G contains the legal group file used to produce Figure 12.1—the minimum, maximum and typical legal requirements were identified for this purpose.

Review the index to determine the longest legal requirement for an applicable jurisdiction. For example, most state and federal laws for payroll records specify a retention period of three years. However, the Internal Revenue Service requires that payroll records be maintained for four years. Bringing all requirements for payroll records together in one group permits you to determine that the longest legal retention period for payroll records is four years.

See Chapter 8 for strategies related to statutes of limitations and the records retention period.

Select the longest legal requirement for records retention purposes. Many so-called "legal requirements," however, are actually "legal considerations." This is particularly true in the case of statutes of limitation, which represent the period of time a legal action can be brought, and may or may not bear on the retention of records. Legal considerations, however, may be added to the legal subject index when appropriate.

See Chapter 10 for details related to personnel records.

Continue the "grouping" process until all legal requirements from the subject index have been covered by one group or another. If you use broad categories of records, 15 to 20 legal groups usually suffice to cover just about every record in the organization. For example, employment hiring records such as applications, resumes, advertising, job descriptions, testing and interviews can all be assigned the same legal retention period of one year. This simplifies the process of categorizing records and reduces the chances of destroying the wrong records.

Appendix G presents the entire Legal Group File used to prepare Figure 12.1.

Once the legal requirements from the subject index have been grouped into categories or legal groups, prepare a new "legal group file" including the 15 to 20 categories of records, and a brief description of each legal group retention period. You might assign a unique number to each legal group to facilitate reference. You could also assign the same reference number to each of the specific laws identified in the subject index which were considered in developing the legal group.

Use the legal group index to categorize each type of record in the organization. The legal group approach, by design, causes some records to be retained longer than required by a specific law. While this is a disadvantage of the legal group approach, the advantages are certainly significant.

Legal requirements can be assigned to records in the retention schedule quickly and accurately; and the review, operation, and update of the retention schedule is simplified.

Keep the legal group file in the legal research notebook with the other records documenting your efforts. Review the legal groups periodically to detect changes in the law. Only rarely will changes in specific laws require you to change the legal group.

THE LEGAL RESEARCH NOTEBOOK

The records retention notebook should contain copies of the original laws with the relevant sections highlighted, the Legal Research Index, and the Legal Group File. Insert tabs for each section of the notebook to facilitate review.

Present the completed legal research notebook to your legal counsel along with the records retention schedules and procedures. If you have followed the recommendations in this book, legal counsel will find it easy to review. Approval of the records retention program, microfilm or other components of the records management program should occur within a relatively short period of time.

CONCLUSION **CHAPTER 22**

☐ You will consider a large number of federal and state legal requirements related to your records program.

☐ You should organize your legal research to facilitate future reference, ensure accuracy, simplify the legal requirements, facilitate future updating, and expedite review and approval by your legal counsel.

☐ The full text of the legal requirements identified by your research should be reproduced for future reference purposes.

☐ Prepare a Legal Research Index to organize similar laws by function or subject and identify jurisdiction, citation, reference number, issuing agency, function or subject, records affected, legal group code, and the recordkeeping requirements.

☐ Prepare a Legal Group File which summarizes the many legal requirements into a few groups. Legal groups are used to help you assign legal requirements to the records quickly and accurately, and simplify the review, operation and update of the records program.

☐ Prepare the Legal Research Notebook to include copies of the original laws (with relevant sections highlighted), the Legal Research Index, and the Legal Group File.

Appendix A   Office of Management and Budget Regulations for the Federal Paperwork Reduction Act

Source:	Code of Federal Regulations
Citation:	5 CFR PART 1320
Agency:	Office of Management and Budget

TITLE 5 — ADMINISTRATIVE PERSONNEL

CHAPTER 3 — OFFICE OF MANAGEMENT AND BUDGET

SUBCHAPTER B — OMB DIRECTIVES

PART 1320 — CONTROLLING PAPERWORK BURDENS ON THE PUBLIC

§ 1320.1 Purpose.

The purpose of this Part is to implement the provisions of the Paperwork Reduction Act of 1980 (Title 44 U.S.C. Chapter 35) (the Act) concerning collections of information. It is issued under the authority of Section 3516 of the Act, which provides that "The Director shall promulgate rules, regulations, or procedures necessary to exercise the authority provided by this Chapter." It is designed to minimize and control burdens associated with the collection of information by Federal agencies from individuals, businesses and other private institutions, and State and local governments. In the case of inter-agency reporting, this Part establishes policy and promulgates regulations to ensure the effective management of inter-agency reporting requirements in the executive branch, and is promulgated under the authority of the Federal Records Act (Title 44 U.S.C. Chapters 21, 25, 27, 29, 31) and Section 104 of the Budget and Accounting Procedures Act of 1950, (Title 31 U.S.C. Section 1111, as well as the Act).

§ 1320.2 Effect.

This Part supersedes and rescinds Circular No. A-40, Revised, dated May 3, 1973, and Transmittal Memorandum No. 1, dated February 10, 1976. This Part will become effective on May 2, 1983.

§ 1320.3 Coverage.

The requirements of this Part apply to all agencies as defined in § 1320.7(a) and to all collections of information conducted or sponsored by those agencies, as defined in § 1320.7(c), wherever conducted or sponsored, except for collections of information:

(a) By compulsory process pursuant to the Anti-trust Civil Process Act or Section 13 of the Federal Trade Commission Improvements Act or Section 13 of the Federal Trade Commission Improvements Act of 1980;

(b) During the conduct of intelligence activities, as defined in Section 4-206 of Executive Order 12036, issued January 24, 1978, or successor orders, including Executive Order 12333, issued December 4, 1981, or during the conduct of cryptologic activities that are communications securities activities; or

(c) During the conduct of a federal criminal investigation or prosecution, during the disposition of a particular criminal matter, during the conduct of a civil action to which the United States or any official or agency thereof is a party, or during the conduct of an administrative action or investigation involving an agency against specific individuals or entities. This exception applies during the entire course of the investigation or action, whether before or after formal charges or complaints are filed or formal administrative action is initiated, but only after a case file or its equivalent is opened with respect to a particular party. General collections of information prepared or undertaken with reference to a category of individuals or entities, such as a class of licensees or an industry, do not fall within this exception.

§ 1320.4 General requirements.

(a) An agency shall not engage in a collection of information without obtaining Office of Management and Budget (OMB) approval of the collection of information and displaying a currently valid OMB control number and, unless OMB determines it to be inappropriate, an expiration date. An agency shall not continue to engage in such collection of such information after the expiration date of the control number, unless OMB has approved an extension. Each agency shall ensure that collections of information required by law or necessary to obtain a benefit, and which are submitted to nine or fewer persons, inform potential respondents that the collection of information is not subject to OMB review under the Act.

(b) To obtain OMB approval of a collection of information, an agency shall demonstrate that it has taken every reasonable step to ensure that:

(1) The collection of information is the least burdensome necessary for the proper performance of the agency's functions to comply with legal requirements and achieve program objectives;

(2) The collection of information is not duplicative of information otherwise accessible to the agency; and

(3) The collection of information has practical utility. The agency shall also seek to minimize the cost to itself of collecting, processing, and using the information, but shall not do so by means of shifting disproportionate costs or burdens onto the public. It shall also comply with the general information collection guidelines set out in § 1320.6, where applicable.

(c) OMB shall determine whether the collection of information, as submitted by the agency, is necessary for the proper performance of the agency's functions. In making this determination, OMB will take into account the criteria listed in § 1320.4(b), and will consider whether the burden of the collection of information is justified by its practical utility. In addition:

(1) OMB will consider necessary any collection of information specifically mandated by statute or court order, but will independently assess any collection of information to the extent that the agency exercises discretion in its implementation; and

(2) OMB will consider necessary any information collection request specifically required by an agency rule approved or not acted upon by OMB pursuant to § § 1320.13 or 1320.14, but will independently assess any such information collection request to the extent that it deviates from the specifications of the rule.

(d) Except as provided in § 1320.19, to the extent that OMB determines that all or any portion of a collection of information by an agency is unnecessary, for any reason, the agency shall not engage in such collection or portion thereof.

§ 1320.5 Public Protection.

(a) Notwithstanding any other provision of law, no person shall be subject to any penalty for failure to comply with any information collection request if the request does not display a currently valid OMB control number, or, in the case of an information collection request which is submitted to nine or fewer persons, the request fails to state that for this reason it is not subject to OMB review under the Act.

(b) Notwithstanding any other provision of law, no person shall be subject to any penalty for failure to comply with any collection of information requirement if the requirement has been disapproved by OMB, unless that disapproval has been overridden by an independent regulatory agency pursuant to § 1320.19. After March 1, 1984, all collection of information requirements that have been submitted to OMB for clearance, and that have not been disapproved by OMB, will display a currently valid OMB control number. The absence of a control number on a collection of information requirement does not, as a legal matter, invalidate such requirement; however, its absence will alert the public that either the agency has failed to comply with applicable legal requirements for the collection of information or the collection of information requirement has been disapproved.

(c) Whenever an agency has imposed an information collection request or collection of information requirement as the means for proving or satisfying a condition to the receipt of a benefit or the avoidance of a penalty, and the information collection request does not display a currently valid OMB control number or statement, as prescribed in § 1320.4(a), or the collection of information requirement has been disapproved by OMB in accordance with the procedures established by this Part (and not overridden by an independent regulatory agency pursuant to § 1320.19), the agency shall not treat a person's failure to comply, in and of itself, as

grounds for withholding the benefit or imposing the penalty. The agency shall instead permit respondents to prove or satisfy the legal conditions in any other reasonable manner.

(1) If such a collection of information is disapproved in whole by OMB (and the disapproval is not overridden pursuant to § 1320.19), the agency shall grant the benefit to (or not impose the penalty on) otherwise qualified persons without requesting further proof concerning the condition.

(2) If such a collection of information is ordered modified by OMB (and the order is not overridden pursuant to § 1320.19), the agency shall permit respondents to prove or satisfy the condition by complying with the collection of information as so modified.

(d) Whenever a member of the public is protected from imposition of a penalty under this section for failure to comply with a collection of information, such penalty may not be imposed by an agency directly, by an agency through judicial process, or by any other person through judicial or administrative process.

§ 1320.6 General information collection guidelines.

Unless the agency is able to demonstrate that such collection of information is necessary to satisfy statutory requirements or other substantial need, OMB will not approve a collection of information:

(a) Requiring respondents to report information to the agency more often than quarterly;

(b) Requiring respondents to prepare a written response to an information collection request or requirement in fewer than 30 days after receipt of it;

(c) Requiring respondents to submit more than an original and two copies of any document;

(d) Requiring grantees to submit or maintain information other than that required under OMB Circular A-102 or A-110;

(e) Providing for renumeration of respondents, other than contractors or grantees;

(f) Requiring respondents to retain records, other than health, medical, or tax records, for more than three years;

(g) In connection with a statistical survey that is not designed to produce results that can be generalized to the universe of study;

(h) Unless the agency has taken all practicable steps to develop separate and simplified requirements for small businesses and other small entities;

(i) Requiring respondents to submit proprietary, trade secret, or other confidential information unless the agency can demonstrate that it has instituted procedures to protect its confidentiality to the extent permitted by law;

(j) Requiring respondents to maintain or provide information in a format other than that in which the information is customarily maintained.

§ 1320.7 Definitions.

For purposes of implementing the Paperwork Reduction Act and this Part, the following terms are defined as follows:

(a) "Agency" means any executive department, military department, government corporation, government controlled corporation, or other establishment in the executive branch of the government, or any independent regulatory agency, but does not include the General Accounting Office, Federal Election Commission, and governments of the District of Columbia and of the territories and possessions of the United States, and their various subdivisions, or government-owned contractor-operated facilities including laboratories engaged in national defense research and production activities.

(b) "Burden" means the total time, effort, or financial resources required to respond to a collection of information, including that to read or hear instructions; to develop, modify, construct, or assemble any materials or equipment; to conduct tests, inspections, polls, observations, or the like necessary to obtain the information; to organize the information into the requested format; to review its accuracy and the appropriateness of its manner of presentation; and to maintain, disclose, or report the information.

(1) The time and financial resources necessary to comply with a collection of information that would be incurred by persons in the normal course of their activities (e.g., in compiling and maintaining business records), will be excluded from the "burden" if the agency demonstrates that the reporting or recordkeeping activities needed to comply are usual and customary.

(2) A collection of information sponsored by a federal agency that it also sponsored by a unit of state or local government is presumed to impose a federal burden except to the extent the agency shows that such state or local requirement would be imposed even in the absence of a federal requirement.

(c) "Collection of information" means the obtaining or soliciting of information by an agency from ten or more persons by means of identical questions, whether such collection of information is mandatory, voluntary, or required to obtain a benefit. For purposes of this definition, the "obtaining or soliciting of information" includes any requirement or request for persons to obtain, maintain, retain, report, or publicly disclose information. "Collections of information" are of two mutually exclusive types: "collection of information requirements" and "information collection requests."

(1) A "collection of information" includes the use of written report forms, application forms, schedules, questionnaires, reporting or recordkeeping requirements, or other similar methods. Similar methods may include contracts, agreements, policy statements, plans, rules or regulations, planning requirements, circulars, directives, instructions, bulletins, requests for proposal or other procurement requirements, interview guides, disclosure requirements, labeling requirements, telegraphic or telephonic requests, and standard questionnaires used to monitor compliance with agency requirements.

(2) Requirements by an agency or a person to obtain or compile information for the purpose of disclosure to members of the public or to the public at large, through posting, notification, labeling, or similar disclosure requirements, constitute the "collection of information" whenever the same requirement to obtain or compile information would be a "collection of information" if the information were directly provided to the agency. The public disclosure of information originally supplied by the Federal government to the recipient for the purpose of disclosure to the public is not included within this definition.

(3) A "collection of information" also includes questions posed to agencies, instrumentalities, or employees of the United States, if the results are to be used for general statistical purposes.

(d) "Collection of information requirement" is the term used for the collection of information by means of agency rule adopted after public notice and comment. The term comprises any form or other written instrument for the collection of information that is published as a part of the rule.

(e) "Director" means the Director of OMB or his designee.

(f) "Display" means:

(1) In the case of forms, questionnaires, instructions, and other written information collection requests individually distributed to potential respondents, to print the OMB control number (and,

unless OMB determines it to be inappropriate, the expiration date) in the upper right hand corner of the front page of the request;

(2) In the case of collections of information published in regulations, guidelines, and other issuances in the FEDERAL REGISTER to publish the OMB control number in the FEDERAL REGISTER (as part of the regulatory text or as a technical amendment) and ensure that it will be included in the Code of Federal Regulations if the issuance is also included therein;

(3) In other cases, and where OMB determines that special circumstances exist, to use other means to inform potential respondents of the OMB control number (and, unless OMB determines it to be inappropriate, the expiration date).

(g) An "Education agency or institution" means any public or private agency or institution with the primary function of education.

(h) "A Federal education program" means any federal activity with a primary purpose of offering instruction or affecting an educational agency's or institution's ability to offer instruction.

(i) "Independent regulatory agency" means the Board of Governors of the Federal Reserve System, the Civil Aeronautics Board, the Commodity Futures Trading Commission, the Consumer Product Safety Commission, the Federal Communications Commission, the Federal Deposit Insurance Corporation, the Federal Energy Regulatory Commission, the Federal Home Loan Bank Board, the Federal Maritime Commission, the Federal Trade Commission, the Interstate Commerce Commission, the Mine Enforcement Safety and Health Review Commission, the National Labor Relations Board, the Nuclear Regulatory Commission, the Occupational Safety and Health Review Commission, the Postal Rate Commission, the Securities and Exchange Commission, National Credit Union Administration, and any other similar agency designated by statute as a Federal independent regulatory agency or commission.

(j) "General purpose statistics" are those collected chiefly for public and general government uses, without primary reference to policy or program operations of the agency collecting the information.

(k) "Information" means any statement of fact or opinion, whether in numerical, graphic, or narrative form, and whether oral or maintained on paper, magnetic tapes, or other media. "Information" does not generally include items in the following categories; however, OMB may determine that any specific item constitutes "information":

(1) Affidavits, oaths, affirmations, certifications, receipts, changes of address, consents, or acknowledgements, provided that they entail no burden other than that necessary to identify the respondent, the date, the respondent's address, and the nature of the instrument;

(2) Samples of products or of any other physical objects;

(3) Facts or opinions obtained through direct observation by an employee or agent of the sponsoring agency or through nonstandardized oral communication in connection with such direct observations;

(4) Facts or opinions submitted in response to general solicitations of comments from the public, published in the FEDERAL REGISTER or other publications, provided that no person is required to supply specific information pertaining to the commenter, other than that necessary for self-identification, as a condition to the agency's full consideration of the comment;

(5) Facts or opinions obtained initially or in follow-on requests, from individuals (including individuals in control groups) under treatment or clinical examination in connection with research on or prophylaxis to prevent a clinical disorder, direct

treatment of that disorder, or the interpretation of biological analyses of body fluids, tissues, or other specimens, or the identification or classification of such specimens;

(6) A request for facts or opinions addressed to a single person;

(7) Examinations designed to test the aptitude, abilities, or knowledge of the persons tested and the collection of information for identification or classification in connection with such examinations;

(8) Facts or opinions obtained or solicited at or in connection with public hearings or meetings;

(9) Facts or opinions obtained or solicited through nonstandardized follow- up questions designed to clarify responses to approved collections of information;

(10) Like items so designated by the Director.

(1) "Information collection request" means the method by which an agency communicates the specifications for a collection of information to potential respondents, including a written report form, application form, schedule, questionnaire, oral communication, reporting or recordkeeping requirement, or other similar method.

(m) "Interagency reporting requirement" means any requirement that an agency report information to another agency or agencies.

(n) "Modify" means to approve in part and disapprove in part.

(o) "Penalty" means the imposition by an agency or court of a fine or other punishment; judgment for monetary damages or equitable relief; or revocation, suspension, reduction, or denial of a license, privilege, right, grant, or benefit.

(p) "Person" means an individual, partnership, association, corporation, (including operations of government owned contractor-operated facilities), business trust, legal representative, organized group of individuals, state, territory, or local government or component thereof. Current employees of the Federal government are excluded from the definition for purposes of the collection of information within the scope of their employment. Military reservists and members of the National Guard are considered Federal employees when on active duty, and for purposes of obtaining information about duty status. Retired and other former federal employees are included entirely within the definition of "person."

(q) "Practical utility" means the actual, not merely the theoretical or potential, usefulness of information to an agency, taking into account its accuracy, adequacy, and reliability, and the agency's ability to process the information in a useful and timely fashion. In determining whether information will have "practical utility," OMB will take into account whether the agency demonstrates actual timely use for the information either to carry out its functions or to make it available to the public, either directly or by means of a public disclosure or labeling requirement, for the use of persons who have an interest in entities or transactions over which the agency has jurisdiction. In the case of general purpose statistics or recordkeeping requirement, "practical utility" means that actual uses can be demonstrated.

(r) "Recordkeeping requirement" means a requirement imposed by an agency on persons to maintain specified records and includes requirements that information be maintained or retained by persons but not necessarily provided to an agency.

(s) "Reporting requirement" means a requirement imposed by an agency on persons to provide information to another person or to the agency. Reporting requirements may implicitly or explicitly include related record- keeping requirements.

(t) "Sponsor." A federal agency is considered to "sponsor" the collection of information if the agency collects the information, causes another agency to collect the information, contracts or enters into a cooperative agreement with a person to collect the information, or requires a person to provide information to another person. A collection of information undertaken by a recipient of a federal grant is considered to be "sponsored" by an agency only if:

(1) The recipient of a grant is collecting information at the specific request of the agency; or

(2) The terms and conditions of the grant require specific approval by the agency of the collection of information or the collection procedures.

(u) "Ten or more persons" refers to the persons to whom an information collection request is addressed by the agency within any 12-month period, and to any independent entities to which the initial addressee may reasonably be expected to transmit the request during that period, including independent state or local entities and separately incorporated subsidiaries or affiliates, but not including employees of the respondent within the scope of their employment, or contractors engaged for the purpose of complying with the information collection request.

(1) Any recordkeeping or reporting requirement contained in a rule of general applicability is deemed to involve ten or more persons.

(2) Any information collection request addressed to all or a substantial majority of an industry is presumed to involve ten or more persons.

§ 1320.8 Agency Head and Senior Official responsibilities.

(a) Except as provided in § 1320.8(b) of this section, each agency head shall designate a Senior Official to carry out the responsibilities of the agency under the Act.

(1) The Senior Official shall report directly to the head of the agency and shall have the authority, subject to that of the agency head, to carry out the responsibilities of the agency under the Act and this Part.

(2) The Senior Official shall independently assess all collections of information to ensure that they meet the criteria specified in § 1320.4(b) and that the agency conducts no collection of information that does not display a currently valid OMB control number.

(b) An agency head may retain full undelegated review authority for any component of the agency which by statute is required to be independent of any agency official below the agency head. For each component for which responsibility under the Act is not delegated to the Senior Official, the agency head shall be responsible for the performance of those functions.

* * * * *

§ 1320.9 Delegation of approval authority.

(a) The Director may, after complying with notice and comment procedures of Title 5 U.S.C. Chapter 5, delegate OMB review of some or all of an agency's collections of information to the Senior Official, or to the agency head with respect to those components of the agency for which he has not delegated authority.

(b) No delegation of review authority shall be made unless the agency demonstrates to OMB that the Senior Official or agency head to whom the authority would be delegated:

(1) Is sufficiently independent of program responsibility to evaluate fairly whether proposed collections of information should be approved, and

(2) Has sufficient resources to carry out this responsibility

effectively.

(c) OMB may limit, condition, or rescind, in whole or in part, at any time, such delegations of authority, and reserves the right to review any individual collection of information, or part thereof, sponsored by an agency, at any time.

(d) Subject to the provisions of this part, and in accord with the terms and conditions of each delegation as specified in Appendix A to this part, the Director delegates review and approval authority to the following agencies:

(1) Board of Governors of the Federal Reserve System.

§ 1320.10 Information collection budget.

Each agency's Senior Official, or agency head in the case of any agency for which the agency head has not delegated responsibility under the Act for any component of the agency to the Senior Official, shall develop and submit to OMB, in such form and in accordance with such procedures as OMB may prescribe, an annual comprehensive budget for all collections of information from the public to be conducted or sponsored by the agency in the succeeding twelve months. If during the course of such year, the agency proposes a collection of information not included in the annual budget, it shall, in accordance with such instructions as OMB may provide, either make offsetting reductions in other items in the budget or obtain supplemental authorization for the additional collection. For good cause, and where it is possible to meets its statutory responsibilities by other means, OMB may exempt any agency from this requirement.

§ 1320.11 Agency submission of collections of information.

(a) Agency submissions of collections of information for OMB review may only be made by the agency head or Senior Official, or their designee. Submissions shall be made in accordance with such procedure and in such form as the Director may prescribe. Submissions shall provide sufficient information to permit consideration of the criteria set out in § 1320.4(b) and (c), shall include an estimate of burden, calculated in a manner prescribed by OMB, shall identify any significant burdens placed on a substantial number of small businesses or other small entities, and shall contain such additional supporting material as the Director may request.

(b) Agencies shall provide copies of the material submitted to OMB for review promptly upon request by any person.

(c) OMB shall review all agency submissions in accordance with the standards set forth in § 1320.4(b) and (c).

(d) In determining whether to approve, disapprove, modify, review, initiate proposals for changes in or stay the effectiveness of its approval of, any collection of information, OMB shall consider any public comments received, and may provide the agency and interested persons additional opportunities to be heard or to submit statements in writing.

(e) Agencies shall submit collections of information contained in proposed rules published for public comment in the FEDERAL REGISTER in accordance with the requirements set forth in § 1320.13. Agencies shall submit collections of information contained in current regulations that were published as final rules in the FEDERAL REGISTER in accordance with the requirements set forth in § 1320.14. Agencies shall submit information collection requests other than those contained in regulations published as final rules in the FEDERAL REGISTER, in accordance with the requirements set forth in § 1320.12. Special rules for clearance and inventory of collections of information pre-

scribed by an agency, but collected by another agency, are set forth in § 1320.15. Special rules for emergency processing of information collection requests are set for in § 1320.17.

(f) Prior to the expiration date assigned to a collection of information, after consultation with the agency, OMB may decide to review the collection of information, and shall so notify the agency. Such decisions will be made only when relevant circumstances have changed or the burden estimates provided by the agency at the time of the initial submission were materially in error. Upon such notification, the agency shall submit the information collection request or requirement for review under the procedures outlined in § 1320.12 or § 1320.14. The agency may continue to sponsor the collection of information while the submission is pending. For good cause, after consultation with the agency, OMB may stay the effectiveness of its approval of any information collection request not specifically required by agency rule, whereupon the agency shall cease sponsoring such request while the submission is pending, and shall publish a notice in the FEDERAL REGISTER to that effect.

(g) Whenever the persons to whom a collection of information is addressed are primarily educational agencies or institutions or whenever the purpose of such activities is primarily to request information needed for the management or formulation of policy related to federal education programs, or research or evaluation studies related to implementation of federal education programs, the collection of information shall be submitted to OMB in accordance with the procedures outlined in this Part. Such request or requirement will be reviewed by the Federal Education Data Acquisition Council (FEDAC), or organizational unit fulfilling the same statutory function within the Department of Education, prior to approval or disapproval by OMB. Collections of information addressed to educational agencies or institutions and submitted to the Secretary of Education under the provisions of Title 20 U.S.C. Section 1221-3 shall be submitted by the Secretary of Education to OMB for approval in accordance with procedures contained in this Part, in time to receive OMB approval and to be announced publicly by the agency by the February 15 preceding the school year in which the information is to be collected.

(h) No substantive or material modification may be made by an agency in an information collection request or requirements after it has been assigned an OMB control number unless the modification has been submitted to OMB for review and approval pursuant to the procedures outlined in this Part.

(i) OMB will reconsider its disapproval of a collection of information upon the written request of an agency head or Senior Official only if the sponsoring agency can provide significant new or additional information relevant to the original decision.

* * * * *

§ 1320.12 Clearance of information collection requests.

Agencies shall submit all collections of information, other than those contained in proposed rules published for public notice and comment, or in current regulations that were published as final rules in the FEDERAL REGISTER, in accordance with the following requirements:

(a) On or before the day of submission to OMB, the agency shall forward a notice to the FEDERAL REGISTER stating that OMB approval is being sought. The notice shall direct requests for information, including copies of the proposed information collection request and supporting documentation, to the agency, and shall direct comments to the Office of Information of Regulatory Affairs of OMB, Attention: Desk Officer for [name of agency]. A copy of the notice submitted to the FEDERAL REGISTER, together with the date of expected publication, shall be included in the agency's submission to OMB.

(b) Within 60 days of its receipt of a proposed information collection request, OMB shall notify the agency involved of its decision to approve, modify, or disapprove the request and shall make such decision publicly available. OMB may extend this 60-day period for an additional 30 days upon notice to the agency. Upon approval of an information collection request, OMB shall assign a control number and an expiration date. OMB shall not approve any information collection request for a period of longer than three years.

(c) If OMB fails to notify the agency of its approval, disapproval, or extension of review within the 60-day period (or 90-day period if notice of an extended review has been given), the agency may request, and OMB shall assign without further delay, a control number, which shall be valid for not more than one year.

(d) No information collection request may become effective until the agency has displayed a valid OMB control number (and, unless OMB determines it to be inappropriate, an expiration date).

§ 1320.13 Clearance of collection of information requirements in proposed rules.

Agencies shall submit collection of information requirements contained in proposed rules published for public comment in the FEDERAL REGISTER in accordance with the following requirements:

(a) The agency shall include in the preamble to the Notice of Proposed Rulemaking a statement that the collection of information requirements contained in the rule have been submitted to OMB for review under Section 3504(h) of the Act. The statement shall direct comments to the Office of Information and Regulatory Affairs of OMB, Attention: Desk Officer for [name of agency].

(b) All such submission shall be made to OMB not later than the day on which the Notice of Proposed Rulemaking is published in the FEDERAL REGISTER, in such form and in accordance with such procedures as the Director may direct. Such submissions shall include a copy of the proposed regulation and preamble.

(c) Within 60 days of publication of the proposed rule, OMB may file public comments on collection of information provisions. Such comments shall be in the form of an OMB Notice of Action, which shall be sent to the Senior Official or agency head, or their designee, and which shall be made a part of the agency's rulemaking record.

(d) If an agency submission is not in compliance with paragraph (b) of this section, OMB may disapprove the collection of information requirement in the proposed rule within 60 days of receipt of the submission. If an agency fails to submit a collection of information requirement subject to this Section, OMB may disapprove it at any time.

(e) When the final rule is published in the FEDERAL REGISTER, the agency shall explain how the final rule responds to any comments received from OMB or the public. The agency shall include an identification and explanation of any modifications made in the rule, or explain why it rejected the comments. If requested by OMB, the agency shall include OMB's comments in the preamble to the final rule.

(f) If OMB has not filed public comments pursuant to § 1320.13(c), or has approved the collection of information requirement contained in a rule before the final rule is published in the FEDERAL REGISTER, OMB may assign a control number

prior to publication of the final rule, and the agency may display the number in its publication of the final rule.

(g) On or before the date of publication of the final rule, the agency shall submit the final rule to OMB, unless it has been approved pursuant to § 1320.13(f) (and not substantively or materially modified by the agency after approval). Not later than 60 days after publication OMB shall approve, modify, or disapprove the collection of information requirement contained in the final rule. Any such disapproval may be based on one or more of the following reasons, as determined by OMB:

(1) The agency failed to comply with paragraph (b) of this section;

(2) The agency had substantially modified the collection of information requirement contained in the final rule from that contained in the proposed rule, without providing OMB with notice of the change of sufficient information to make a determination concerning the modified collection of information requirement, at least 60 days before publication of the final rule; or

(3) In cases where OMB had filed public comments pursuant to paragraph (c) of this section, the agency's response to such comments was unreasonable, and the collection of information is unnecessary for the proper performance of the agency's functions.

(h) After making such decision to approve, modify, or disapprove a collection of information requirement, OMB shall so notify the agency. If OMB approves the collection of information requirement, or if it has not acted upon the submission within the time limits of this Section, OMB shall assign a control number. If OMB disapproves the collection of information requirement, it shall make the reasons for its decision publicly available.

(i) OMB shall not approve any collection of information requirement for a period longer than three years. Approval of any collection of information submitted under this Section will be for the full three-year period, unless the Director determines that there are special circumstances requiring approval for a shorter period.

(j) After receipt of notification of OMB's approval, disapproval, or failure to act, and prior to the effective date of the rule, the agency shall publish a notice in the FEDERAL REGISTER to inform the public of OMB's decision. If OMB has approved or failed to act upon the collection of information requirement, the agency shall include the OMB control number in such notice. A collection of information requirement may not become effective until OMB has assigned a control number, and such number is displayed.

§ 1320.14 Clearance of collections of information in current rules.

Agencies shall submit reporting and recordkeeping requirements contained in current regulations that were published as final rules in the FEDERAL REGISTER in accordance with the following procedures:

(a) Collections of information not previously reviewed by OMB or the General Accounting Office, and not assigned currently valid control numbers, shall be submitted to OMB for review prior to December 31, 1983 in accordance with an orderly schedule to be developed by the agency with OMB concurrence. Previously approved collections of information subject to this section shall be submitted not later than 90 days before the expiration date of the OMB control number assigned to the collection.

(b) On or before the day of submission to OMB, the agency shall forward a notice to the FEDERAL REGISTER stating that OMB review is being sought. The notice shall direct requests for information, including copies of the collection of information and supporting documentation, to the agency, and shall direct comments to the Office of Information and Regulatory Affairs of OMB, Attention: Desk Officer for [name of agency]. A copy of the notice submitted to the FEDERAL REGISTER, together with the date of expected publication, shall be included in the agency's submission to OMB.

(c) Within 60 days of its receipt of a collection of information submission, OMB shall notify the agency involved of its decision whether to approve or to initiate proposals for change in the collection and shall make such decision publicly available. OMB may extend this 60-day period for an additional 30 days upon notice to the agency. Upon approval of a collection of information, OMB shall assign a control number and an expiration date.

(d) OMB shall not approve any collection of information for a period longer than three years. Approval of any collection of information submitted under this Section will be for the full three year period, unless the Director determines that there are special circumstances requiring approval for a shorter period.

(e) If OMB fails to notify the agency of its approval, decision to initiate proposals for change, or extension of review within the 60-day period (or 90 — day period if notice of an extended review has been given), the agency may request, and OMB shall assign without further delay, a control number, which shall be valid for not more than one year. Upon assignment of a control number by OMB, the agency shall display such number in accordance with § 1320.7(f)(2).

(f) If OMB has notified the agency of a decision to initiate proposals for change in the collection of information it shall extend the existing approval of the collection for the duration of the period required for consideration of proposed changes, including that required for OMB approval or disapproval of the collection of information under § 1320.12(b) or § 1320.13(g), as appropriate. In the case of a collection of information not previously approved, a control number shall be granted for such period. The agency shall publish a notice on the agency's next practicable publication date in the FEDERAL REGISTER to inform the public that OMB has initiated proposals for change in the collection, and has granted or extended its approval of the collection of information.

(g) Thereafter, the agency shall, within a reasonable period of time not to exceed 120 days, undertake such procedures as are necessary in compliance with the Administrative Procedure Act and other applicable law to amend or rescind the collection of information, and shall notify the public through the FEDERAL REGISTER. Such notice shall identify the proposed changes in the collections of information and shall solicit public comment on retention, modification, or rescission of such collections of information. If the agency employs notice and comment rulemaking procedures for amendment or rescission of the requirement, publication of the above in the FEDERAL REGISTER and submission to OMB shall initiate OMB clearance procedures under § 3504(h) of the Act and § 1320.13. If the agency does not employ notice and comment rulemaking procedures for amendment or rescission of the collection of information, publication of such notice and submission to OMB shall initiate OMB clearance procedures under Section 3507 of the Act and § 1320.12. All procedures shall be completed within a reasonable period of time to be determined by OMB in consultation with the agency.

(h) OMB may disapprove in whole or in part, any collection of information subject to the procedures of this section if the agency:

(1) Has refused within a reasonable time to comply with an OMB directive to submit the collection of information for review;

(2) Has refused within a reasonable time to initiate procedures to change the collection of information; or

(3) Has refused within a reasonable time to publish a final rule containing the collection of information, with such changes as may be appropriate, or otherwise complete the procedures for amendment or rescission of the collection of information.

(i) Upon disapproval by OMB of a collection of information subject to this section, the OMB control number assigned to such collection shall immediately expire, and no agency shall conduct or sponsor such collection of information. Any such disapproval shall constitute disapproval of the collection of information request or requirement contained in the Notice of Proposed Rulemaking or other submissions, and also of the preexisting request or requirement directed at the same collection of information and therefore constituting essentially the same request or requirement.

§ 1320.15 Collections of information prescribed by another agency.

(a) Any collection of information prescribed by an agency and to be adopted as a Standard or Optional Form after approval by the General Services Administration (GSA) shall be submitted to OMB for approval through GSA in accordance with such procedures and in such form as the Director may prescribe.

(1) Standard and Optional Forms used for the collection of information must be approved by OMB and assigned a currently valid control number before they can be used.

(2) GSA, with the assistance of the agencies using the forms, shall submit annually to OMB a list of all Standard and Optional Forms in use during that year for the collection of information from the public, stating which agencies use these forms, the number of each form used by each agency, and an estimate of the burden required to complete each form. Burden estimates developed by GSA will be counted as burden imposed by each agency in proportion to the use of the information.

(b) Any other collections of information prescribed by an agency but collected by another agency or agencies shall be submitted to OMB for approval by the agency that prescribes the collection, in accordance with such procedures and in such form as the Director may prescribe. With the assistance of the agencies collecting the information, the agency making the submission shall inform OMB of which agencies collect the information and an estimate of the burden of the collection of information. Burden estimates developed by the submitting agency will be counted as burden imposed by each agency in proportion to their use of the information.

(c) In other respects, collections of information under this Section shall be treated under the standards and procedures of § 1320.11-14, as appropriate.

* * * * *

§ 1320.17 Emergency and expedited processing.

An agency head or the Senior Official may request emergency processing of submissions of information collection requests.

(a) Any such request shall be accompanied by a written determination that the collection of information is essential to the mission of the agency, and that public harm will result if normal clearance procedures are followed, or that an unanticipated event has occurred which will prevent or disrupt the collection of information or cause a statutory or judicial deadline to be missed if normal procedures are followed.

(b) The agency shall state the time period within which OMB should approve or disapprove the collection of information.

(c) The agency shall submit information indicating that is has taken all practicable steps to consult with interested agencies and members of the public in order to minimize the burden of the collection of information.

(d) OMB shall approve or disapprove each such submission within the time period stated under § 1320.17(b), provided such time period is consistent with the purposes of the Act.

(e) If OMB approves the collection of information it shall assign a control number valid for a maximum of 90 days after receipt of the agency submission.

(f) Upon request by an agency, OMB may agree to act on a collection of information submission on an expedited schedule, even though such submission may not qualify for emergency processing under this section.

§ 1320.18 Public access.

(a) In order to enable the public to participate in and provide comments during the clearance process, OMB will ordinarily make its paperwork docket files available for public inspection during normal business hours. Notwithstanding other provisions of this rule, requirements to publish public notices or to provide materials to the public may be modified or waived by the Director to the extent that public participation in the approval process would defeat the purpose of the collection of information; jeopardize the confidentiality of proprietary, trade secret, or other confidential information; violate state or federal law; or substantially interfere with an agency's ability to perform its statutory obligations. Provisions of this paragraph guaranteeing public availability of comments on agency collections of information will not be waived or modified.

(b) Agencies conducting or sponsoring an information collection request shall take reasonable steps to inform potential respondents of the identity of the federal agency sponsoring any collection of information, why the information is being collected, how it is to be used, whether responses to the request are voluntary, required to obtain or retain a benefit (citing authority), or mandatory (citing authority), and the nature and extent of confidentiality to be provided, if any (citing authority).

§ 1320.19 Independent regulatory agency override authority.

An independent regulatory agency may override OMB's disapproval or stay of effectiveness of approval of a collection of information by a majority vote of its members or commissioners. The agency shall certify any such override to the Director, and shall explain in writing its reasons for exercising the override authority. OMB shall promptly assign an OMB control number, valid for the length of time requested by the agency, up to three years, to any information collection request or collection of information requirement as to which this authority is exercised. No override shall become effective until the independent regulatory agency has displayed the OMB control number.

§ 1320.20 Other authority.

(a) The Director shall determine whether any collection of information or other matter is within the scope of the Act, or of this Part.

(b) In appropriate cases, after consultation with the agency, the Director may initiate a rulemaking proceeding to determine whether an agency's collection of information is consistent with statutory standards. Such proceedings shall be in accordance with informal rulemaking procedures under Title 5 U.S.C. Chapter 5.

(c) Each agency is responsible for complying with the information policies, principles, standards, and guidelines prescribed by the Director.

(d) To the extent permitted by law, the Director may waive any requirements contained in this Part.

(e) Nothing in this Part shall be interpreted to limit the authority of the Director under the Paperwork Reduction Act of 1980 or any other law. Nothing in this Part or the Paperwork Reduction Act shall be interpreted as increasing or decreasing the authority of OMB with respect to the substantive policies and programs of the agencies.

Appendix B   State Statutes of Limitation Affecting Records

Abbreviations:

SL: Statute of limitations, limitations of action or prescription. Time period begins from starting time stated below.

All periods are in "years."

Statute of Limitations Starting Periods

General Contracts: starts from date of the breach.

Sales Contracts: starts from date of the breach

Personal Injury: starts from date of injury

Property Damage: starts from date of damage

Medical Malpractice: starts from date of alleged act. Actual law suit must generally start within one to three years after the malpractice is recognized but will be barred forever after the stated period. Some states extend the period if the malpractice could not be detected during the period stated.

Legal Malpractice: starts from date of alleged act. Actual law suit must generally start within one to three years after the malpractice is recognized but will be barred forever after the stated period.

Product Liability: starts from date of first sales of product to consumer. Actual law suit must generally start within two to three years after the injury occurs but will be barred forever after the stated period

Improvements to Real Property: starts from date of substantial completion of improvements to real property. Actual law suit must generally start within two years after the defect is recognized but will be barred forever after the stated period

State	General Contracts	Sales Contracts	Personal Injury	Property Injury	Medical Malpractice	Legal Malpractice	Product Liability	Improvements Real Property
Alabama	SL6	SL4	SL2	SL2	SL4	-	SL10	-
Alaska	SL6	SL4	SL2	SL6	-	-	-	SL6
American Samoa	SL10	-	SL2	SL3	-	-	-	-
Arizona	SL6	SL4	SL2	SL2	SL2	-	SL12	SL8
Arkansas	SL3	SL4	SL3	SL3	SL3	SL3	SL3	SL3
California	SL4	SL4	SL4	SL3	SL3	SL4	SL4	SL10
Colorado	SL3	SL3	SL2	SL2	SL2	-	SL2	SL8
Connecticut	SL6	SL4	SL3	SL3	SL2	SL2	-	SL10
Delaware	SL3	SL4	SL2	SL2	SL2	-	-	SL6
District of Columbia	SL3	SL4	SL3	SL3	SL3	SL3	SL3	SL10
Florida	SL5	SL4	SL4	SL4	SL7	SL2	SL4	SL15
Georgia	SL6	SL4	SL2	SL4	SL5	SL2	-	SL10
Guam	SL4	SL4	SL4	SL3	SL4	SL4	SL4	SL4
Hawaii	SL6	SL4	SL2	SL2	SL6	SL6	SL6	SL6
Idaho	SL5	SL4	SL4	SL3	SL2	SL2	SL10	SL6
Illinois	SL10	SL4	SL2	SL5	SL5	-	SL12	SL4
Indiana	SL20	SL4	SL2	SL2	SL15	SL15	SL15	SL12
Iowa	SL10	SL4	SL2	SL5	SL6	-	-	SL15
Kansas	SL5	SL4	SL2	SL2	SL2	SL2	SL2	SL2
Kentucky	SL15	SL4	SL5	SL5	SL1	SL1	SL10	SL7
Louisiana	SL10	SL3	SL10	SL10	SL3	SL3	-	SL10
Maine	SL6	SL4	SL6	SL6	-	-	-	SL10
Maryland	SL3	SL4	SL3	SL3	SL5	-	-	SL20
Massachusetts	SL6	SL4	SL3	SL3	SL7	SL3	SL4	SL6
Michigan	SL6	SL4	SL3	SL3	SL6	SL6	SL6	SL6
Minnesota	SL6	SL4	SL2	SL6	SL2	-	SL4	-
Mississippi	SL3	SL6	SL3	SL3	SL2	SL3	SL3	SL6
Missouri	SL10	SL4	SL5	SL5	SL2	-	-	SL10
Montana	SL8	SL4	SL3	SL2	SL5	SL10	-	SL10
Nebraska	SL5	SL4	SL4	SL4	SL10	SL10	SL10	SL10
Nevada	SL6	SL4	SL2	SL3	SL4	SL4	SL4	SL12
New Hampshire	SL3	SL4	SL3	SL3	SL2	SL3	SL12	SL8
New Jersey	SL6	SL4	SL2	SL6	-	-	-	SL10
New Mexico	SL6	SL4	SL3	SL4	-	-	-	SL10
New York	SL6	SL4	SL3	SL3	SL2.5	-	-	-
North Carolina	SL3	SL4	SL3	SL3	SL4	-	SL6	SL6
North Dakota	SL6	SL4	SL6	SL6	SL6	SL10	SL11	SL10
Ohio	SL15	SL4	SL2	SL2	SL1	SL10	SL10	SL10
Oklahoma	SL5	SL5	SL2	SL2	SL5	SL5	SL5	SL5
Oregon	SL6	SL4	SL10	SL10	SL5	SL10	SL8	SL10

State	General Contracts	Sales Contracts	Personal Injury	Property Injury	Medical Malpractice	Legal Malpractice	Product Liability	Improvements Real Property
Pennsylvania	SL4	SL4	SL2	SL2	SL6	SL6	SL6	SL12
Puerto Rico	-	-	-	-	-	-	-	-
Rhode Island	SL10	SL4	SL10	SL10	SL3	SL10	SL10	SL10
South Carolina	SL6	SL6	SL3	SL3	SL3	SL6	SL6	SL13
South Dakota	SL6	SL4	SL3	SL6	SL2	SL3	SL3	SL11
Tennessee	SL10	SL4	SL1	SL3	-	SL1	-	SL5
Texas	SL4	SL4	SL2	SL2	SL4	SL4	SL4	SL12
Utah	SL6	SL4	SL4	SL3	SL4	SL4	SL2	SL12
Vermont	SL6	SL4	SL3	SL3	SL7	SL6	SL6	SL6
Virgin Islands	SL6	SL4	SL2	SL6	SL10	SL10	SL10	SL10
Virginia	SL5	SL4	SL2	SL5	SL10	SL1	SL1	SL5
Washington	SL6	SL4	SL3	SL3	SL3	SL2	SL12	SL6
West Virginia	SL10	SL4	SL2	SL2	SL2	SL2	SL2	SL10
Wisconsin	SL6	SL6	SL3	SL6	SL5	SL10	SL10	SL6
Wyoming	SL10	-	SL4	SL4	SL2	SL4	SL4	SL4

Appendix C Federal Tax Recordkeeping Requirements

Source: United States Code

TITLE 26 - INTERNAL REVENUE

CHAPTER 61 - INFORMATION AND RETURNS

PART I - RECORDS, STATEMENTS, AND SPECIAL
        RETURNS

Citation: 26 USC 6001

§ 6001. Notice or regulations requiring records, statements, and special returns

Every person liable for any tax imposed by this title, or for the collection thereof, shall keep such records, render such statements, make such returns, and comply with such rules and regulations as the Secretary may from time to time prescribe. Whenever in the judgment of the Secretary it is necessary, he may require any person, by notice served upon such person or by regulations, to make such returns, render such statements, or keep such records, as the Secretary deems sufficient to show whether or not such person is liable for tax under this title. The only records which an employer shall be required to keep under this section in connection with charged tips shall be charge receipts, records necessary to comply with section 6053(c), and copies of statements furnished by employees under section 6053(a).

CHAPTER 66 - LIMITATIONS

SUBCHAPTER A - LIMITATIONS ON ASSESSMENT AND
               COLLECTION

Citation: 26 USC 6501

§ 6501. Limitations on assessment and collection

(a) General rule

Except as otherwise provided in this section, the amount of any tax imposed by this title shall be assessed within 3 years after the return was filed (whether or not such return was filed on or after the date prescribed) or, if the tax is payable by stamp, at any time after such tax became due and before the expiration of 3 years after the date on which any part of such tax was paid, and no proceeding in court without assessment for the collection of such tax shall be begun after the expiration of such period.

* * * * *

(c) Exceptions

(1) False return

In the case of a false or fraudulent return with the intent to evade tax, the tax may be assessed, or a proceeding in court for collection of such tax may be begun without assessment, at any time.

(2) Willful attempt to evade tax

In case of a willful attempt in any manner to defeat or evade tax imposed by this title (other than tax imposed by subtitle A or B), the tax may be assessed, or a proceeding in court for the collection of such tax may be begun without assessment, at any time.

(3) No return

In the case of failure to file a return, the tax may be assessed, or a proceeding in court for the collection of such tax may be begun without assessment, at any time.

(4) Extension by agreement

Where, before the expiration of the time prescribed in this section for the assessment of any tax imposed by this title, except the estate tax provided in chapter 11, both the Secretary and the taxpayer have consented in writing to its assessment after such time, the tax may be assessed at any time prior to the expiration of the period agreed upon. The period so agreed upon may be extended by subsequent agreements in writing made before the expiration of the period previously agreed upon.

(5) Tax resulting from changes in certain income tax or estate tax credits

For special rules applicable in cases where the adjustment of certain taxes allowed as a credit against income taxes or estate taxes results in additional tax, see section 905(c) (relating to the foreign tax credit for income tax purposes) and section 2016 (relating to taxes of foreign countries, States, etc., claimed as credit against estate taxes).

(6) Tax resulting from certain distributions or from termination as life insurance company

In the case of any tax imposed under section 802(a) by reason of section 802(b)(3) on account of a termination of the taxpayer as an insurance company or as a life insurance company to which section 815(d)(2)(A) applies, or on account of a distribution by the taxpayer to which section 815(d)(2)(B) applies, such tax may be assessed within 3 years after the return was filed whether or not such return was filed on or after the date prescribed) for the taxable year for which the taxpayer ceases to be an insurance company, the second taxable year for which the taxpayer is not a life insurance company, or the taxable year in which the distribution is actually made, as the case may be.

(7) Termination of private foundation status

In the case of a tax on termination of private foundation status under section 507, such tax may be assessed, or a proceeding in court for the collection of such tax may be begun without assessment, at any time.

* * * * *

(e) Substantial omission of items

Except as otherwise provided in subsection (c)-

(1) Income taxes

In the case of any tax imposed by subtitle A-

(A) General rule

If the taxpayer omits from gross income an amount properly includible therein which is in excess of 25 percent of the amount of gross income stated in the return, the tax may be assessed, or a proceeding in court for the collection of such tax may be begun without assessment, at any time within 6 years after the return was filed. For purposes of this subparagraph-

(i) In the case of a trade or business, the term "gross income" means the total of the amounts received or accrued from the sale of goods or services (if such amounts are required to be shown on the return) prior to diminution by the cost of such sales or services; and

(ii) In determining the amount omitted from gross income, there shall not be taken into account any amount which is omitted from gross income stated in the return if such amount is disclosed in the return, or in a statement attached to the return, in a manner adequate to apprise the Secretary of the nature and amount of such item.

(B) Constructive dividends

If the taxpayer omits from gross income an amount properly includible therein under section 551(b) (relating to the inclusion in the gross income of United States shareholders of their distributive shares of the undistributed foreign personal holding company income), the tax may be assessed, or a proceeding in court for the collection of such tax may be begun without assessment, at any time within 6 years after the return was filed.

(2) Estate and gift taxes

In the case of a return of estate tax under chapter 11 or a return of gift tax under chapter 12, if the taxpayer omits from the gross estate or from the total amount of the gifts made during the period for which the return was filed items includible in such gross estate or such total gifts, as the case may be, as exceed in amount 25 percent of the gross estate stated in the return or the total amount of gifts stated in the return, the tax may be assessed, or a proceeding in court for the collection of such tax may be begun without assessment, at any time within 6 years after the return was filed. In determining the items omitted from the gross estate or the total gifts, there shall not be taken into account any item which is omitted from the gross estate or from the total gifts stated in the return if such item is disclosed in the return, or in a statement attached to the return, in a manner adequate to apprise the Secretary of the nature and amount of such item.

(3) Excise taxes

In the case of a return of a tax imposed under a provision of subtitle D, if the return omits an amount of such tax properly includible thereon which exceeds 25 percent of the amount of such tax reported thereon, the tax may be assessed, or a proceeding in court for the collection of such tax may be begun without assessment, at any time within 6 years after the return is filed. In

determining the amount of tax omitted on a return, there shall not be taken into account any amount of tax imposed by chapter 41, 42, 43, or 44 which is omitted from the return if the transaction giving rise to such tax is disclosed in the return, or in a statement attached to the return, in a manner adequate to apprise the Secretary of the existence and nature of such item.

(f) Personal holding company tax

If a corporation which is a personal holding company for any taxable year fails to file with its return under chapter 1 for such year a schedule setting forth -

(1) the items of gross income and adjusted ordinary gross income, described in section 543, received by the corporation during such year, and

(2) the names and addresses of the individuals who owned, within the meaning of section 544 (relating to rules for determining stock ownership), at any time during the last half of such year more than 50 percent in value of the outstanding capital stock of the corporation,

the personal holding company tax for such year may be assessed, or a proceeding in court for the collection of such tax may be begun without assessment, at any time within 6 years after the return for such year was filed.

* * * * *

Citation: 26 USC 6502

---

§ 6502. Collection after assessment

(a) Length of period

Where the assessment of any tax imposed by this title has been made within the period of limitation properly applicable thereto, such tax may be collected by levy or by a proceeding in court, but only if the levy is made or the proceeding begun-

(1) within 6 years after the assessment of the tax, or

(2) prior to the expiration of any period for collection agreed upon in writing by the Secretary and the taxpayer before the expiration of such 6-year period (or, if there is a release of levy under section 6343 after such 6-year period, then before such release).

The period so agreed upon may be extended by subsequent agreements in writing made before the expiration of the period previously agreed upon. The period provided by this subsection during which a tax may be collected by levy shall not be extended or curtailed by reason of a judgment against the taxpayer.

* * * * *

SUBCHAPTER B - LIMITATIONS ON CREDIT OR REFUND

Citation: 26 USC 6511

---

§ 6511. Limitations on credit or refund

(a) Period of limitation on filing claim

Claim for credit or refund of an overpayment of any tax imposed by this title in respect of which tax the taxpayer is required to file a return shall be filed by the taxpayer within 3 years from the time the return was filed or 2 years from the time the tax was paid, whichever of such periods expires the later, or if no return was filed by the taxpayer, within 2 years from the time the tax was paid. Claim for credit or refund of an overpayment of any tax imposed by this title which is required to be paid by means of a stamp shall be filed by the taxpayer within 3 years from the time the tax was paid.

* * * * *

(d) Special rules applicable to income taxes

(1) Seven-year period of limitation with respect to bad debts and worthless securities

If the claim for credit or refund relates to an overpayment of tax imposed by subtitle A on account of -

(A) The deductibility by the taxpayer, under section 166 or section 832(c), of a debt as a debt which became worthless, or, under section 165(g), of a loss from worthlessness of a security, or

(B) The effect that the deductibility of a debt or loss described in subparagraph (A) has on the application to the taxpayer of a carryover, in lieu of the 3-year period of limitation prescribed in subsection (a), the period shall be 7 years from the date prescribed by law for filing the return for the year with respect to which the claim is made. If the claim for credit or refund relates to an overpayment on account of the effect that the deductibility of such a debt or loss has on the application to the taxpayer of a carryback, the period shall be either 7 years from the date prescribed by law for filing the return for the year of the net operating loss which results in such carryback or the period prescribed in paragraph (2) of this subsection, whichever expires the later. In the case of a claim described in this paragraph the amount of the credit or refund may exceed the portion of the tax paid within the period prescribed in subsection (b)(2) or (c), whichever is applicable, to the extent of the amount of the overpayment attributable to the deductibility of items described in this paragraph.

* * * * *

SUBCHAPTER D - PERIODS OF LIMITATION IN JUDICIAL PROCEEDINGS

Citation: 26 USC 6531

§ 6531. Periods of limitation on criminal prosecutions

No person shall be prosecuted, tried, or punished for any of the various offenses arising under the internal revenue laws unless the indictment is found or the information instituted within 3 years next after the commission of the offense, except that the period of limitation shall be 6 years -

(1) for offenses involving the defrauding or attempting to defraud the United States or any agency thereof, whether by conspiracy or not, and in any manner;

(2) for the offense of willfully attempting in any manner to evade or defeat any tax or the payment thereof;

(3) for the offense of willfully aiding or assisting in, or procuring, counseling, or advising, the preparation or presentation under, or in connection with any matter arising under, the internal revenue laws, of a false or fraudulent return, affidavit, claim, or document (whether or not such falsity or fraud is with the knowledge or consent of the person authorized or required to present such return, affidavit, claim, or document);

(4) for the offense of willfully failing to pay any tax, or make any return (other than a return required under authority of part III of subchapter A of chapter 61) at the time or times required by law or regulations;

(5) for offenses described in sections 7206(1) and 7207 (re-

lating to false statements and fraudulent documents);

(6) for the offense described in section 7212(a) (relating to intimidation of officers and employees of the United States);

(7) for offenses described in section 7214(a) committed by officers and employees of the United States; and

(8) for offenses arising under section 371 of Title 18 of the United States Code, where the object of the conspiracy is to attempt in any manner to evade or defeat any tax or the payment thereof.

The time during which the person committing any of the various offenses arising under the internal revenue laws is outside the United States or is a fugitive from justice within the meaning of section 3290 of Title 18 of the United States Code, shall not be taken as any part of the time limited by law for the commencement of such proceedings. (The preceding sentence shall also be deemed an amendment to section 3748(a) of the Internal Revenue Code of 1939, and shall apply in lieu of the sentence in section 3748(a) which relates to the time during which a person committing an offense is absent from the district wherein the same is committed, except that such amendment shall apply only if the period of limitations under section 3748 would, without the application of such amendment, expire more than 3 years after the date of enactment of this title, and except that such period shall not, with the application of this amendment, expire prior to the date which is 3 years after the date of enactment of this title.) Where a complaint is instituted before a commissioner of the United States within the period above limited, the time shall be extended until the date which is 9 months after the date of the making of the complaint before the commissioner of the United States. For the purpose of determining the periods of limitation on criminal prosecutions, the rules of section 6513 shall be applicable.

Citation: 26 USC 6532

§ 6532. Periods of limitation on suits

(a) Suits by taxpayers for refund

(1) General rule

No suit or proceeding under section 7422(a) for the recovery of any internal revenue tax, penalty, or other sum, shall be begun before the expiration of 6 months from the date of filing the claim required under such section unless the Secretary renders a decision thereon within that time, nor after the expiration of 2 years from the date of mailing by certified mail or registered mail by the Secretary to the taxpayer of a notice of the disallowance of the part of the claim to which the suit or proceeding relates.

* * * * *

(b) Suits by United States for recovery of erroneous refunds

Recovery of an erroneous refund by suit under section 7405 shall be allowed only if such suit is begun within 2 years after the making of such refund, except that such suit may be brought at any time within 5 years from the making of the refund if it appears that any part of the refund was induced by fraud or misrepresentation of a material fact.

(c) Suit by persons other than taxpayers

(1) General rule

Except as provided by paragraph (2), no suit or proceeding under section 7426 shall be begun after the expiration of 9 months from the date of the levy or agreement giving rise to such action.

* * * * *

CHAPTER 75 - CRIMES, OTHER OFFENSES, AND FORFEITURES

Citation: 26 USC 7203

§ 7203. Willful failure to file return, supply information, or pay tax

Any person required under this title to pay any estimated tax or tax, or required by this title or by regulations made under authority thereof to make a return (other than a return required under authority of section 6015), keep any records, or supply any information, who willfully fails to pay such estimated tax or tax, make such return, keep such records, or supply such information, at the time or times required by law or regulations, shall, in addition to other penalties provided by law, be guilty of a misdemeanor and, upon conviction thereof, shall be fined not more than $25,000 ($100,000 in the case of a corporation), or imprisoned not more than 1 year, or both, together with the costs of prosecution. In the case of any person with respect to whom there is a failure to pay any estimated tax, this section shall not apply to such person with respect to such failure if there is no addition to tax under section 6654 or 6655 with respect to such failure.

Source:	Code of Federal Regulations
Agency:	Department of the Treasury
	Internal Revenue Service

COMPUTATION OF TAXABLE INCOME

Itemized Deductions for Individuals and Corporations

Citation: 26 CFR 1.162-17

§ 1.162-17 Reporting and substantiation of certain business expenses of employees.

* * * * *

(d) *Substantiation of items of expense.* * * *

* * * * *

(2) The Code contemplates that taxpayers keep such records as will be sufficient to enable the Commissioner to correctly determine income tax liability. Accordingly, it is to the advantage of taxpayers who may be called upon to substantiate expense account information to maintain as adequate and detailed records of travel, transportation, entertainment, and similar business expenses as practical since the burden of proof is upon the taxpayer to show that such expenses were not only paid or incurred but also that they constitute ordinary and necessary business expenses. One method for substantiating expenses incurred by an employee in connection with his employment is through the preparation of a daily diary or record of expenditures, maintained in sufficient detail to enable him to readily identify the amount and nature of any expenditure, and the preservation of supporting documents, especially in connection with large or exceptional expenditures. Nevertheless, it is recognized that by reason of the nature of certain expenses or the circumstances under which they are incurred, it is often difficult for an employee to maintain detailed records or to preserve supporting documents for all his expenses. Detailed records of small expenditures incurred in traveling or for trans-

portation, as for example, tips, will not be required.

(3) Where records are incomplete or documentary proof is unavailable, it may be possible to establish the amount of the expenditures by approximations based upon reliable secondary sources of information and collateral evidence. For example, in connection with an item of traveling expense a taxpayer might establish that he was in a travel status a certain number of days but that it was impracticable for him to establish the details of all his various items of travel expense. In such a case rail fares or plane fares can usually be ascertained with exactness and automobile costs approximated on the basis of mileage covered. A reasonable approximation of meals and lodging might be based upon receipted hotel bills or upon average daily rates for such accommodations and meals prevailing in the particular community for comparable accommodations. Since detailed records of incidental items are not required, deductions for these items may be based upon a reasonable approximation. In cases where a taxpayer is called upon to substantiate expense account information, the burden is on the taxpayer to establish that the amounts claimed as a deduction are reasonably accurate and constitute ordinary and necessary business expenses paid or incurred by him in connection with his trade or business. In connection with the determination of factual matters of this type, due consideration will be given to the reasonableness of the stated expenditures for the claimed purposes in relation to the taxpayer's circumstances (such as his income and the nature of his occupation), to the reliability and accuracy of records in connection with other items more readily lending themselves to detailed recordkeeping, and to all of the facts and circumstances in the particular case.

* * * * *

Citation: 26 CFR 1.167(a)-7

§ 1.167(a)-7 Accounting for depreciable property.

* * * * *

(c) A taxpayer may establish as many accounts for depreciable property as he desires. Depreciation allowances shall be computed separately for each account. Such depreciation preferably should be recorded in a depreciation reserve account; however, in appropriate cases it may be recorded directly in the asset account. Where depreciation reserves are maintained, a separate reserve account shall be maintained for each asset account. The regular books of account or permanent auxiliary records shall show for each account the basis of the property, including adjustments necessary to conform to the requirements of section 1016 and other provisions of law relating to adjustments to basis, and the depreciation allowances for tax purposes. In the event that reserves for book purposes do not correspond with reserves maintained for tax purposes, permanent auxiliary records shall be maintained with the regular books of accounts reconciling the differences in depreciation for tax and book purposes because of different methods of depreciation, bases, rates, salvage, or other factors. Depreciation schedules filed with the income tax return shall show the accumulated reserves computed in accordance with the allowances for income tax purposes.

* * * * *

Procedure and Administration

INFORMATION AND RETURNS

Records, Statements, and Special Returns

Citation: 26 CFR 1.6001-1

---

§ 1.6001-1 Records.

(a) *In general.* Except as provided in paragraph (b) of this section, any person subject to tax under subtitle A of the Code (including a qualified State individual income tax which is treated pursuant to section 6361(a) as if it were imposed by chapter 1 of subtitle A), or any person required to file a return of information with respect to income, shall keep such permanent books of account or records, including inventories, as are sufficient to establish the amount of gross income, deductions, credits, or other matters required to be shown by such person in any return of such tax or information.

(b) *Farmers and wage-earners.* Individuals deriving gross income from the business of farming, and individuals whose gross income includes salaries, wages, or similar compensation for personal services rendered, are required with respect to such income to keep such records as will enable the district director to determine the correct amount of income subject to the tax. It is not necessary, however, that with respect to such income individuals keep the books of account or records required by paragraph (a) of this section. For rules with respect to the records to be kept in substantiation of traveling and other business expenses of employees, see § 1.162-17.

(c) *Exempt organizations.* In addition to such permanent books and records as are required by paragraph (a) of this section with respect to the tax imposed by section 511 on unrelated business income of certain exempt organizations, every organization exempt from tax under section 501(a) shall keep such permanent books of account or records, including inventories, as are sufficient to show specifically the items of gross income, receipts and disbursements. Such organizations shall also keep such books and records as are required to substantiate the information required by section 6033. See section 6033 and § 1.6033-1.

(d) *Notice by district director requiring returns statements, or the keeping of records.* The district director may require any person, by notice served upon him, to make such returns, render such statements, or keep such specific records as will enable the district director to determine whether or not such person is liable for tax under subtitle A of the Code, including qualified State individual income taxes, which are treated pursuant to section 6361(a) as if they were imposed by chapter 1 of subtitle A.

(e) *Retention of records.* The books or records required by this section shall be kept at all times available for inspection by authorized internal revenue officers or employees, and shall be retained so long as the contents thereof may become material in the administration of any internal revenue law.

SUBCHAPTER C - EMPLOYMENT TAXES AND COLLECTION OF INCOME TAX AT SOURCE

PART 31 - EMPLOYMENT TAXES AND COLLECTION OF INCOME TAX AT SOURCE

Subpart G - Administrative Provisions of Special Application to Employment Taxes (Selected Provisions of Subtitle F, Internal Revenue Code of 1954)

Citation: 26 CFR 31.6001-1

---

§ 31.6001-1 Records in general.

(a) *Form of records.* The records required by the regulations in this part shall be kept accurately, but no particular form is required for keeping the records. Such forms and systems of accounting shall be used as will enable the district director to ascertain whether liability for tax is incurred and, if so, the amount thereof.

(b) *Copies of returns, schedules, and statements.* Every person who is required, by the regulations in this part or by instructions applicable to any form prescribed thereunder, to keep any copy of any return, schedule, statement, or other document, shall keep such copy as a part of his records.

(c) *Records of claimants.* Any person (including an employee) who, pursuant to the regulations in this part, claims a refund, credit or abatement, shall keep a complete and detailed record with respect to the tax, interest, addition to the tax, additional amount, or assessable penalty to which the claim relates. Such record shall include any records required of the claimant by paragraph (b) of this section and by §31.6001-2 to 31.6001-5, inclusive, which relate to the claim.

(d) *Records of employees.* While not mandatory (except in the case of claims), it is advisable for each employee to keep permanent, accurate records showing the name and address of each employer for whom he performs services as an employee, the dates of beginning and termination of such services, the information with respect to himself which is required by the regulations in this subpart to be kept by employers, and the statements furnished in accordance with the provisions of § 31.6051-1.

(e) *Place and period for keeping records.* (1) All records required by the regulations in this part shall be kept, by the person required to keep them, at one or more convenient and safe locations accessible to internal revenue officers, and shall at all times be available for inspection by such officers.

(2) Except as otherwise provided in the following sentence, every person required by the regulations in this part to keep records in respect of a tax (whether or not such person incurs liability for such tax) shall maintain such records for at least four years after the due date of such tax for the return period to which the records relate, or the date such tax is paid, whichever is the later. The records of claimants required by paragraph (c) of this section shall be maintained for a period of at least four years after the date the claim is filed.

(f) *Cross reference.* See §31.6001-2 to 31.6001-5, inclusive, for additional records required with respect to the Federal Insurance Contributions Act, the Railroad Retirement Tax Act, the Federal Unemployment Tax act, and the collection of income tax at source on wages, respectively.

Citation:　　26 CFR 31.6001-2

§ 31.6001-2 Additional records under Federal Insurance Contributions Act.

(a) *In general.* (1) Every employer liable for tax under the Federal Insurance Contributions Act shall keep records of all remuneration, whether in cash or in a medium other than cash, paid to his employees after 1954 for services (other than agricultural labor which constitutes or is deemed to constitute employment, domestic service in a private home of the employer, or service not in the course of the employer's trade or business) performed for him after 1936. Such records shall show with respect to each employee receiving such remuneration -

(i) The name, address, and account number of the employee and such additional information with respect to the employee as is required by paragraph (c) of § 31.6011(b)-2 when the employee does not advise the employer what his account number and name are as shown on an account number card issued to the employee by the Social Security Administration.

(ii) The total amount and date of each payment of remuneration (including any sum withheld therefrom as tax or for any other reason) and the period of services covered by such payment.

(iii) The amount of each such remuneration payment which constitutes wages subject to tax. See §31.3121(a)-1 to 31.3121(a)(12)-1, inclusive.

(iv) The amount of employee tax, or any amount equivalent to employee tax, collected with respect to such payment, and, if collected at a time other than the time such payment was made, the date collected. See paragraph (b) of § 31.3102-1 for provisions relating to collection of amounts equivalent to employee tax.

(v) If the total remuneration payment (paragraph (a)(1)(ii) of this section) and the amount thereof which is taxable (paragraph (a)(1)(iii) of this section) are not equal, the reason therefor.

(2) Every employer shall keep records of the details of each adjustment or settlement of taxes under the Federal Insurance Contributions Act made pursuant to the regulations in this part. The employer shall keep as a part of his records a copy of each statement furnished pursuant to paragraph (c) of § 31.6011(a)-1.

(3) Every employer shall keep records of all remuneration in the form of tips received by his employees after 1965 in the course of their employment and reported to him pursuant to section 6053(a). The employer shall keep as part of his records employee statements of tips furnished him pursuant to section 6053(a) (unless the information disclosed by such statements is recorded on another document retained by the employer pursuant to paragraph (a)(1) of this section) and copies of employer statements furnished employees pursuant to section 6053(b).

(b) *Agricultural labor, domestic service, and service not in the course of employer's trade or business.* (1) Every employer who pays cash remuneration after 1954 for the performance for him after 1950 of agricultural labor which constitutes or is deemed to constitute employment, of domestic service in a private home of the employer not on a farm operated for profit, or of service not in the course of his trade or business shall keep records of all such cash remuneration with respect to which he incurs, or expects to incur, liability for the taxes imposed by the Federal Insurance Contributions Act, or with respect to which amounts equivalent to employee tax are deducted pursuant to section 3102(a). See §31.3101-3, 31.3111-3, and 31.3121(a)-2 for provisions relating, respectively, to the liability for employee tax which is incurred when wages are received, the liability for employer tax which is incurred when wages are paid, and the time when wages are paid

and received. Such records shall show with respect to each employee receiving such cash remuneration -

(i) The name of the employee.

(ii) The account number of each employee to whom wages for such services are paid within the meaning of § 31.3121(a)-2, and such additional information as is required by paragraph (c) of § 31.6011(b)-2 when the employee does not advise the employer what his account number and name are as shown on an account number card issued to the employee by the Social Security Administration.

(iii) The amount of such cash remuneration paid to the employee (including any sum withheld therefrom as tax or for any other reason) for agricultural labor which constitutes or is deemed to constitute employment, for domestic service in a private home of the employer not on a farm operated for profit, or for service not in the course of the employer's trade or business; the calendar month in which such cash remuneration was paid; and the character of the services for which such cash remuneration was paid. When the employer incurs liability for the taxes imposed by the Federal Insurance Contributions Act with respect to any such cash remuneration which he did not previously expect would be subject to the taxes, the amount of any such cash remuneration not previously made a matter of record shall be determined by the employer to the best of his knowledge and belief.

(iv) The amount of employee tax, or any amount equivalent to employee tax, collected with respect to such cash remuneration and the calendar month in which collected. See paragraph (b) of § 31.3102-1 for provisions relating to collection of amounts equivalent to employee tax.

(v) To the extent material to a determination of tax liability, the number of days during each calendar year after 1956 on which agricultural labor which constitutes or is deemed to constitute employment is performed by the employee for cash remuneration computed on a time basis.

(2) Every person to whom a "crew leader", as that term is defined in section 3121(i), furnishes individuals for the performance of agricultural labor after December 31, 1958, shall keep records of the name; permanent mailing address, or if none, present address; and identification number, if any, of such "crew leader".

§ 31.6001-4 Additional records under Federal Unemployment Tax Act.

(a) *Records of employers.* Every employer liable for tax under the Federal Unemployment Tax Act for any calendar year shall, with respect to each such year, keep such records as are necessary to establish -

(1) The total amount of remuneration (including any sum withheld therefrom as tax or for any other reason) paid to his employees during the calendar year for services performed after 1938.

(2) The amount of such remuneration which constitutes wages subject to the tax. See § 31.3306(b)-1 through § 31.3306(b)(8)-1.

(3) The amount of contributions paid by him into each State unemployment fund, with respect to services subject to the law of such State, showing separately (i) payments made and neither deducted nor to be deducted from the remuneration of his employees, and (ii) payments made and deducted or to be deducted from the remuneration of his employees.

(4) The information required to be shown on the prescribed return and the extent to which the employer is liable for the tax.

(5) If the total remuneration paid (paragraph (a)(1) of this section) and the amount thereof which is subject to the tax (paragraph (a)(2) of this section) are not equal, the reason therefor.

(6) To the extent material to a determination of tax liability, the dates, in each calendar quarter, on which each employee performed services not in the course of the employer's trade or business, and the amount of cash remuneration paid at any time for such services performed within such quarter See § 31.3306(c)(3)-1.

The term "remuneration," as used in this paragraph, includes all payments whether in cash or in a medium other than cash, except that the term does not include payments in a medium other than cash for services not in the course of the employer's trade or business. See § 31.3306(b)(7)-1.

(b) *Records of persons who are not employers.* Any person who employs individuals in employment (see §31.3306(c)-1 to 31.3306(c)-3, inclusive) during any calendar year but who considers that he is not an employer subject to the tax (see § 31.3306(a)-1) shall, with respect to each such year, be prepared to establish by proper records (including, where necessary, records of the number of employees employed each day) that he is not an employer subject to the tax.

Citation: 26 CFR 31.6001-5

---

§ 31.6001-5 Additional records in connection with collection of income tax at source on wages.

(a) Every employer required under section 3402 to deduct and withhold income tax upon the wages of employees shall keep records of all remuneration paid to (including tips reported by) such employees. Such records shall show with respect to each employee -

(1) The name and address of the employee, and after December 31, 1962, the account number of the employee.

(2) The total amount and date of each payment of remuneration (including any sum withheld therefrom as tax or for any other reason) and the period of services covered by such payment.

(3) The amount of such remuneration payment which constitutes wages subject to withholding.

(4) The amount of tax collected with respect to such remuneration payment, and, if collected at a time other than the time such payment was made, the date collected.

(5) If the total remuneration payment (paragraph (a)(2) of this section) and the amount thereof which is taxable (paragraph (a)(3) of this section) are not equal, the reason therefor.

(6) Copies of any statements furnished by the employee pursuant to paragraph (b)(12) of § 31.3401(a)-1 (relating to permanent residents of the Virgin Islands).

(7) Copies of any statements furnished by the employee pursuant to §31.3401(a)(6)-1 and 31.3401(a)(7)-1, relating to nonresident alien individuals.

(8) Copies of any statements furnished by the employee pursuant to § 31.3401(a)(8)(A)-1 (relating to residence or physical presence in a foreign country).

(9) Copies of any statements furnished by the employee pursuant to § 31.3401(a)(8)(C)-1 (relating to citizens resident in Puerto Rico).

(10) The fair market value and date of each payment of noncash remuneration, made to an employee after August 9, 1955, for services performed as a retail commission salesman, with respect to which no income tax is withheld by reason of § 31.3402(j)-1.

(11) With respect to payments made in 1955 under a wage continuation plan (as defined in paragraph (a)(2)(i) of § 1.105-4 and § 1.105-5 of this chapter (Income Tax Regulations)), the

records required to be kept in respect of such payments are those prescribed under paragraph (b)(8)(i) of § 31.3401(a)-1.

(12) In the case of the employer for whom services are performed, with respect to payments made directly by him after December 31, 1955, under a wage continuation plan (as defined in paragraph (a)(2)(i) of § 1.105-4 and § 1.105-5 of this chapter (Income Tax Regulations.)) -

(i) The beginning and ending dates of each period of absence from work for which any such payment was made; and

(ii) Sufficient information to establish the amount and weekly rate of each such payment.

(13) The withholding exemption certificates (Forms W-4 and W-4E) filed with the employer by the employee.

(14) The agreement, if any, between the employer and the employee for the withholding of additional amounts of tax pursuant to § 31.3402(i)-1.

(15) To the extent material to a determination of a tax liability, the dates, in each calendar quarter, on which the employee performed services not in the course of the employer's trade or business, and the amount of cash remuneration paid at any time for such services performed within such quarter. (See § 31.3401(a)(4)-1.)

(16) In the case of tips received by an employee after 1965 in the course of his employment, copies of any statements furnished by the employee pursuant to section 6053(a) unless the information disclosed by such statements is recorded on another document retained by the employer pursuant to the provisions of this paragraph.

(17) Any request of an employee under section 3402(h)(3) and § 31.3402(h)(3)-1 to have the amount of tax to be withheld from his wages computed on the basis of his cumulative wages, and any notice of revocation thereof.

The term "remuneration," as used in this paragraph, includes all payments whether in cash or in a medium other than cash, except that the term does not include payments in a medium other than cash for services not in the course of the employer's trade or business, and does not include tips received by an employee in any medium other than cash or in cash if such tips amount to less than $20 for any cal-endar month. See §31.3401(a)(11)-1 and 31.3401(a)(16)-1, respectively

(b) The employer shall keep records of the details of each adjustment or settlement of income tax withheld under section 3402 made pursuant to the regulations in this part.

SUBCHAPTER F - PROCEDURE AND ADMINISTRATION

PART 301 - PROCEDURE AND ADMINISTRATION

INFORMATION AND RETURNS

Tax Returns or Statements.

Information Regarding Wages Paid Employees

Citation: 26 CFR 301.6058-1

---

§ 301.6058-1 Information required in connection with certain plans of deferred compensation.

* * * * *

(c) *Other rules applicable to annual returns*

* * * * *

(4) *Records.* Records substantiating all data and information required by this section to be filed must be kept at all times available for inspection by internal revenue officers at the principal office or place of business of the employer or plan administrator.

* * * * *

COLLECTION

Citation:	26 CFR 301.6316-6

§ 301.6316-6 Declarations of estimated tax.

(a) *Filing of declaration.* A declaration of estimated tax in respect of amounts on which the tax is to be paid in foreign currency under the provisions of § 301.6316-1 shall be filed with the Director of International Operations, Internal Revenue Service, Washington, D.C. 20225, and shall have attached thereto the statements required by paragraph (b)(1) and (2) (i) of § 301.6316-4 in respect of the tax return except that the statement certified by the foundation, commission, or other person having control of the payments to the taxpayer in nonconvertible foreign currency may be based upon amounts expected to be received by the taxpayer during the taxable year if they are not in fact known at the time of certification. A copy of this certified statement shall be retained by the taxpayer for the purpose of exhibiting it to the disbursing officer when making installment deposits of foreign currency under the provisions of paragraph (c) of this section. For the time for filing declarations of estimated tax, see sections 6073 and 6081 and §1.6073-1 to 1.6073-4, inclusive, and §1.6081-1 and 1.6081-2 of this chapter (Income Tax Regulations).

* * * * *

LIMITATIONS ON ASSESSMENT AND COLLECTION

Citation:26 CFR 301.6501(a)-1

§ 301.6501(a)-1 Period of limitations upon assessment and collection.

(a) The amount of any tax imposed by the Code (other than a tax collected by means of stamps) shall be assessed within 3 years after the return was filed. For rules applicable in cases where the return is filed prior to the due date thereof, see section 6501(b). In the case of taxes payable by stamp, assessment shall be made at any time after the tax became due and before the expiration of 3 years after the date on which any part of the tax was paid. For exceptions and additional rules, see subsections (b) to (g) of section 6501, and for cross references to other provisions relating to limitations on assessment and collection, see section 6501(h) and 6504.

(b) No proceeding in court without assessment for the collection of any tax shall be begun after the expiration of the applicable period for the assessment of such tax.

Citation:26 CFR 301.6501(c)-1

§ 301.6501(c)-1 Exceptions to general period of limitations on assessment and collection.

(a) *False return.* In the case of a false or fraudulent return with intent to evade any tax, the tax may be assessed, or a proceeding in court for the collection of such tax may be begun without assessment, at any time after such false or fraudulent return is filed.

(b) *Willful attempt to evade tax.* In the case of a willful attempt in any manner to defeat or evade any tax imposed by the Code (other than a tax imposed by subtitle A or B, relating to income, estate, or gift taxes), the tax may be assessed, or a proceeding in court for the collection of such tax may be begun without assessment, at any time.

(c) *No return.* In the case of a failure to file a return, the tax may be assessed, or a proceeding in court for the collection of such tax may be begun without assessment, at any time after the date prescribed for filing the return. For special rules relating to filing a return for chapter 42 and similar taxes, see §301.6501(n)-1, 301.6501(n)-2, and 301.6501(n)-3.

(d) *Extension by agreement.* The time prescribed by section 6501 for the assessment of any tax (other than the estate tax imposed by chapter 11 of the Code) may, prior to the expiration of such time, be extended for any period of time agreed upon in writing by the taxpayer and the district director or an assistant regional commissioner. The extension shall become effective when the agreement has been executed by both parties. The period agreed upon may be extended by subsequent agreements in writing made before the expiration of the period previously agreed upon.

Citation:26 CFR 301.6501(e)-1

§ 301.6501(e)-1 Omission from return.

(a) *Income taxes* - (1) *General rule.* (i) If the taxpayer omits from the gross income stated in the return of a tax imposed by subtitle A of the Code an amount properly includible therein which is in excess of 25 percent of the gross income so stated, the tax may be assessed, or a proceeding in court for the collection of such tax may be begun without assessment, at any time within 6 years after the return was filed.

* * * * *

(b) *Estate and gift taxes.* - (1) If the taxpayer omits from the gross estate as stated in the estate tax return, or from the total amount of the gifts made during the period for which the gift tax return was filed (see § 25.6019 - 1 of this chapter) as stated in such return, an item or items properly includible therein the amount of which is in excess of 25 percent of the gross estate as stated in the return, or 25 percent of the total amount of the gifts as stated in the return, the tax may be assessed, or a proceeding in court for the collection thereof may be begun without assessment, at any time within 6 years after the return was filed.

* * * * *

(c) *Excise Taxes* - (1) *In general.* If the taxpayer omits from a return of a tax imposed under a provision of subtitle D an amount properly includible thereon, which amount is in excess of 25 percent of the amount of tax reported thereon, the tax may be assessed or a proceeding in court for the collection thereof may be begun without assessment, at any time within 6 years after the return was filed. For special rules relating to chapter 41, 42, 43, and 44 taxes, see subparagraphs (2), (3), (4), and (5) of this paragraph.

* * * * *

Citation: 26 CFR 301.6501(f)-1

---

§ 301.6501(f)-1 Personal holding company tax.

If a corporation which is a personal holding company for any taxable year fails to file with its income tax return for such year a schedule setting forth the items of gross income described in section 543(a) received by the corporation during such year, and the names and addresses of the individuals who owned, within the meaning of section 544, at any time during the last half of such taxable year, more than 50 percent in value of the outstanding capital stock of the corporation, the personal holding company tax for such year may be assessed, or a proceeding in court for the collection thereof may be begun without assessment, at any time within 6 years after the return for such year was filed.

Limitations on Credit or Refund

Citation: 26 CFR 301.6511(a)-1

---

§ 301.6511(a)-1 Period of limitation on filing claim.

(a) In the case of any tax (other than a tax payable by stamp):

(1) If a return is filed, a claim for credit or refund of an overpayment must be filed by the taxpayer within 3 years from the time the return was filed or within 2 years from the time the tax was paid, whichever of such periods expires the later.

(2) If no return is filed, the claim for credit or refund of an overpayment must be filed by the taxpayer within 2 years from the time the tax was paid.

(b) In the case of any tax payable by means of a stamp, a claim for credit or refund of an overpayment of such tax must be filed by the taxpayer within 3 years from the time the tax was paid. For provisions relating to redemption of unused stamps, see section 6805.

(c) For limitations on allowance of credit or refund, special rules, and exceptions, see subsections (b) through (e) of section 6511. For limitations in the case of a petition to the Tax Court, see section 6512. For rules as to time return is deemed filed and tax considered paid, see section 6513.

Citation: 26 CFR 301.6511(d)-1

---

§ 301.6511(d)-1 Overpayment of income tax on account of bad debts, worthless securities, etc.

(a)(1) If the claim for credit or refund relates to an overpayment of income tax on account of-

(i) The deductibility by the taxpayer, under section 166, or section 832(c), of a debt as a debt which became worthless, or, under section 165(g), of a loss from the worthlessness of a security, or

(ii) The effect that the deductibility of a debt or loss described in subdivision (i) of this subparagraph has on the application to

the taxpayer of a carryover, then in lieu of the 3-year period from the time the return was filed in which claim may be filed or credit or refund allowed, as prescribed in section 6511 (a) or (b), the period shall be 7 years from the date prescribed by law for filing the return (determined without regard to any extension of time for filing such return) for the taxable year for which the claim is made or the credit or refund allowed or made.

* * * * *

Periods of Limitation in Judicial Proceedings

Citation: 26 CFR 301.6532-1

---

§ 301.6532-1 Periods of limitation on suits by taxpayers.

(a) No suit or proceeding under section 7422(a) for the recovery of any internal revenue tax, penalty, or other sum shall be begun until whichever of the following first occurs:

(1) The expiration of 6 months from the date of the filing of the claim for credit or refund, or

(2) A decision is rendered on such claim prior to the expiration of 6 months after the filing thereof.

Except as provided in paragraph (b) of this section, no suit or proceeding for the recovery of any internal revenue tax, penalty, or other sum may be brought after the expiration of 2 years from the date of mailing by registered mail prior to September 3, 1958, or by either registered or certified mail on or after September 3, 1958, by a district director, a director of an internal revenue service center, or an assistant regional commissioner to a taxpayer of a notice of disallowance of the part of the claim to which the suit or proceeding relates.

* * * * *

Citation: 26 CFR 301.6532-2

---

§ 301.6532-2 Periods of limitation on suits by the United States.

The United States may not recover any erroneous refund by civil action under section 7405 unless such action is begun within 2 years after the making of such refund. However, if any part of the refund was induced by fraud or misrepresentation of a material fact, the action to recover the erroneous refund may be brought at any time within 5 years from the date the refund was made.

Citation: 26 CFR 301.6532-3

---

§ 301.6532-3 Periods of limitation on suits by persons other than taxpayers.

(a) *General rule.* No suit or proceeding, except as otherwise provided in section 6532(c)(2) and paragraph (b) of this section, under section 7426 and § 301.7426-1 relating to civil actions by persons other than taxpayers, shall be begun after the expiration of 9 months from the date of levy or agreement under section 6325(b)(3) giving rise to such action.

* * * * *

Source:	Revenue Procedures
Agency:	Department of the Treasury
	Internal Revenue Service
Citation:	Rev. Proc. 81-46

§ 1. Purpose.

.01 The purpose of this revenue procedure is to update Rev. Proc. 76-43, 1976-2 C.B. 667, which sets forth the conditions under which microfilm (including microfiche) reproduction of general books of account will be considered books and records within the meaning of section 6001 of the Internal Revenue Code. General books of account include cash books, journals, voucher registers, ledgers, etc., and supporting records of detail.

§ 2. Changes.

.01 Previous sections 3.02 and 3.03 requiring (1) permission from the Internal Revenue Service to establish a microfilm system and (2) the Service's review of such system have been eliminated.

.02 Section 5.01 revises previous section 4.01 to eliminate specific standards of microfilm systems.

.03 Section 4.03 has been added to provide that those taxpayers considered not in compliance with this revenue procedure may be subject to all applicable penalties under sub-title F of the Code.

§ 3. Background.

.01 Rev. Rul. 75-265, 1975-2 C.B. 460, holds that microfilm reproduction of general books of account and supporting records of detail will be considered books and records within the meaning of section 6001 of the Code when such books are maintained in accordance with Rev. Proc. 75-33, 1975-2 C.B. 559. Rev. Proc. 75-33 was superseded by Rev. Proc. 76-43.

.02 In undertaking a system of micrographic reproduction of books and records, the taxpayer is responsible for the integrity and availability of the books and records, and for a quality that is sufficient to establish the amount of gross income, deductions, credits, or other matters required to be shown in any return of tax or information.

.03 If a taxpayer uses microfilm, books, records, statements, and returns to which section 6001 of the Code applies, they are required to be authentic, accessible, and readable.

§ 4. Procedure.

.01 Taxpayers who want to keep books and records on microfilm must meet the requirements set forth in section 5 of this revenue procedure (1) if they have a micrographic system that includes the ability to produce records on microfilm directly on-line from the computer or off-line from magnetic tape, or (2) if they have records photographed onto microfilm from original documents, "hard copy" printouts, etc.

.02 Taxpayers whose micrographic systems do not meet the requirements of section 5 will be considered not in compliance with section 6001 of the Code and section 1.6001 of the Income Tax Regulations

.03 Taxpayers whose micrographic systems are found to be not in compliance with this revenue procedure may be subject to all applicable penalties under subtitle F of the Code.

§ 5. Requirements.

.01 The following requirements apply to microfilm:

1. Taxpayers must set forth in writing the procedures governing the establishment of a microfilm system, and the individuals who are responsible for maintaining and operating the microfilm system with appropriate authorization from the Board of Directors, general partner(s), or owner, whichever is applicable;

2. The microfilm system must be complete and must be used consistently in the regularly conducted activity of the business;

3. Taxpayers must establish procedures with appropriate documentation so the original document can be followed through the micrographic system;

4. Taxpayers must establish internal procedures for inspection and quality assurance;

5. Taxpayers are responsible for the effective identification, processing, storage, and preservation of microfilm, making it readily available for as long as the contents may become material in the administration of any Internal Revenue law;

6. Taxpayers must keep a record of where, when, by whom, and on what equipment the microfilm was produced;

7. When displayed on a microfilm reader (viewer) or reproduced on paper, the material must exhibit a high degree of legibility and readability. For this purpose, legibility is defined as the quality of a letter or numeral that enables the observer to identify it positively and quickly to the exclusion of all other letters or numerals. Readability is defined as the quality of a group of letters or numerals being recognizable as words or complete numbers;

8. A detailed index of all microfilmed data must be maintained and arranged in a manner that permits the immediate location of any particular record;

9. All microfilming and processing duplication, quality control, storage, identification, and inspection must meet industry standards as set forth by the American National Standards Institute, National Micrographics Association, or National Bureau of Standards;

10. The taxpayer must make available upon the Service's request a reader/printer in good working order at the examination site for reading, locating, and reproducing any record maintained on microfilm; and

11. If any part of the taxpayer's books and records are maintained in any machine-sensible data medium (for example, magnetic tape or magnetic disk) prior to microfilming, the taxpayer must contact the local District Director to get an automatic data processing records evaluation under Rev. Rul. 71-20, 1971-1 C.B. 392.

§ 6. Effect on other documents.

.01 Microfilm books of account are another class of records added to those described in Rev. Proc. 64-12, 1964-1 (Part 1) C.B. 672, if produced by an automatic data processing system. Rev. Proc. 64-12 is amplified. Rev. Proc. 76-43 is superseded.

| Citation: | Rev. Proc. 91-59 |

§ 1. Purpose

.01 The purpose of this revenue procedure is to update Rev. Proc. 86-19, 1986-1 C.B. 558, and to specify the basic requirements that the Internal Revenue Service considers to be essential in cases where a taxpayer's records are maintained within an

Automatic Data Processing (ADP) system. Rev. Proc. 86-19 provides guidelines for record requirements to be followed in cases where part or all of the accounting records are maintained within an ADP system. References to ADP systems include all accounting and/or financial systems and subsystems that process all or part of a taxpayer's transactions, records, or data by other than manual methods.

.02 The technology of automatic data processing has evolved rapidly, and new methods and techniques are constantly being devised and adopted. The requirements set forth in Section 5 of this revenue procedure are intended to ensure that all machine-sensible records generated by a taxpayer's ADP system are retained so long as they may become material in the administration of any internal revenue law. These requirements will be modified and amended as needed to keep pace with developments in ADP systems.

§ 2. Background.

.01 Section 6001 of the Code provides that every person liable for any tax imposed by the Code, or for the collection thereof, shall keep such records as the Secretary may from time to time prescribe.

.02 Rev. Rul. 71-20, 1971-1 C.B. 392, establishes that all machine-sensible data media used for recording, consolidating, and summarizing accounting transactions and records within a taxpayer's ADP system are records within the meaning of section 6001 of the Code and section 1.6001-1 of the Income Tax Regulations, and are required to be retained so long as the contents may be material in the administration of any internal revenue law.

§ 3. Scope.

.01 This revenue procedure encompasses all types of data processing systems, including, but not limited to, microcomputer systems, Data Base Management Systems (DBMS), and all systems using Electronic Data Interchange (EDI) technology. For purposes of this revenue procedure: DBMS means a software system that creates, controls, retrieves, and provides accessibility to data stored in a data base; and EDI technology means the computer-to-computer exchange of business information.

.02 The utilization of a service bureau, time-sharing service, or value-added network does not relieve the taxpayer of the responsibilities described in this revenue procedure.

.03 A taxpayer with assets of $10 million or more at the end of its taxable year shall comply with the record retention requirements of Rev. Rul. 71-20 and the provisions of this revenue procedure. For purposes of this revenue procedure, a controlled group of corporations, as defined in section 1563 of the Code, will be considered to be one corporation and all assets of all members of the group will be aggregated

.04 A taxpayer that has assets of less than $10 million shall comply with the record retention requirements of Rev. Rul. 71-20 and the provisions of this revenue procedure if any of the following conditions exist:

(1) information required by section 6001 of the Code is not in the hardcopy books and records, but is available in machine-sensible records;

(2) machine-sensible records were used for computations that cannot be reasonably verified or recomputed without using a computer (e.g., Last-In, First-Out (LIFO) inventories); or

(3) the taxpayer is notified by the District Director that machine-sensible records must be retained to meet the requirements of section 6001 of the Code.

.05 The requirements of this revenue procedure pertain to all matters under the jurisdiction of the Commissioner of Internal Revenue including, but not limited to, income, excise, employment, and estate and gift taxes, as well as employee plans and exempt organizations.

.06 The requirements of this revenue procedure are applicable to the machine-sensible records generated by a Controlled Foreign Corporation (CFC), a domestic corporation that is 25 percent foreign-owned, and foreign corporation engaged in a trade or business within the United States at any time during a taxable year because the definition of "records" in section 964(c), 982(d), 6038A, and 6038C of the Code and the regulations thereunder has the same meaning as "records" as used in section 6001 of the Code and section 1.6001-1(a) of the regulations.

.07 Machine-sensible records used by an insurance company to determine losses incurred under section 832(b)(5) of the Code shall be retained in accordance with the requirements of this revenue procedure and Rev. Proc. 75- 56, 1975-2 C.B. 596. For this purpose, the machine- sensible files for a particular taxable year include the files for that year and the seven preceding years, all of which must be retained so long as they are material to the examination of the return. *See* section 5.06 for a discussion of materiality.

.08 The requirements of this revenue procedure are applicable to any sections of the Code that have unique or specific record-keeping requirements. For example, machine-sensible records maintained by the taxpayer to meet the requirements of section 274(d) relating to the amount, time, and place of a business expense must meet the requirements of this revenue procedure.

§ 4. District Director Authority.

.01 In the case of a taxpayer that has less than $10 million in assets at the end of its taxable year, the District Director may notify a taxpayer that machine-sensible records must be retained to meet the requirements of section 6001 of the Code, and that Rev. Rul. 71-20 and the provisions of this revenue procedure apply to that taxpayer. Subsequent failure to comply with this notification may result in the imposition of the penalties described in section 7.

.02 The District Director has the authority to enter into or revoke a record retention limitation agreement with the taxpayer to modify or waive all or any of the specific requirements in this revenue procedure. The taxpayer remains subject to all requirements of this revenue procedure that are not specifically modified or waived by a record retention limitation agreement. A taxpayer that has questions regarding the application of this revenue procedure to a specific factual situation should contact the appropriate District Director.

(1) A record retention limitation agreement does not apply to a subsidiary company acquired, or accounting and tax systems added, subsequent to the completion of the record evaluation (see section 3.03 below) upon which the agreement is based. All machine-sensible records produced by a subsequently acquired company or a subsequently added accounting and tax system whose contents may be or may become material in the administration of the Code shall be retained by the taxpayer who signed the agreement until a new evaluation is conducted by the District Director.

(2) Upon the disposition of a subsidiary, the files being retained for the Service by, or for, the disposed subsidiary shall be retained by the taxpayer until a new evaluation can be made by the District Director.

.03 To determine if a taxpayer may limit its retention of machine-sensible records, a record evaluation may be conducted by the District Director. This evaluation of the data processing and accounting systems may be initiated by the District Director or requested by the taxpayer, and is not an "examination," "investigation," or "inspection" of the books and records within the meaning of section 7605(b) of the Code because the evaluation is not directly related to the determination of tax liability for a particular taxable period.

,04 The District Director may periodically initiate tests to establish the authenticity, readability, completeness, and integrity of the machine-sensible records retained as required by this revenue procedure. These tests may include the testing of EDI and/or other procedures, and a review of the internal controls and security procedures associated with the creation and storage of the records. These tests are not an "examination," "investigation," or "inspection" of the books and records within the meaning of section 7605(b) of the Code because these tests are not directly related to the determination of tax liability for a particular taxable period.

§ 5. Machine-Sensible Recordkeeping Requirements.

.01 All machine-sensible records whose contents may be or may become material to the administration of the Code shall be retained by the taxpayer. The retained records shall be in a retrievable format that provides the information necessary to determine the correct tax liability. The taxpayer shall ensure that the details and the source documents underlying any summary accounting data may be easily identified and made available to the Service upon request.

.02 Documentation that provides a complete description of the ADP portion of the accounting system, including all subsystems and files that feed into the accounting system, shall be retained and made available to the Service upon request. The statements and illustrations as to the scope of operations shall be sufficiently detailed to indicate:

(1) the application being performed;

(2) the procedures employed in each application;

(3) the controls used to ensure accurate and reliable processing; and

(4) the controls used to prevent the unauthorized addition, alteration, or deletion of retained records.

.03 The following specific documentation for all retained files shall also be kept:

(1) record formats (including the meaning of all "codes" used to represent information);

(2) flowcharts for a system and a program;

(3) label descriptions;

(4) source program listings of programs that created the retained files;

(5) detailed charts of accounts (for specific periods);

(6) evidence that periodic checks of the retained records that are prescribed in section 5.08 were performed; and

(7) evidence that the retained records reconcile to the books and the tax return. This reconciliation shall establish the relationship between the total of the amounts in the retained records by account to the account totals in the books and to the tax return.

04. Any changes to the ADP system which affects the accounting system and/or subsystems, together with their effective dates, shall be documented in order to preserve an accurate chronological record. This documentation shall include any changes to software or systems and any changes to the formats of files.

Audit trails should be designed to insure that details underlying the summary accounting data, such as invoices and vouchers, may be easily identified and made available to the Service upon request.

.05 In addition to the documentation described in section 5.02 through 5.04, the Service may require that the taxpayer furnish any other evidence (e.g., internal audit reports) that pertains to the authenticity and integrity of the records.

.06 Machine-sensible records are required to be retained until their contents are no longer material to the administration of the Code. At a minimum, this materiality continues until the expiration of the statute of limitations, including extensions, for each tax year. In certain situations, records should be kept for a longer period of time. For example, records that pertain to fixed assets, loses incurred under section 832(b)(5) of the Code, and LIFO inventories should be kept for longer period of time.

.07 All machine-sensible records that must be retained shall be clearly labeled and stored in a secure environment. For example, supplemental labels with the statement "Tax Year 19XX Records - Retain for IRS until _____" or "Retain for IRS, Consult Tax Manager Before Releasing" should be used and affixed to each tape reel, cartridge, disk pack, diskette, or other device being retained, and a retention date should be written on the internal label. Back-up copies of machine-sensible records retained for the service should be stored at an off-site location. The Service recommends that taxpayers refer to the National Archives and Record Administration's (NARA) standards for additional guidance on the maintenance and storage of electronic records. See, Standards for the Creation, Use, Preservation, and Disposition of Electronic Records, 36 C.F.R. Ch. XII, Part 1234, Subpart C (1990).

.08 The taxpayer shall make periodic checks on all records retained for the Service. The Service recommends using the NARA standard for making periodic checks of retained machine-sensible records. See, 36 C.F.R. § 1234.28(g)(4) (199). In general, this standard requires a recordkeeper to annually select and test a random sample of all reels of magnetic tape to identify any loss of data, and to discover and correct the causes of the data loss. In libraries with 1800 or fewer storage units (e.g., magnetic tape reels), a 20 percent random sample or a sample size of 50 units, whichever is larger, shall be read. In libraries with more than 1800 units, a sample of 384 units shall be read.

.09 If any machine-sensible records required to be retained are lost, destroyed, damaged, or found to be incomplete or materially inaccurate, the taxpayer shall report this to the District Director and recreate the files within a reasonable period of time.

.10 Although the NARA sampling standard referred to in section 5.08 is specifically for magnetic computer tape, the Service recommends that all retained machine-sensible media be randomly sampled and tested as described by NARA. A taxpayer whose data maintenance practices conform with the NARA standards and who loses only a portion of the data from a particular storage unit will not be subject to the penalties described in section 7. However, this taxpayer remains responsible for substantiating the information on its return as required by section 6001 of the Code.

.11 The taxpayer must be able to process the retained records at the time of a Service examination. Processing shall include the ability to print a hardcopy of any record. When the data processing system that created the records is being replaced by a system with which the records would be incompatible, the taxpayer shall convert pre-existing records to a format that is compatible with the new system. Any changes in the ability to process the retained records shall be reported to the District Director.

.12 The taxpayer shall provide the Service, at the time of an examination, with computer resources (e.g., terminal access, computer time, personnel, etc.) that are necessary for the processing of the retained records. Failure to provide these resources will be a failure to maintain books and records under section 6001 of the Code.

.13 The use of a DBMS necessitates the implementation of procedures to ensure that appropriate records and documentation are retained. A taxpayer is in compliance with the provisions of this revenue procedure if a sequential file exists and is available to the Service. The sequential file shall contain the detail necessary to identify the underlying source documents. The process to create a sequential file should be reviewed by the District Director prior to destruction of the DBMS records. Section 5.01 through 5.12 of this procedure shall apply to the resultant sequential file(s).

.14 In addition to the documentation described in section 5.02 through 5.05, the following documentation pertaining to each DBMS system shall be retained:

(1) Data Base Description (DBD);

(2) Record layout of each segment with respect to the fields in the segment;

(3) Systems Control Language;

(4) Program Specification Block (PSB); and

(5) Program Communication Block (PCB).

.15 In order to be in compliance with this revenue procedure, a taxpayer that uses EDI technology must retain machine-sensible records that, in combination with any other records (*e.g.*, the underlying contracts, price lists, and price changes), contain all of the detailed information required by section 6001 of the Code. The extent of the detail in the retained electronic and other records, if any, must be equivalent to the level of detail contained in an acceptable paper record. For example, the retained records for an electronic invoice must contain identification of the vendor by name, invoice date, product description, quantity purchased, price, etc. The taxpayer may capture this information at any level within the accounting system provided that the audit trail, authenticity, and integrity of the retained records can be established.

§ 6. Impact on Hardcopy Recordkeeping Requirements.

.01 Except as otherwise provided in this section, the provisions of this revenue procedure do not relieve taxpayers of the responsibility to retain hardcopy records that are created or received in the ordinary course of business as required by existing law and regulations. Hardcopy records may be retained in microfiche or microfilm format in accordance with the requirements outlined in Rev. Proc. 81-46, 1981-2 C.B. 621. These records are not a substitute for the machine-sensible records required to be retained by this revenue procedure.

.02 Hardcopy records generated at the time of a transaction (*e.g., credit card receipts*) *need not be retained if all the details relating to the transaction are subsequently received by the taxpayer in an EDI transaction and are retained by the taxpayer in accordance with this revenue procedure.*

.03 If hardcopy records are not produced or received in the ordinary course of transacting business (as may be the case when utilizing EDI technology), or are not retained pursuant to section 6.02, hardcopy printouts of computerized records need not be created unless requested by the Service. These requests may be made either at the time of an examination or in conjunction with the testing described in section 4.04.

.04 Computer printouts that are created for validation, control, or other temporary purposes need not be retained.

§ 7. Penalties.

The District Director may issue a Notice of Inadequate Records pursuant to section 1.6001-1(d) of the regulations if machine-sensible records are not properly retained as required by this revenue procedure. Failure to comply with the provisions of this revenue procedure may also result in the imposition of an accuracy related civil penalty under section 6662(a) of the Code that is attributable to negligence or disregard of rules or regulations as provided under section 6662(b)(1). A criminal penalty under section 7203 may also be applicable. See Rev. Rul. 81-205, 1981-2 C.B. 225, which explains the applicability of the predecessor of section 6662(a) civil penalty and the section 7203 criminal penalty.

§ 8. Effect on Other Revenue Procedures.

Rev. Proc. 86-19 is superseded for taxable years beginning after December 31, 1991. However, if a taxpayer complies with this revenue procedure for prior taxable years, the taxpayer will be treated as having complied with Rev. Proc. 86-19 for those years.

§ 9. Effective date.

This revenue procedure is effective for taxable years beginning after December 31, 1991.

Source:	Revenue Rulings
Agency:	Department of the Treasury
	Internal Revenue Service
Citation:	Rev. Rul. 71-20

Advice has been requested whether punched cards, magnetic tapes, disks, and other machine-sensible data media used in the automatic data processing of accounting transactions constitute records within the meaning of section 6001 of the Internal Revenue Code of 1954 and section 1.6001-1 of the Income Tax Regulations.

In the typical situation the taxpayer maintains records within his automatic data processing (ADP) system. Daily transactions are recorded on punched cards and processed by the taxpayer's computer which prints daily listings and accumulates the individual transaction records for a month's business on magnetic tapes. At the month's end the tapes are used to print out monthly journals, registers, and subsidiary ledgers and to prepare account summary totals entered on punched cards. The summary data from these cards is posted to the general ledger and a monthly printout is generated to reflect opening balances, summary total postings, and closing balances. At the year's end several closing ledger runs are made to record adjusting entries. In other situations taxpayers use punched cards, disks, or other machine-sensible data media to store accounting information.

Section 6001 of the Code provides that every person liable for any tax imposed by the Code, or for the collection thereof, shall keep such records as the Secretary of the Treasury or his delegate may from time to time prescribe.

Section 1.6001-1(a) of the Income Tax Regulations provides that any person subject to income tax shall keep such permanent books of account of records, including inventories, as are sufficient to establish the amount of gross income, deductions, credits, or other matters required to be shown by such person in any return of such tax.

Section 1.6001-1(e) of the regulations provides that the books and records required by this section shall be retained so long as the contents thereof may become material in the administration of any internal revenue law.

It is held that punched cards, magnetic tapes, disks, and other machine- sensible data media used for recording, consolidating, and summarizing accounting transactions and records within a taxpayer's automatic data processing system are records within the meaning of section 6001 of the Code and section 1.6001-1 of the regulations and are required to be retained so long as the contents may become material in the administration of any internal revenue law.

However, where punched cards are used merely as a means of input to the system and the information is duplicated on magnetic tapes, disks, or other machine-sensible records, such punched cards need not be retained.

It is recognized that ADP accounting systems will vary from taxpayer to taxpayer and, usually, will be designed to fit the specific needs of the taxpayer. Accordingly, taxpayers who are in doubt as to which records are to be retained or who desire further information should contact their District Director for assistance.

See Revenue Procedure 64-12, C.B. 1964-1 (Part 1), 672, which sets forth guidelines for keeping records within an ADP system.

Appendix D   State Tax Records Retention Requirements

State	Limitation of Assessment for General Tax Records		Specific Retention Requirements	
	Lowest	Highest	Income Tax	Sales/Use
Alabama	LA3	LA5	-	-
Alaska	LA3	LA3	-	-
American Samoa	-	-	-	-
Arizona	LA4	LA7	-	2
Arkansas	LA3	LA8	6	6
California	LA4	LA4	-	4
Colorado	LA3	LA4	-	3
Connecticut	LA3	LA3	-	-
Delaware	LA3	LA3	-	-
District of Columbia	LA3	LA5	-	-
Florida	LA3	LA5	-	3
Georgia	LA3	LA6	-	3
Guam	LA3	LA3	-	-
Hawaii	LA3	LA3	3	3
Idaho	LA3	LA6	-	4
Illinois	LA3	LA6	-	3
Indiana	LA3	LA3	-	-
Iowa	LA3	LA6	-	5
Kansas	LA3	LA4	-	3
Kentucky	LA4	LA6	7	4
Louisiana	LA3	LA3	-	-
Maine	LA3	LA6	-	6
Maryland	LA4	LA7	-	4
Massachusetts	LA3	LA3	3	3
Michigan	LA4	LA4	6	4

State	Limitation of Assessment for General Tax Records		Specific Retention Requirements	
	Lowest	Highest	Income Tax	Sales/Use
Minnesota	LA3.5	LA6.5	-	-
Mississippi	LA3	LA3	-	3
Missouri	LA3	LA6	-	3
Montana	LA5	LA7	-	-
Nebraska	LA3	LA3	-	-
Nevada	LA3	LA3	-	4
New Hampshire	LA3	LA3	3	-
New Jersey	LA5	LA5	5	3
New Mexico	LA3	LA10	-	-
New York	LA3	LA6	-	3
North Carolina	LA3	LA3	3	3
North Dakota	LA3	LA6	-	3.25
Ohio	LA4	LA4	4	4
Oklahoma	LA3	LA3	-	3
Oregon	LA3	LA5	-	-
Pennsylvania	LA3	LA6	3	3
Puerto Rico	-	-	-	-
Rhode Island	LA3	LA6	-	3
South Carolina	LA3	LA3	-	3
South Dakota	-	-	6	3
Tennessee	LA3	LA5	6	3
Texas	LA3	LA3	4	4
Utah	LA3	LA3	-	3
Vermont	LA3	LA6	-	3
Virgin Islands	LA3	LA7	-	-
Virginia	LA3	LA6	3	3
Washington	-	LA4	-	5
West Virginia	LA3	LA3	3	3
Wisconsin	LA4	LA6	-	4
Wyoming	LA10	LA10	-	3

Appendix E   Federal Employment Recordkeeping Requirements

Source:	United States Code

TITLE 29 — LABOR

CHAPTER 8 — FAIR LABOR STANDARDS

Citation:	29 USC 211

§ 211. Collection of data

* * * * *

(c) Records

Every employer subject to any provision of this chapter or of any order issued under this chapter shall make, keep, and preserve such records of the persons employed by him and of the wages, hours, and other conditions and practices of employment maintained by him, and shall preserve such records for such periods of time, and shall make such reports therefrom to the Administrator as he shall prescribe by regulation or order as necessary or appropriate for the enforcement of the provisions of this chapter or the regulations or orders thereunder.

* * * * *

CHAPTER 9 — PORTAL-TO-PORTAL PAY

Citation:	29 USC 255

§ 255. Statute of limitations

Any action commenced on or after May 14, 1947, to enforce any cause of action for unpaid minimum wages, unpaid overtime compensation, or liquidated damages, under the Fair Labor Standards Act of 1938, as amended [29 U.S.C. 201 et seq.], the WALSH-HEALEY Act [41 U.S.C. 35 et seq.], or the BACON-DAVIS Act [40 U.S.C. 276a et seq.] −

(a) if the cause of action accrues on or after May 14, 1947 — may be commenced within two years after the cause of action accrued, and every such action shall be forever barred unless commenced within two years after the cause of action accrued, except that a cause of action arising out of a willful violation may be commenced within three years after the cause of action accrued;

* * * * *

CHAPTER 11 — LABOR-MANAGEMENT REPORTING AND DISCLOSURE PROCEDURE

SUBCHAPTER III — REPORTING BY LABOR ORGANIZATIONS, OFFICERS AND EMPLOYEES OF LABOR ORGANIZATIONS, AND EMPLOYERS

Citation:	29 USC 436

§ 436. Retention of records

Every person required to file any report under this subchapter shall maintain records on the matters required to be reported which will provide in sufficient detail the necessary basic information and data from which the documents filed with the Secretary may be verified, explained, or clarified, and checked for accuracy and completeness, and shall include vouchers, worksheets, receipts, and applicable resolutions, and shall keep such records available for examination for a period of not less than five years after the filing of the documents based on the information which they contain.

CHAPTER 18 — EMPLOYEE RETIREMENT INCOME SECURITY PROGRAM

SUBCHAPTER I — PROTECTION OF EMPLOYEE BENEFIT RIGHTS

Citation:	29 USC 1022

§ 1022. Plan description and summary plan description

(a)(1) A summary plan description of any employee benefit plan shall be furnished to participants and beneficiaries as provided in section 1024(b) of this title. The summary plan description shall include the information described in subsection (b) of this section, shall be written in a manner calculated to be understood by the average plan participant, and shall be sufficiently accurate and comprehensive to reasonably apprise such participants and beneficiaries of their rights and obligations under the plan. A summary of any material modification in the terms of the plan and any change in the information required under subsection (b) of this section shall be written in a manner calculated to be understood by the average plan participant and shall be furnished in accordance with section 1024(b)(1) of this title.

(2) A plan description (containing the information required by subsection (b) of this section) of any employee benefit plan shall be prepared on forms prescribed by the Secretary, and shall be filed with the Secretary as required by section 1024(a)(1) of this title. Any material modification in the terms of the plan and any change in the information described in subsection (b) of this section shall be filed in accordance with section 1024(a)(1)(D) of this title.

(b) The plan description and summary plan description shall contain the following information: The name and type of administration of the plan; the name and address of the person designated as agent for the service of legal process, if such person is not the administrator; the name and address of the administrator; names, titles, and addresses of any trustee or trustees (if they are persons different from the administrator); a description of the relevant provisions of any applicable collective bargaining agreement; the plan's requirements respecting eligibility for participation and benefits; a description of the provisions providing for nonforfeitable pension benefits; circumstances which may result in disqualification, ineligibility, or denial or loss of benefits; the source of financing of the plan and the identity of any organization through which benefits are provided; the date of the end of the plan year and whether the records of the plan are kept on a calendar, policy, or fiscal year basis; the procedures to be followed in presenting claims for benefits under the plan and the remedies available under the plan for the redress of claims which are denied in whole or in part (including procedures required under section 1133 of this title).

Citation: 29 USC 1027

---

§ 1027. Retention of records

Every person subject to a requirement to file any description or report or to certify any information therefor under this subchapter or who would be subject to such a requirement but for an exemption or simplified reporting requirement under section 1024(a)(2) or (3) of this title shall maintain records on the matters of which disclosure is required which will provide in sufficient detail the necessary basic information and data from which the documents thus required may be verified, explained, or clarified, and checked for accuracy and completeness, and shall include vouchers, worksheets, receipts, and applicable resolutions, and shall keep such records available for examination for a period of not less than six years after the filing date of the documents based on the information which they contain, or six years after the date on which such documents would have been filed but for an exemption or simplified reporting requirement under section 1024(a)(2) or (3) of this title.

PART 2 — PARTICIPATION AND VESTING

Citation: 29 USC 1059

---

§ 1059. Recordkeeping and reporting requirements

(a)(1) Except as provided by paragraph (2) every employer shall, in accordance with regulations prescribed by the Secretary, maintain records with respect to each of his employees sufficient to determine the benefits due or which may become due to such employees. The plan administrator shall make a report, in such manner and at such time as may be provided in regulations

prescribed by the Secretary, to each employee who is a participant under the plan and who —

(A) requests such report, in such manner and at such time as may be provided in such regulations,

(B) terminates his service with the employer, or

(C) has a 1-year break in service (as defined in section 1053(b)(3)(A) of this title).

The employer shall furnish to the plan administrator the information necessary for the administrator to make the reports required by the preceding sentence. Not more than one report shall be required under subparagraph (A) in any 12- month period. Not more than one report shall be required under subparagraph (C) with respect to consecutive 1-year breaks in service. The report required under this paragraph shall be sufficient to inform the employee of his accrued benefits under the plan and the percentage of such benefits which are nonforfeitable under the plan.

(2) If more than one employer adopts a plan, each such employer shall, in accordance with regulations prescribed by the Secretary, furnish to the plan administrator the information necessary for the administrator to maintain the records and make the reports required by paragraph (1). Such administrator shall maintain the records and, to the extent provided under regulations prescribed by the Secretary, make the reports, required by paragraph (1).

(b) If any person who is required, under subsection (a) of this section, to furnish information or maintain records for any plan year fails to comply with such requirement, he shall pay to the Secretary a civil penalty of $10 for each employee with respect to whom such failure occurs, unless it is shown that such failure is due to reasonable cause.

* * * * *

PART 4 — FIDUCIARY RESPONSIBILITY

Citation: 29 USC 1113

---

§ 1113. Limitation of actions

(a) No action may be commenced under this subchapter with respect to a fiduciary's breach of any responsibility, duty, or obligation under this part, or with respect to a violation of this part, after the earlier of —

(1) six years after (A) the date of the last action which constituted a part of the breach or violation, or (B) in the case of an omission the latest date on which the fiduciary could have cured the breach or violation, or

(2) three years after the earliest date (A) on which the plaintiff had actual knowledge of the breach or violation, or (B) on which a report from which he could reasonably be expected to have obtained knowledge of such breach or violation was filed with the Secretary under this subchapter; except that in the case of fraud or concealment, such action may be commenced not later than six years after the date of discovery of such breach or violation.

PART 6 — ENFORCEMENT

Citation: 29 USC 1451

---

§ 1451. Civil actions

* * * * *

(f) Time limitations

An action under this section may not be brought after the later of —

(1) 6 years after the date on which the cause of action arose, or

(2) 3 years after the earliest date on which the plaintiff acquired or should have acquired actual knowledge of the existence of such cause of action; except that in the case of fraud or concealment, such action may be brought not later than 6 years after the date of discovery of the existence of such cause of action.

* * * * *

Source:	Code of Federal Regulations
Agency:	Department of Labor
	Wage and Hour Division

TITLE 9 — LABOR

SUBCHAPTER A — REGULATIONS

PART 516 — RECORDS TO BE KEPT BY EMPLOYERS

Citation:	29 CFR 516.1

§ 516.1 Form of records; scope of regulations.

(a) *Form of records.* No particular order or form of records is prescribed by the regulations in this part. However, every employer subject to any provisions of the Fair Labor Standards Act of 1938, as amended (hereinafter referred to as the "Act"), is required to maintain records containing the information and data required by the specific sections of this part. The records may be maintained and preserved on microfilm or other basic source document of an automatic word or data processing memory provided that adequate projection or viewing equipment is available, that the reproductions are clear and identifiable by date or pay period and that extensions or transcriptions of the information required by this part are made available upon request.

(b) *Scope of regulations.* The regulations in this part are divided into two subparts. (1) Subpart A of this part contains the requirements generally applicable to all employers employing covered employees, including the requirements relating to the posting of notices, the preservation and location of records, and the recordkeeping requirements for employers of employees to whom both the minimum wage provision of section 6 or the minimum wage provisions of section 6 and the overtime pay provisions of section 7(a) of the Act apply. In addition, section 516.3 contains the requirements relating to executive, administrative, and professional employees (including academic administrative personnel or teachers in elementary or secondary schools), and outside sales employees.

(2) Subpart B of this part deals with the information and data which must be kept for employees (other than executive, administrative, etc., employees) who are subject to any of the exemptions provided in the Act. This section also specifies the records needed for deductions from and additions to wages for "board, lodging, and other facilities," industrial homeworkers and employees whose tips are credited toward wages. The sections in Subpart B of this part require the recording of more, less, or different items of information or data than required under the generally applicable recordkeeping requirements of Subpart A.

(c) *Relationship to other recordkeeping and reporting requirements.* Nothing in 29 CFR Part 516 shall excuse any party from complying with any recordkeeping or reporting requirement imposed by any other Federal, State or local law, ordinance, regulation or rule.

Subpart A — General Requirements

Citation:	29 CFR 516.2

§ 516.2 Employees subject to minimum wage or minimum wage and overtime provisions pursuant to section 6 or sections 6 and 7(a) of the Act.

(a) *Items required.* Every employer shall maintain and preserve payroll or other records containing the following information and data with respect to each employee to whom section 6 or both section 6 and 7(a) of the Act apply:

(1) Name in full, as used for Social Security recordkeeping purposes, and on the same record, the employee's identifying symbol or number if such is used in place of name on any time, work, or payroll records,

(2) Home address, including zip code,

(3) Date of birth, if under 19,

(4) Sex and occupation in which employed (sex may be indicated by use of the prefixes Mr., Mrs., Miss, or Ms.) (Employee's sex identification is related to the equal pay provisions of the Act which are administered by the Equal Employment Opportunity Commission. Other equal pay recordkeeping requirements are contained in 29 CFR Part 1620.)

(5) Time of day and day of week on which the employee's workweek begins (or for employees employed under section 7(k) of the Act, the starting time and length of each employee's work period). If the employee is part of a workforce or employed in or by an establishment all of whose workers have a workweek beginning at the same time on the same day, a single notation of the time of the day and beginning day of the workweek for the whole workforce or establishment will suffice,

(6)(i) Regular hourly rate of pay for any workweek in which overtime compensation is due under section 7(a) of the Act, (ii) explain basis of pay by indicating the monetary amount paid on a per hour, per day, per week, per piece, commission on sales, or other basis, and (iii) the amount and nature of each payment which, pursuant to section 7(e) of the Act, is excluded from the "regular rate" (these records may be in the form of vouchers or other payment data),

(7) Hours worked each workday and total hours worked each workweek (for purposes of this section, a "workday" is any fixed period of 24 consecutive hours and a "workweek" is any fixed and regularly recurring period of 7 consecutive workdays),

(8) Total daily or weekly straight-time earnings or wages due for hours worked during the workday or workweek, exclusive of premium overtime compensation,

(9) Total premium pay for overtime hours. This amount excludes the straight-time earnings for overtime hours recorded under item (8) above,

(10) Total additions to or deductions from wages paid each pay period including employee purchase orders or wage assignments. Also, in individual employee records, the dates, amounts, and nature of the items which make up the total additions and deductions,

(11) Total wages paid each pay period,

(12) Date of payment and the pay period covered by payment.

(b) *Records of retroactive payment of wages.* Every employer who makes retroactive payment of wages or compensation under the supervision of the Administrator of the Wage and Hour Division pursuant to section 16(c) and/or section 17 of the Act, shall:

(1) Record and preserve, as an entry on the pay records, the amount of such payment to each employee, the period covered by such payment, and the date of payment.

(2) Prepare a report of each such payment on a receipt form provided by or authorized by the Wage and Hour Division, and (i) preserve a copy as part of the records, (ii) deliver a copy to the employee, and (iii) file the original, as evidence of payment by the employer and receipt by the employee, with the Administrator or an authorized representative within 10 days after payment is made.

(c) *Employees working on fixed schedules.* With respect to employees working on fixed schedules, an employer may maintain records showing instead of the hours worked each day and each workweek as required by paragraph (a)(7) of this section, the schedule of daily and weekly hours the employee normally works. Also,

(1) In weeks in which an employee adheres to this schedule, indicates by check mark, statement or other method that such hours were in fact actually worked by him, and

(2) In weeks in which more or less than the scheduled hours are worked, shows that exact number of hours worked each day and each week.

Citation:	29 CFR 516.3

---

§ 516.3 Bona fide executive, administrative, and professional employees (including academic administrative personnel and teachers in elementary or secondary schools), and outside sales employees employed pursuant to section 13(a)(1) of the Act.

With respect to each employee in a bona fide executive, administrative, or professional capacity (including employees employed in the capacity of academic administrative personnel or teachers in elementary or secondary schools), or in outside sales, as defined in Part 541 of this chapter (pertaining to so-called "white collar" employee exemptions), employers shall maintain and preserve records containing all the information and data required by § 516.2(a) except paragraphs (a)(6) through (10) and, in addition, the basis on which wages are paid in sufficient detail to permit calculation for each pay period of the employee's total remuneration for employment including fringe benefits and prerequisites. (This may be shown as the dollar amount of earnings per month, per week, per month plus commissions, etc. with appropriate addenda such as "plus hospitalization and insurance plan A," "benefit package B," "2 weeks paid vacation," etc.)

Citation:	29 CFR 516.4

---

§ 516.4 Posting of notices.

Every employer employing any employees subject to the Act's minimum wage provisions shall post and keep posted a notice explaining the Act, as prescribed by the Wage and Hour Division, in conspicuous places in every establishment where such employees are employed so as to permit them to observe readily a copy. Any employer of employees to whom section 7 of the Act does not apply because of an exemption of broad application to an establishment may alter or modify the poster with a legible

notation to show that the overtime provisions do not apply. For example: "Overtime Provisions Not Applicable to Taxicab Drivers (Sec. 13(b)(17))".

Citation:	29 CFR 516.5

---

§ 516.5 Records to be preserved 3 years.

Each employer shall preserve for at least 3 years:

(a) *Payroll records.* From the last date of entry, all payroll or other records containing the employee information and data required under any of the applicable sections of this part, and

(b) *Certificates, agreements, plans, notices, etc.* From their last effective date, all written:

(1) Collective bargaining agreements relied upon for the exclusion of certain costs under section 3(m) of the Act,

(2) Collective bargaining agreements, under section 7(b)(1) or 7(b)(2) of the Act, and any amendments or additions thereto,

(3) Plans, trusts, employment contracts, and collective bargaining agreements under section 7(e) of the Act,

(4) Individual contracts or collective bargaining agreements under section 7(f) of the Act. Where such contracts or agreements are not in writing, a written memorandum summarizing the terms of each such contract or agreement,

(5) Written agreements or memoranda summarizing the terms of oral agreements or understandings under section 7(g) or 7(j) of the Act, and

(6) Certificates and notices listed or named in any applicable section of this part.

(c) *Sales and purchase records.* A record of (1) total dollar volume of sales or business, and (2) total volume of goods purchased or received during such periods (weekly, monthly, quarterly, etc.), in such form as the employer maintains records in the ordinary course of business.

Citation:	29 CFR 516.6

---

§ 516.6 Records to be preserved 2 years.

(a) Supplementary basic records: Each employer required to maintain record under this part shall preserve for a period of at least 2 years.

(1) *Basic employment and earnings records.* From the date of last entry, all basic time and earning cards or sheets on which are entered the daily starting and stopping time of individual employees, or of separate work forces, or the amounts of work accomplished by individual employees on a daily, weekly, or pay period basis (for example, units produced) when those amounts determine in whole or in part the pay period earnings or wages of those employees.

(2) *Wage rate tables.* From their last effective date, all tables or schedules of the employer which provide the piece rates or other rates used in computing straight-time earnings, wages, or salary, or overtime pay computation.

(b) Order, shipping, and billing records: From the last date of entry, the originals or true copies of all customer orders or invoices received, incoming or outgoing shipping or delivery records, as well as all bills of lading and all billings to customers (not including individual sales slips, cash register tapes or the like) which the employer retains or makes in the usual course of business operations.

(c) Records of additions to or deductions from wages paid:

(1) Those records relating to individual employees referred to

in § 516.2(a)(10) and

(2) All records used by the employer in determining the original cost, operating and maintenance cost, and depreciation and interest charges, if such costs and charges are involved in the additions to or deductions from wages paid.

Citation: 29 CFR 516.7

---

§ 516.7 Place for keeping records and their availability for inspection.

(a) *Place of records.* Each employer shall keep records required by this part safe and accessible at the place or places of employment, or at one or more established central recordkeeping offices where such records are customarily maintained. Where the records are maintained at a central recordkeeping office, other than in the place or places of employment, such records shall be made available within 72 hours following notice from the Administrator or a duly authorized and designated representative.

(b) *Inspection of records.* All records shall be available for inspection and transcription by the Administrator or a duly authorized and designated representative.

Citation: 29 CFR 516.8

---

§ 516.8 Computations and reports.

Each employer required to maintain records under this part shall make such extension, recomputation, or transcription of the records and shall submit to the Wage and Hour Division such reports concerning persons employed and the wages, hours, and other conditions and practices of employment set forth in the records as the Administrator or a duly authorized and designated representative may request in writing.

Citation: 29 CFR 516.9

---

§ 516.9 Petitions for exceptions.

(a) *Submission of petitions for relief.* Any employer or group of employers who, due to peculiar conditions under which they must operate, desire authority to maintain records in a manner other than required in this part, or to be relieved of preserving certain records for the period specified in this part, may submit a written petition to the Administrator requesting such authority, setting forth the reasons therefore.

(b) *Action on petitions.* If, after review of the petition, the Administrator finds that the authority requested will not hinder enforcement of the Act, the Administrator may grant such authority limited by any conditions determined necessary and subject to subsequent revocation. Prior to revocation of such authority because of noncompliance with any of the prescribed conditions, the employer will be notified of the reasons and given an opportunity to come into compliance.

(c) *Compliance after submission of petitions.* The submission of a petition or the delay of the Administrator in acting upon such petition will not relieve any employer or group of employers from any obligations to comply with all the applicable requirements of the regulations in this part. However, the Administrator will provide a response to all petitions as soon as possible.

Subpart B — Records Pertaining to Employees Subject to Miscellaneous Exemptions Under the Act; Other Special Requirements

---

Citation: 29 CFR 516.11

---

§ 516.11 Employees exempt from both minimum wage and overtime pay requirements under section 13(a), (2), (3), (4), (5), (8), (10), (12), or 13(d) of the Act.

With respect to each and every employee exempt from both the minimum wage and overtime pay requirements of the Act pursuant to the provisions of section 13(a), (2), (3), (4), (5), (8), (10), (12), or 13(d) of the Act, employers shall maintain and preserve records containing the information and data required by § 516.2(a)(1) through (4).

Citation: 29 CFR 516.12

---

§ 516.12 Employees exempt from overtime pay requirements pursuant to section 13(b)(1), (2),(3), (5), (9), (10), (15), (16), (17), (20), (21), (24), (27), or (28) of the Act.

With respect to each employee exempt from the overtime pay requirements of the Act pursuant to the provisions of section 13(b)(1), (2),(3), (5), (9), (10), (15), (16), (17), (20), (21), (24), (27), or (28) of the Act, shall maintain and preserve payroll or other records, containing all the information and data required by § 516.2(a) except paragraphs (a)(6) and (9) and, in addition, information and data regarding the basis on which wages are paid (such as the monetary amount paid, expressed as earnings per hour, per day, per week, etc.).

Agency: Department of Labor
Equal Employment Opportunity Commission

PART 1602 — RECORDS AND REPORTS

Subpart C — Recordkeeping by Employers

Citation: 29 CFR 1602.12

---

§ 1602.12 Records to be made or kept.

The Commission has not adopted any requirement, generally applicable to employers, that records be made or kept. It reserves the right to impose recordkeeping requirements upon individual employers or groups of employers subject to its jurisdiction whenever, in its judgment, such records (a) are necessary for the effective operation of the EEO-1 reporting system or of any special or supplemental reporting system as described above; or (b) are further required to accomplish the purposes of Title VII. Such recordkeeping requirements will be adopted in accordance with the procedures referred to in section 709(c), and otherwise prescribed by law.

Citation: 29 CFR 1602.13

§ 1602.13 Records as to racial or ethnic identify of employees.

Employers may acquire the information necessary for completion of Items 5 and 6 of Report EEO-1 either by visual surveys of the work force, or at their option, by the maintenance of post-employment records as to the identity of employees where the same is permitted by State law. In the latter case, however, the Commission recommends the maintenance of a permanent record as to the racial or ethnic identity of an individual for purpose of completing the report form only where the employer keeps such records separately from the employee's basic personnel form or other records available to those responsible for personnel decisions, e.g. as part of an automatic data processing system in the payroll department.

Citation: 29 CFR 1602.14

§ 1602.14 Preservation of records made or kept.

(a) Any personnel or employment record made or kept by an employer (including but not necessarily limited to application forms submitted by applicants and other records having to do with hiring, promotion, demotion, transfer, layoff or termination, rates of pay or other terms of compensation, and selection for training or apprenticeship) shall be preserved by the employer for a period of 6 months from the date of the making of the record or the personnel action involved, whichever occurs later. In the case of involuntary termination of an employee, the personnel records of the individual terminated shall be kept for a period of 6 months from the date of termination. Where a charge of discrimination has been filed, or an action brought by the Commission or the Attorney General, against an employer under title VII, the respondent employer shall preserve all personnel records relevant to the charge or action until final disposition of the charge or the action. The term "personnel records relevant to the charge," for example, would include personnel or employment records relating to the aggrieved person and to all other employees holding positions similar to that held or sought by the aggrieved person and application forms or test papers completed by an unsuccessful applicant and by all other candidates for the same position as that for which the aggrieved person applied and was rejected. The date of "final disposition of the charge or the action" means the date of expiration of the statutory period within which the aggrieved person may bring an action in a U.S. District Court or, where an action is brought against an employer either by the aggrieved person, the Commission, or by the Attorney General, the date on which such litigation is terminated.

(b) The requirements of this section shall not apply to application forms and other preemployment records of applicants for positions known to applicants to be of a temporary or seasonal nature.

PART 1607 — UNIFORM GUIDELINES ON EMPLOYEE SELECTION PROCEDURES (1978)

Documentation of Impact and Validity Evidence

Citation: 29 CFR 1607.15

§ 1607.15 Documentation of impact and validity evidence.

A. *Required information.* Users of selection procedures other than those users complying with section 15A(1) below should maintain and have available for each job information on adverse impact of the selection process for that job and, where it is determined a selection process has an adverse impact, evidence of validity as set forth below.

(1) *Simplified recordkeeping for users with less than 100 employees.* In order to minimize recordkeeping burdens on employers who employ one hundred (100) or fewer employees, and other users not required to file EEO-1, et seq., reports, such users may satisfy the requirements of this section 15 if they maintain and have available records showing, for each year:

(a) The number of persons hired, promoted, and terminated for each job, by sex, and where appropriate by race and national origin:

(b) The number of applicants for hire and promotion by sex and where appropriate by race and national origin; and

(c) The selection procedures utilized (either standardized or not standardized).

These records should be maintained for each race or national origin group (see section 4 above) constituting more than two percent (2%) of the labor force in the relevant labor area. However, it is not necessary to maintain records by race and/or national origin (see § 4 above) if one race or national origin group in the relevant labor area constitutes more than ninety-eight percent (98%) of the labor force in the area. If the user has reason to believe that a selection procedure has an adverse impact, the user should maintain any available evidence of validity for that procedure (see sections 7A and 8).

(2) *Information on impact* — (a) *Collection of information on impact.* Users of selection procedures other than those complying with section 15A(1) above should maintain and have available for each job records or other information showing whether the total selection process for that job has an adverse impact on any of the groups for which records are called for by sections 4B above.

* * * * *

(c) *When data is insufficient to determine impact.* Where there has been an insufficient number of selections to determine whether there is an adverse impact of the total selection process for a particular job, the user should continue to collect, maintain and have available the information on individual components of the selection process required in section 15(A)(2)(a) above until the information is sufficient to determine that the overall selection process does not have an adverse impact as defined in section 4 above, or until the job has changed substantially.

(3) *Documentation of validity evidence.* — (a) *Types of evidence.* Where a total selection process has an adverse impact (see section 4 above) the user should maintain and have available for each component of that process which has an adverse impact, one or more of the following types of documentation evidence:

(i) Documentation evidence showing criterion-related validity of the selection procedure (see section 15B, below).

(ii) Documentation evidence showing content validity of the selection procedure (see section 15C, below).

(iii) Documentation evidence showing construct validity of the selection procedure (see section 15D, below)

(iv) Documentation evidence from other studies showing validity of the selection procedure in the user's facility (see section 15E, below).

(v) Documentation evidence showing why a validity study cannot or need not be performed and why continued use of the procedure is consistent with Federal law.

* * * * *

PART 1620 — THE EQUAL PAY ACT

Citation: 29 CFR 1620.32

§ 1620.32 Recordkeeping requirements.

(a) Employers having employees subject to the Act are required to keep records in accordance with U.S. Department of Labor regulations found at 29 CFR Part 516 (Records To Be Kept by Employers Under the FLSA). The regulations of that part are adopted herein by reference.

(b) Every employer subject to the equal pay provisions of the Act shall maintain and preserve all records required by the applicable sections of 29 CFR Part 516 and in addition, shall preserve any records which he makes in the regular course of his business operation which relate to the payment of wages, wage rates, job evaluations, job descriptions, merit systems, seniority systems, collective bargaining agreements, description of practices or other matters which describe or explain the basis for payment of any wage differential to employees of the opposite sex in the same establishment, and which may be pertinent to a determination whether such differential is based on a factor other than sex.

(c) Each employer shall preserve for at least two years the records he makes of the kind described in § 1620.21(b) which explain the basis for payment of any wage differential to employees of the opposite sex in the same establishment.

Citation: 29 CFR 1620.33

§ 1620.33 Recovery of wages due; injunctions; penalties for willful violations.

* * * * *

(b) The following methods are provided under sections 16 and 17 of the FLSA for recovery of unpaid wages: The Commission may supervise payment of the back wages and may bring suit for back pay and an equal amount as liquidated damages. The employee may sue for back pay and an additional sum, up to the amount of back pay, as liquidated damages, plus attorney's fees and court costs. The employee may not bring suit if he or she has been paid back wages in full under supervision of the Commission, or if the Commission has filed suit under the Act to collect the wages due the employee. The Commission may also obtain a court injunction to restrain any person from violating the law, including the unlawful withholding by an employer of proper compensation. A 2-year statute of limitations applies to the recovery of unpaid wages, except that an action on a cause of action arising out of a willful violation may be commenced within 3 years after the cause of action accrued.

* * * * *

PART 1627 — RECORDS TO BE MADE OR KEPT RELATING TO AGE: NOTICES TO BE POSTED: ADMINISTRATIVE EXEMPTIONS

Subpart B — Records To Be Made or Kept Relating to Age; Notices To Be Posted

Citation: 29 CFR 1627.2

§ 1627.2 Forms of records.

No particular order or form of records is required by the regulations in this Part 1627. It is required only that the records contain in some form the information specified. If the information required is available in records kept for other purposes, or can be obtained readily by recomputing or extending data recorded in some other form, no further records are required to be made or kept on a routine basis by this Part 1627.

Citation: 29 CFR 1627.3

§ 1627.3 Records to be kept by employers.

(a) Every employer shall make and keep for 3 years payroll or other records for each of his employees which contain:

(1) Name;

(2) Address;

(3) Date of birth;

(4) Occupation;

(5) Rate of pay, and

(6) Compensation earned each week.

(b)(1) Every employer who, in the regular course of his business, makes, obtains, or uses, any personnel or employment records related to the following, shall, except as provided in paragraphs (b)(3) and (4) of this section, keep them for a period of 1 year from the date of the personnel action to which any records relate:

(i) Job applications, resumes, or any other form of employment inquiry whenever submitted to the employer in response to his advertisement or other notice of existing or anticipated job openings, including records pertaining to the failure or refusal to hire any individual,

(ii) Promotion, demotion, transfer, selection for training, layoff, recall, or discharge of any employee,

(iii) Job orders submitted by the employer to an employment agency or labor organization for recruitment of personnel for job openings,

(iv) Test papers completed by applicants or candidates for any position which disclose the results of any employer-administered aptitude or other employment test considered by the employer in connection with any personnel action,

(v) The results of any physical examination where such examination is considered by the employer in connection with any personnel action,

(vi) Any advertisements or notices to the public or to employees relating to job openings, promotions, training programs, or opportunities for overtime work.

(2) Every employer shall keep on file any employee benefit plans such as pension and insurance plans, as well as copies of any seniority systems and merit systems which are in writing, for the full period the plan or system is in effect, and for at least 1 year after its termination. If the plan or system is not in writing, a

memorandum fully outlining the terms of such plan or system and the manner in which it has been communicated to the affected employees, together with notations relating to any changes or revisions thereto, shall be kept on file for a like period.

(3) In the case of application forms and other preemployment records of applicants for positions which are, and are known by applicants to be, of a temporary nature, every record required to be kept under paragraph (b)(1) of this section shall be kept for a period of 90 days from the date of the personnel action to which the record relates

(4) When an enforcement action is commenced under section 7 of the Act regarding a particular applicant or employee, the Commission or its authorized representative may require the employer to retain any record required to be kept under paragraph (b)(1), (2), or (3) of this section which is relative to such action until the final disposition thereof.

Citation: 29 CFR 1627.6

§ 1627.6 Availability of records for inspection.

(a) *Place records are to be kept.* The records required to be kept by this part shall be kept safe and accessible at the place of employment or business at which the individual to whom they relate is employed or has applied for employment or membership, or at one or more established central recordkeeping offices.

(b) *Inspection of records.* All records required by this part to be kept shall be made available for inspection and transcription by authorized representatives of the Commission during business hours generally observed by the office at which they are kept or in the community generally. Where records are maintained at a central recordkeeping office pursuant to paragraph (a) of this section, such records shall be made available at the office at which they would otherwise be required to be kept within 72 hours following request from the Commission or its authorized representative.

Citation: 29 CFR 1627.7

§ 1627.7 Transcriptions and reports.

Every person required to maintain records under the Act shall make such extension, recomputation or transcriptions of his records and shall submit such reports concerning actions taken and limitations and classifications of individuals set forth in records as the Commission or its authorized representative may request in writing.

Citation: 29 CFR 1627.11

§ 1627.11 Petitions for recordkeeping exceptions.

(a) *Submission of petitions for relief.* Each employer, employment agency, or labor organization who for good cause wishes to maintain records in a manner other than required in this part, or to be relieved of preserving certain records for the period or periods prescribed in this part, may submit in writing a petition to the Commission requesting such relief setting forth the reasons therefor and proposing alternative recordkeeping or record-retention procedures.

* * * * *

Agency: Department of Labor
                Occupational Safety and
                Health Administration

PART 1904 — RECORDING AND REPORTING
              OCCUPATIONAL INJURIES AND ILLNESSES

Citation: 29 CFR 1904.2

§ 1904.2 Log and summary of occupational injuries and illnesses.

(a) Each employer shall, except as provided in paragraph (b) of this section, (1) maintain in each establishment a log and summary of all recordable occupational injuries and illnesses for that establishment; and (2) enter each recordable injury and illness on the log and summary as early as practicable but no later than 6 working days after receiving information that a recordable injury or illness has occurred. For this purpose form OSHA No. 200 or an equivalent which is as readable and comprehensible to a person not familiar with it shall be used. The log and summary shall be completed in the detail provided in the form and instructions on form OSHA No. 200.

(b) Any employer may maintain the log of occupational injuries and illnesses at a place other than the establishment or by means of data-processing equipment, or both, under the following circumstances:

(1) There is available at the place where the log is maintained sufficient information to complete the log to a date within 6 working days after receiving information that a recordable case has occurred, as required by paragraph (a) of this section.

(2) At each of the employer's establishments, there is available a copy of the log which reflects separately the injury and illness experience of that establishment complete and current to a date within 45 calendar days.

Citation: 29 CFR 1904.3

§ 1904.3 Period covered.

Records shall be established on a calendar year basis.

Citation: 29 CFR 1904.4

§ 1904.4 Supplementary record.

In addition to the log of occupational injuries and illnesses provided for under § 1904.2, each employer shall have available for inspection at each establishment within 6 working days after receiving information that a recordable case has occurred, a supplementary record for each occupational injury or illness for that establishment. The record shall be completed in the detail prescribed in the instructions accompanying Occupational Safety and Health Administration Form OSHA No. 101. Workmen's compensation, insurance, or other reports are acceptable alternative records if they contain the information required by Form OSHA No. 101. If no acceptable alternative record is maintained for other purposes, Form OSHA No. 101 shall be used or the necessary information shall be otherwise maintained.

Citation: 29 CFR 1904.6

§ 1904.6 Retention of records.

Records provided for in § § 1904.2, 1904.4, and 1904.5 (including form OSHA No. 200 and its predecessor forms OSHA No. 100 and OSHA No. 102) shall be retained in each establishment for 5 years following the end of the year to which they relate.

Citation: 29 CFR 1904.7

§ 1904.7 Access to records.

(a) Each employer shall provide, upon request, records provided for in § § 1904.2, 1904.4, and 1904.5, for inspection and copying by any representative of the Secretary of Labor for the purpose of carrying out the provisions of the Act, and by representatives of the Secretary of Health, Education, and Welfare during any investigation under section 20(b) of the Act, or by any representative of a State accorded jurisdiction for occupational safety and health inspections or for statistical compilation under sections 18 and 24 of the Act.

(b)(1) The log and summary of all recordable occupational injuries and illnesses (OSHA No. 200) (the log) provided for in § 1904.2 shall, upon request, be made available by the employer to any employee, former employee, and to their representatives for examination and copying in a reasonable manner and at reasonable times. The employee, former employee, and their representatives shall have access to the log for any establishment in which the employee is or has been employed.

(2) Nothing in this section shall be deemed to preclude employees and employee representatives from collectively bargaining to obtain access to information relating to occupational injuries and illnesses in addition to the information made available under this section.

(3) Access to the log provided under this section shall pertain to all logs retained under the requirements of § 1904.6.

Citation: 29 CFR 1904.9

§ 1904.9 Falsification, or failure to keep records or reports.

(a) Section 17(g) of the Act provides that "Whoever knowingly makes any false statement, representation, or certification in any application, record, report, plan or other document filed or required to be maintained pursuant to this Act shall, upon conviction, be punished by a fine of not more than $10,000 or by imprisonment, for not more than 6 months or both."

(b) Failure to maintain records or file reports required by this part, or in the details required by forms and instructions issued under this part, may result in the issuance of citations and assessment of penalties as provided for in sections 9, 10, and 17 of the Act.

Citation: 29 CFR 1904.13

§ 1904.13 Petitions for recordkeeping exceptions.

(a) *Submission of petition.* Any employer who wishes to maintain records in a manner different from that required by this part may submit a petition containing the information specified in paragraph (c) of this section to the Regional Commissioner of the Bureau of Labor Statistics wherein the establishment involved is located.

* * * * *

PART 1910 — OCCUPATIONAL SAFETY AND HEALTH STANDARDS

Subpart C — General Safety and Health Provisions

Citation: 29 CFR 1910.20

§ 1910.20 Access to employee exposure and medical records.

(a) *Purpose.* The purpose of this section is to provide employees and their designated representatives a right of access to relevant exposure and medical records; and to provide representatives of the Assistant Secretary a right of access to these records in order to fulfill responsibilities under the Occupational Safety and Health Act. Access by employees, their representatives, and the Assistant Secretary is necessary to yield both direct and indirect improvements in the detection, treatment, and prevention of occupational disease. Each employer is responsible for assuring compliance with this section, but the activities involved in complying with the access to medical records provisions can be carried out, on behalf of the employer, by the physician or other health care personnel in charge of employee medical records. Except as expressly provided, nothing in this section is intended to affect existing legal and ethical obligations concerning the maintenance and confidentiality of employee medical information, the duty to disclose information to a patient/employee or any other aspect of the medical-care relationship, or affect existing legal obligations concerning the protection of trade secret information.

(b) *Scope and application.* (1) This section applies to each general industry, maritime, and construction employer who makes, maintains, contracts for, or has access to employee exposure or medical records, or analyses thereof, pertaining to employees exposed to toxic substances or harmful physical agents.

(2) This section applies to all employee exposure and medical records, and analyses thereof, of employees exposed to toxic substances or harmful physical agents, whether or not the records are related to specific occupational safety and health standards.

(3) This section applies to all employee exposure and medical records, and analyses thereof, made or maintained in any manner, including on an in-house or contractual (e.g., fee-for-service) basis. Each employer shall assure that the preservation and access requirements of this section are complied with regardless of the manner in which records are made or maintained.

(c) *Definitions.* (1) "Access" means the right and opportunity to examine and copy.

(2) "Analysis using exposure or medical records" means any compilation of data, or any research, statistical or other study based at least in part on information collected from individual employee exposure or medical records or information collected from health insurance claims records, provided that either the analysis has been reported to the employer or no further work is currently being done by the person responsible for preparing the analysis.

(3) "Designated representative" means any individual or organization to whom an employee gives written authorization to exercise a right of access. For the purposes of access to employee

exposure records and analyses using exposure or medical records, a recognized or certified collective bargaining agent shall be treated automatically as a designated representative without regard to written employee authorization.

(4) "Employee" means a current employee, a former employee, or an employee being assigned or transferred to work where there will be exposure to toxic substances or harmful physical agents. In the case of a deceased or legally incapacitated employee, the employee's legal representative may directly exercise all the employee's rights under this section.

(5) "Employee exposure record" means a record containing any of the following kinds of information concerning employee exposure to toxic substances or harmful physical agents:

(i) Environmental (workplace) monitoring or measuring, including personal, area, grab, wipe, or other form of sampling, as well as related collection and analytical methodologies, calculations, and other background data relevant to interpretation of the results obtained;

(ii) Biological monitoring results which directly assess the absorption of a substance or agent by body systems (e.g., the level of a chemical in the blood, urine, breath, hair, fingernails, etc.) but not including results which assess the biological effect of a substance or agent;

(iii) Material safety data sheets; or

(iv) In the absence of the above, any other record which reveals the identity (e.g., chemical, common, or trade name) of a toxic substance or harmful physical agent.

(6)(i) "Employee medical record" means a record concerning the health status of an employee which is made or maintained by a physician, nurse, or other health care personnel, or technician, including:

(A) Medical and employment questionnaires or histories (including job description and occupational exposures),

(B) The results of medical examinations (pre-employment, pre-assignment, periodic, or episodic) and laboratory tests (including X-ray examinations and all biological monitoring),

(C) Medical opinions, diagnoses, progress notes, and recommendations,

(D) Descriptions of treatments and prescriptions, and

(E) Employee medical complaints.

(ii) "Employee medical record" does not include the following:

(A) Physical specimens (e.g., blood or urine samples) which are routinely discarded as a part of normal medical practice, and are not required to be maintained by other legal requirements,

(B) Records concerning health insurance claims if maintained separately from the employer's medical program and its records, and not accessible to the employer by employee name or other direct personal identifier (e.g., social security number, payroll number, etc.), or

(C) Records concerning voluntary employee assistance programs (alcohol, drug abuse, or personal counseling programs) if maintained separately from the employer's medical program and its records.

(7) "Employer" means a current employer, a former employer, or a successor employer.

(8) "Exposure" or "exposed" means that an employee is subjected to a toxic substance or harmful physical agent in the course of employment through any route of entry (inhalation, ingestion, skin contact or absorption, etc.), and includes past exposure and potential (e.g., accidental or possible) exposure, but does not include situations where the employer can demonstrate that the toxic substance or harmful physical agent is not used, handled, stored, generated, or present in the workplace in any manner different from typical non-occupational situations.

(9) "Record" means any item, collection, or grouping of information regardless of the form or process by which it is maintained (e.g., paper document, microfiche, microfilm, X-ray film, or automated data processing).

(10) "Specific written consent" (i) means a written authorization containing the following:

(A) The name and signature of the employee authorizing the release of medical information,

(B) The date of the written authorization,

(C) The name of the individual or organization that is authorized to release the medical information,

(D) The name of the designated representative (individual or organization) that is authorized to receive the released information,

(E) A general description of the medical information that is authorized to be released,

(F) A general description of the purpose for the release of the medical information, and

(G) A date or condition upon which the written authorization will expire (if less than one year).

(ii) A written authorization does not operate to authorize the release of medical information not in existence on the date of written authorization, unless this is expressly authorized, and does not operate for more than one year from the date of written authorization.

(iii) A written authorization may be revoked in writing prospectively at any time.

(11) "Toxic substance or harmful physical agent" means any chemical substance, biological agent (bacteria, virus, fungus, etc.) or physical stress (noise, heat, cold, vibration, repetitive motion, ionizing and non-ionizing radiation, hypo- or hyperbaric pressure, etc.) which:

(i) Is regulated by any Federal law or rule due to a hazard to health,

(ii) Is listed in the latest printed edition of the National Institute for Occupational Safety and Health (NIOSH) Registry of Toxic Effects of Chemical Substances (RTECS) (*See* Appendix B),

(iii) Has yielded positive evidence of an acute or chronic health hazard in human, animal, or other biological testing conducted by, or known to, the employer, or

(iv) Has a material safety data sheet available to the employer indicating that the material may pose a hazard to human health.

(d) *Preservation of records.* (1) Unless a specific occupational safety and health standard provides a different period of time, each employer shall assure the preservation and retention of records as follows:

(i) *Employee medical records.* Each employee medical record shall be preserved and maintained for at least the duration of employment plus thirty (30) years, except that health insurance claims records maintained separately from the employer's medical program and its records need not be retained for any specified period;

(ii) *Employee exposure records.* Each employee exposure record shall be preserved and maintained for at least thirty (30) years, except that:

(A) Background data to environmental (workplace) monitoring or measuring, such as laboratory reports and worksheets, need only be retained for one (1) year so long as the sampling results, the collection methodology (sampling plan), a description of the analytical and mathematical methods used, and a summary of other background data relevant to interpretation of the results obtained, are retained for at least thirty (30) years; and

(B) Material safety data sheets and paragraph (c)(5)(iv) records concerning the identity of a substance or agent need not be retained for any specified period as long as some record of the identity (chemical name if known) of the substance or agent, where it was used, and when it was used is retained for at least thirty (30) years; and

(iii) *Analyses using exposure or medical records.* Each analysis using exposure or medical records shall be preserved and maintained for at least thirty (30) years.

(2) Nothing in this section is intended to mandate the form, manner, or process by which an employer preserves a record so long as the information contained in the record is preserved and retrievable, except that X-ray films shall be preserved in their original state.

(e) *Access to records (1) General.* (i) Whenever an employee or designated representative requests access to a record, the employer shall assure that access is provided in a reasonable time, place, and manner, but in no event later than fifteen (15) days after the request for access is made.

(ii) Whenever an employee or designated representative requests a copy of a record, the employer shall, within the period of time previously specified, assure that either:

(A) A copy of the record is provided without cost to the employee or representative,

(B) The necessary mechanical copying facilities (e.g., photocopying) are made available without cost to the employee or representative for copying the record, or

(C) The record is loaned to the employee or representative for a reasonable time to enable a copy to be made.

(iii) Whenever a record has been previously provided without cost to an employee or designated representative, the employer may charge reasonable, non-discriminatory administrative costs (i.e., search and copying expenses but not including overhead expenses) for a request by the employee or designated representative for additional copies of the record, except that

(A) An employer shall not charge for an initial request for a copy of new information that has been added to a record which was previously provided; and

(B) An employer shall not charge for an initial request by a recognized or certified collective bargaining agent for a copy of an employee exposure record or an analysis using exposure or medical records.

(iv) Nothing in this section in intended to preclude employees and collective bargaining agents from collectively bargaining to obtain access to information in addition to that available under this section.

(2) *Employee and designated representative access — (i) Employee exposure records.* Each employer shall, upon request, assure the access of each employee and designated representative to employee exposure records relevant to the employee. For the purpose of this section, exposure records relevant to the employee consist of:

(A) Records of the employee's past or present exposure to toxic substances or harmful physical agents,

(B) Exposure records of other employees with past or present job duties or working conditions related to or similar to those of the employee,

(C) Records containing exposure information concerning the employee's workplace or working conditions, and

(D) Exposure records pertaining to workplaces or working conditions to which the employee is being assigned or transferred.

(ii) *Employee medical records.* (A) Each employer shall, upon request, assure the access of each employee to employee medical records of which the employee is the subject, except as provided in paragraph (e)(2)(ii)(D) below.

(B) Each employer shall, upon request, assure the access of each designated representative to the employee medical records of any employee who has given the designated representative specific written consent. Appendix A to this section contains a sample form which may be used to establish specific written consent for access to employee medical records.

(C) Whenever access to employee medical records is requested, a physician representing the employer may recommend that the employee or designated representative:

(*1*) Consult with the physician for the purposes of reviewing and discussing the records requested,

(*2*) Accept a summary of material facts and opinions in lieu of the records requested, or

(*3*) Accept release of the requested records only to a physician or other designated representative.

(D) Whenever an employee requests access to his or her employee medical records, and a physician representing the employer believes that direct employee access to information contained in the records regarding a specific diagnosis of a terminal illness or a psychiatric condition could be detrimental to the employee's health, the employer may inform the employee that access will only be provided to a designated representative of the employee having specific written consent, and deny the employee's request for direct access to this information only. Where a designated representative with specific written consent requests access to information so withheld, the employer shall assure the access of the designated representative to this information, even when it is known that the designated representative will give the information to the employee.

(E) Nothing in this section precludes a physician, nurse, or other responsible health care personnel maintaining employee medical records from deleting from requested medical records the identity of a family member, personal friend, or fellow employee who has provided confidential information concerning an employee's health status.

(iii) *Analyses using exposure or medical records.* (A) Each employer shall, upon request, assure the access of each employee and designated representative to each analysis using exposure or medical records concerning the employee's working conditions or workplace.

(B) Whenever access is requested to an analysis which reports the contents of employee medical records by either direct identifier (name, address, social security number, payroll number, etc.) or by information which could reasonably be used under the circumstances indirectly to identify specific employees (exact age, height, weight, race, sex, date of initial employment, job title, etc.), the employer shall assure that personal identifiers are removed before access is provided. If the employer can demonstrate that removal of personal identifiers from an analysis is not feasible, access to the personally identifiable portions of the analysis need not be provided.

(3) *OSHA access.* (i) Each employer shall, upon request, assure the immediate access of representatives of the Assistant Secretary of Labor for Occupation Safety and Health to employee exposure and medical records and to analyses using exposure or medical records. Rules of agency practice and procedure governing OSHA access to employee medical records are contained in 29 CFR 1913.10.

(ii) Whenever OSHA seeks access to personally identifiable employee medical information by presenting to the employer a written access order pursuant to 29 CFR 1913.10(d), the employer shall prominently post a copy of the written access order and its accompanying cover letter for at least fifteen (15) working days.

(f) *Trade secrets.* (1) Except as provided in paragraph (f)(2) of this section, nothing in this section precludes an employer from deleting from records requested by an employee or designated representative any trade secret data which discloses manufacturing processes, or discloses the percentage of a chemical substance in a mixture, as long as the employee or designated representative is notified that information has been deleted. Whenever deletion of trade secret information substantially impairs evaluation of the place where or the time when exposure to a toxic substance or harmful physical agent occurred, the employer shall provide alternate information which is sufficient to permit the employee to identify where and when exposure occurred.

(2) Notwithstanding any trade secret claims, whenever access to records is requested, the employer shall provide access to chemical or physical agent identities including chemical names, levels of exposure, and employee health status data contained in the requested records.

(3) Whenever trade secret information is provided to an employee or designated representative, the employer may require, as a condition of access, that the employee or designated representative agree in writing not to use the trade secret information for the purpose of commercial gain and not to permit misuse of the trade secret information by a competitor or potential competitor of the employer.

(g) *Employee information.* (1) Upon an employee's first entering into employment, and at least annually thereafter, each employer shall inform employees exposed to toxic substances or harmful physical agents of the following:

(i) The existence, location, and availability of any records covered by this section;

(ii) The person responsible for maintaining and providing access to records; and

(iii) Each employee's rights of access to these records.

(2) Each employer shall make readily available to employees a copy of this standard and its appendices, and shall distribute to employees any informational materials concerning this standard which are made available to the employer by the Assistant Secretary of Labor for Occupational Safety and Health.

(h) *Transfer of records.* (1) Whenever an employer is ceasing to do business, the employer shall transfer all records subject to this section to the successor employer. The successor employer shall receive and maintain these records.

(2) Whenever an employer is ceasing to do business and there is no successor employer to receive and maintain the records subject to this standard, the employer shall notify affected employees of their rights of access to records at least three (3) months prior to the cessation of the employer's business.

(3) Whenever an employer either is ceasing to do business and there is no successor employer to receive and maintain the records, or intends to dispose of any records required to be preserved for at least thirty (30) years, the employer shall:

(i) Transfer the records to the Director of the National Institute for Occupational Safety and Health (NIOSH) if so required by a specific occupational safety and health standard: or

(ii) Notify the Director of NIOSH in writing of the impending disposal of records at least three (3) months prior to the disposal of the records.

(4) Where an employer regularly disposes of records required to be preserved for at least thirty (30) years, the employer may, with at least three (3) months notice, notify the Director of NIOSH on an annual basis of the records intended to be disposed of in the coming year.

(i) *Appendices.* The information contained in the appendices to this section is not intended, by itself, to create any additional obligations not otherwise imposed by this section nor detract from any existing obligation.

(j) *Effective date.* This section shall become effective on August 21, 1980. All obligations of this section commence on the effective date except that the employer shall provide the information required under paragraph (g)(1) of this section to all current employees within sixty (60) days after the effective date.

Subpart E — Means of Egress

Citation:	29 CFR 1910.38

§ 1910.38 Employee emergency plans and fire prevention plans.

(a) *Emergency action plan.* (1) *Scope and application.* This paragraph (a) applies to all emergency action plans required by a particular OSHA standard. The emergency action plan shall be in writing (except as provided in the last sentence of paragraph (a)(5)(iii) of this section) and shall cover those designated actions employers and employees must take to ensure employee safety from fire and other emergencies.

* * * * *

(iii) The employer shall review with each employee upon initial assignment those parts of the plan which the employee must know to protect the employee in the event of an emergency. The written plan shall be kept at the workplace and made available for employee review. For those employers with 10 or fewer employees the plan must be communicated orally to employees and the employer need not maintain a written plan.

(b) *Fire prevention plan.* * * *

* * * * *

(5) *Maintenance.* The employer shall regularly and properly maintain, according to established procedures, equipment and systems installed on heat producing equipment to prevent accidental ignition of combustible materials. The maintenance procedures shall be included in the written fire prevention plan.

Subpart G — Occupational Health and Environmental Control

Citation:	29 CFR 1910.95

§ 1910.95 Occupational noise exposure.

* * * * *

(m) *Recordkeeping* — (1) *Exposure measurements.* The employer shall maintain an accurate record of all employee exposure measurements required by paragraph (d) of this section.

(2) *Audiometric tests.* (i) The employer shall retain all employee audiometric test records obtained pursuant to paragraph (g) of this section:

(ii) This record shall include:

(A) Name and job classification of the employee;

(B) Date of the audiogram;

(C) The examiner's name;

(D) Date of the last acoustic or exhaustive calibration of the audiometer; and

(E) Employee's most recent noise exposure assessment.

(F) The employer shall maintain accurate records of the measurements of the background sound pressure levels in audiometric test rooms.

(3) *Record retention.* The employer shall retain records re-

quired in this paragraph (m) for at least the following periods.

(i) Noise exposure measurement records shall be retained for two years.

(ii) Audiometric test records shall be retained for the duration of the affected employee's employment.

(4) *Access to records.* All records required by this section shall be provided upon request to employees, former employees, representatives designated by the individual employee, and the Assistant Secretary. The provisions of 29 CFR 1910.20 (a)-(e) and (g)-(i) apply to access to records under this section.

(5) *Transfer of records.* If the employer ceases to do business, the employer shall transfer to the successor employer all records required to be maintained by this section, and the successor employer shall retain them for the remainder of the period prescribed in paragraph (m) (3) of this section.

* * * * *

Subpart L — Fire Protection

Citation: 29 CFR 1910.156

§ 1910.156 Fire brigades.

* * * * *

(c) *Training and education.*

* * * * *

(4) The employer shall inform fire brigade members about special hazards such as storage and use of flammable liquids and gases, toxic chemicals, radioactive sources, and water reactive substances, to which they may be exposed during fire and other emergencies. The fire brigade members shall also be advised of any changes that occur in relation to the special hazards. The employer shall develop and make available for inspection by fire brigade members, written procedures that describe the actions to be taken in situations involving the special hazards and shall include these in the training and education program.

* * * * *

Portable Fire Suppression Equipment

Citation: 29 CFR 1910.157

§ 1910.157 Portable fire extinguishers.

* * * * *

(e) *Inspection, maintenance and testing.*

* * * * *

(3) The employer shall assure that portable fire extinguishers are subjected to an annual maintenance check. Stored pressure extinguishers do not require an internal examination. The employer shall record the annual maintenance date and retain this record for one year after the last entry or the life of the shell, whichever is less. The record shall be available to the Assistant Secretary upon request.

* * * * *

(16) The employer shall maintain and provide upon request

to the Assistant Secretary evidence that the required hydrostatic testing of fire extinguishers has been performed at the time intervals shown in Table L-1. Such evidence shall include the date of test, the test pressure used, and the person or agency performing the test. Such records shall be kept until the extinguisher is hydrostatically retested at the time interval specified in Table L-1 or until the extinguisher is taken out of service, whichever is less.

* * * * *

Fixed Fire Suppression Equipment

Citation: 29 CFR 1910.159

§ 1910.159 Automatic sprinkler systems.

* * * * *

(c) *General requirements.*

* * * * *

(3) *Acceptance tests.* The employer shall conduct proper acceptance tests on sprinkler systems installed for employee protection after January 1, 1981, and record the dates of such tests.

* * * * *

Citation: 29 CFR 1910.160

§ 1910.160 Fixed extinguishing systems, general.

* * * * *

(b) *General requirements.*

* * * * *

(9) The employer shall assure that inspection and maintenance dates are recorded on the container, on a tag attached to the container, or in a central location. A record of the last semiannual check shall be maintained until the container is checked again or for the life of the container, whichever is less.

* * * * *

Citation: 29 CFR 1910.1200

§ 1910.1200 Hazardous communication.

* * * * *

(g) *Material safety data sheets.* (1) Chemical manufacturers and importers shall obtain or develop a material safety data sheet for each hazardous chemical they produce or import. Employers shall have a material safety data sheet for each hazardous chemical which they use.

(2) Each material safety data sheet shall be in English and shall contain at least the following information:

(i) The identity used on the label, and, except as provided for in paragraph (i) of this section on trade secrets:

(A) If the hazardous chemical is a single substance, its chemical and common name(s):

(B) If the hazardous chemical is a mixture which has been tested as a whole to determine its hazards, the chemical and common name(s) of the ingredients which contribute to these known hazards, and the common name(s) of the mixture itself; or,

(C) If the hazardous chemical is a mixture which has not been tested as a whole:

(1) The chemical and common name(s) of all ingredients which have been determined to be health hazards, and which comprise 1% or greater of the composition, except that chemicals identified as carcinogens under paragraph (d)(4) of this section shall be listed if the concentrations are 0.1% or greater; and

(2) The chemical and common name(s) of all ingredients which have been determined to be health hazards, and which comprise less than 1% (0.1% for carcinogens) of the mixture, if there is evidence that the ingredient(s) could be released from the mixture in concentrations which would exceed an established OSHA permissible exposure limit or ACGIH Threshold Limit Value, or could present a health hazard to employees; and,

(3) The chemical and common name(s) of all ingredients which have been determined to present a physical hazard when present in the mixture;

(ii) Physical and chemical characteristics of the hazardous chemical (such as vapor pressure, flash point);

(iii) The physical hazards of the hazardous chemical, including the potential for fire, explosion, and reactivity;

(iv) The health hazards of the hazardous chemical, including signs and symptoms of exposure, and any medical conditions which are generally recognized as being aggravated by exposure to the chemical;

(v) The primary route(s) of entry;

(vi) The OSHA permissible exposure limit, ACGIH Threshold Limit Value, and any other exposure limit used or recommended by the chemical manufacturer, importer, or employer preparing the material safety data sheet, where available;

(vii) Whether the hazardous chemical is listed in the National Toxicology Program (NTP) *Annual Report on Carcinogens* (latest edition) or has been found to be a potential carcinogen in the International Agency for Research on Cancer (IARC) *Monographs* (latest editions), or by OSHA;

(viii) Any generally applicable precautions for safe handling and use which are known to the chemical manufacturer, importer or employer preparing the material safety data sheet, including appropriate hygienic practices, protective measures during repair and maintenance of contaminated equipment, and procedures for clean-up of spills and leaks;

(ix) Any generally applicable control measures which are known to the chemical manufacturer, importer or employer preparing the material safety data sheet, such as appropriate engineering controls, work practices, or personal protective equipment;

(x) Emergency and first aid procedures;

(xi) The date of preparation of the material safety data sheets or the last change to it; and

(xii) The name, address and telephone number of the chemical manufacturer, import, employer or other responsible party preparing or distributing the material safety data sheet, who can provide additional information on the hazardous chemical and appropriate emergency procedures, if necessary.

(3) If no relevant information is found for any given category on the material safety data sheet, the chemical manufacturer, importer or employer preparing the material safety data sheet shall mark it to indicate that no applicable information was found.

(4) Where complex mixtures have similar hazards and contents (i.e., the chemical ingredients are essentially the same, but the specific composition varies from mixture to mixture), the chemical manufacturer, importer or employer may prepare one material safety data sheet to apply to all of these similar mixtures.

(5) The chemical manufacturer, importer or employer preparing the material safety data sheet shall ensure that the information recorded accurately reflects the scientific evidence used in making the hazard determination. If the chemical manufacturer, importer or employer preparing the material safety data sheet becomes newly aware of any significant information regarding the hazards of the chemical, or ways to protect against the hazards, this new information shall be added to the material safety data sheet within three months. If the chemical is not currently being produced or imported the chemical manufacturer or importer shall add the information to the material safety data sheet before the chemical is introduced into the workplace again.

(6) Chemical manufacturers or importers shall ensure that distributors and employers are provided an appropriate material safety data sheet with their initial shipment, and with the first shipment after a material safety data sheet is updated. The chemical manufacturer or importer shall either provide material safety data sheets with the shipped containers or send them to the employer prior to or at the time of the shipment. If the material safety data sheet is not provided with a shipment that has been labeled as a hazardous chemical, the employer shall obtain one from the chemical manufacturer, importer, or distributor as soon as possible.

(7) Distributors shall ensure that material safety data sheets, and updated information, are provided to other distributors and employers. Retail distributors which sell hazardous chemicals to commercial customers shall provide a material safety data sheet to such employers upon request, and shall post a sign or otherwise inform them that a material safety data sheet is available. Chemical manufacturers, importers, and distributors need not provide material safety data sheets to retail distributors which have informed them the retail distributor does not sell the product to commercial customers or open the sealed container to use it in their own workplaces.

(8) The employer shall maintain copies of the required material safety data sheet for each hazardous chemical in the workplace, and shall ensure that they are readily accessible during each work shift to employees when they are in their work area(s).

(9) Where employees must travel between workplaces during a workshift, *i.e.,* their work is carried out at more than one geographical location, the material safety data sheets may be kept at a central location at the primary workplace facility. In this situation, the employer shall ensure that employees can immediately obtain the required information in an emergency.

(10) Material safety data sheets may be kept in any form, including operating procedures, and may be designed to cover groups of hazardous chemicals in a work area where it may be more appropriate to address the hazards of a process rather than individual hazardous chemicals. However, the employer shall ensure that in all cases the required information is provided for each hazardous chemical, and is readily accessible during each work shift to employees when they are in their work area(s).

(11) Material safety data sheets shall also be made readily available, upon request, to designated representatives and to the Assistant Secretary, in accordance with the requirements of 29 CFR 1910.20(e). The Director shall also be given access to material safety data sheets in the same manner.

* * * * *

Appendix F   Federal Acquisition Regulations

Source: Code of Federal Regulations
Citation: 48 CFR Part 4

Title 48 — Federal Acquisition Regulations System

PART 4 — ADMINISTRATIVE MATTERS

Subpart 4.7 — Contractor Record Retention

§ 4.700 Scope of subpart.

This subpart provides policies and procedures for retention of records by contractors to meet the records review requirements of the Government. In this subpart, the terms "contracts" and "contractors" include "subcontracts" and "subcontractors."

§ 4.701 Purpose.

The purpose of this subpart is to generally describe record retention requirements and to allow reductions in the retention period for specific classes of records under prescribed circumstances.

§ 4.702 Applicability.

(a) This subpart applies to records generated under contracts that contain one of the following clauses:
(1) Examination of Records by Comptroller General (52.215-1).
(2) Audit—Sealed bidding (52.214-26).
(3) Audit—Negotiation (52.215-2).
(b) This subpart is not mandatory on Department of Energy contracts for which the Comptroller General allows alternative records retention periods. Apart from this exception, this subpart applies to records retention periods under contract that are subject to Chapter 137, Title 10, U.S.C., and the Federal Property and Administrative Services Act of 1949, as amended, 40 U.S.C. 471 et seq.

§ 4.703 Policy.

(a) Except as stated in 4.703(b), contractors shall make available books, records, documents, and other supporting evidence to satisfy contract negotiation, administration, and audit requirements of the contracting agencies and the Comptroller General for (1) 3 years after final payment or, for certain records, (2) the period specified in 4.705 and 4.704, whichever of these periods expires first.

(b) Contractors shall make available the foregoing documents and supporting evidence for a longer period of time than is required is 4.703(a) if —
(1) A retention period longer than that cited in 4703(a) is specified in any contract clause; or
(2) The contractor, for its own purposes, retains the foregoing documents and supporting evidence for a longer period. Under this circumstance, the retention period shall be the period of the contractor's retention or 3 years after final payment, whichever period expires first.

(c) Contractors need not retain duplicate copies of records or supporting documents unless they contain significant information not shown on the record copy.

(d) Contractors need not retain intermediate data records consisting of punched cards, electronic tape, or comparable media if printouts or listings are prepared and maintained. The printouts or listing must show the details of the transactions charged or allocated to individual Government contracts and must identify the supporting source documents.

§ 4.704 Calculation of retention periods.

(a) The retention periods in 4.705 are calculated from the end of the contractor's fiscal year in which an entry is made charging or allocating a cost to a government contract or subcontract. If a specific record contains a series of entries, the retention period is calculated from the end of the contractor's fiscal year in which the final entry is made. The contractor should cut off the records in annual blocks and retain them for block disposal under the prescribed retention periods.

(b) When records generated during a prior contract are relied upon by a contractor for cost or pricing data in negotiating a succeeding contract, the prescribed periods shall run from the date of the succeeding contract.

(c) If two or more of the record categories described in 4.705 are interfiled and screening for disposal is not practical, the contractor shall retain the entire records series for the longest period prescribed for any category of record.

§ 4.705 Specific retention periods.

The contractor shall retain the records identified in 4.705-1 through 4.705-3 for the periods designated, provided retention is required under 4.702. Records are identified in this subpart in terms of their purpose or use and not by specific name or form number. Although the descriptive identifications may not conform to normal contractor usage or filing practices, these identifications apply to all contractor records that come within the description.

§ 4.705-1 Financial and cost accounting records.

(a) Accounts receivable invoices, adjustments to the accounts, invoices registers, carrier freight bills, shipping orders, and other documents which detail the material or services billed on the related invoices: Retain 4 years.

(b) Material, work order, or service order files, consisting of purchase requisitions or purchase orders for material or services, or orders for transfer of material or supplies: Retain 4 years.

(c) Cash advance recapitulations, prepared as posting entries to accounts receivable ledgers for amounts of expense vouchers prepared for employees' travel and related expenses: Retain 4 years.

(d) Paid, canceled, and voided checks, other than those issued for the payment of salary and wages: Retain 4 years.

(e) Accounts payable records to support disbursement of funds for materials, equipment, supplies, and services, containing originals or copies of the following and related documents: remittance advices and statements, vendors' invoices, invoice audits and distribution slips, receiving and inspection reports or comparable certifications of receipt and inspection of material or services, and debit and credit memoranda: Retain 4 years.

(f) Labor cost distribution cards or equivalent documents: Retain 2 years.

(g) Petty cash records showing description of expenditures, to whom paid, name of person authorizing payment, and date, including copies of vouchers and other supporting documents: Retain 2 years.

§ 4.705-2 Pay administration records.

(a) Payroll sheets, registers, or their equivalent, of salaries and wages paid to individual employees for each payroll period; change slips; and tax withholding statements. Retain 4 years.

(b) Clock cards or other time and attendance cards: Retain 2 years.

(c) Paid checks, receipts for wages paid in cash, or other evidence of payments for services rendered by employees: Retain 2 years.

§ 4.705-3 Acquisition and supply records.

(a) Store requisitions for materials, supplies, equipment, and services: Retain 2 years.

(b) Work orders for maintenance and other services: Retain 4 years.

(c) Equipment records, consisting of equipment usage and status reports and equipment repair orders: Retain 4 years.

(d) Expendable property records, reflecting accountability for the receipt and use of material in the performance of a contract: Retain 4 years.

(e) Receiving and inspection report records, consisting of reports reflecting receipt and inspection of supplies, equipment, and materials: Retain 4 years.

(f) Purchase order files for supplies, equipment, material, or services used in the performance of a contract; supporting documentation and backup files including, but not limited to, invoices, and memoranda; e.g., memoranda of negotiations showing the principal elements of subcontract price negotiations (see 52.244-1

and 52.244-2): Retain 4 years.

(g) Production records of quality control, reliability, and inspection: Retain 4 years.

§ 4.706 Microfilming records.

§ 4.706-1 General.

(a) Contractors may use microfilm (e.g., film chips, jackets, aperture cards, microprints, roll film, and microfiche) for record-keeping, subject to the limitations in this subpart.

(b) In the process of microfilming documents, the contractor shall also microfilm all relevant notes, worksheets, and other papers necessary for reconstructing or understanding the records.

(c) The contractor shall review all microfilm before destroying the hardcopy documents to ensure legibility and reproducibility of the microfilm.

(d) Unless earlier retirement of records is permitted by 4.705, or the administrative contracting officer agrees to a lesser retention period when the contractor has established adequate internal controls including continuing surveillance over the microfilm system, the contractor shall not destroy original records that have been microfilmed, until—

(1) All claims under the contract are settled;

(2) Eighteen months have passed since final payment; or

(3) The time original records are required to be kept by other laws or regulations has elapsed.

§ 4.706-2 Filing and retrieval.

The contractor shall —

(a) Maintain an effective indexing system to permit timely and convenient access to the microfilmed records by the Government;

(b) Provide strict security measures to prevent the loss of microfilm and to safeguard classified information;

(c) Store microfilm in a fireproof cabinet in an environment ensuring the safety of these records for the specified retention periods; and

(d) Have adequate viewing equipment and provide printouts the approximate size of the original material.

§ 4.706-3 Quality control.

(a) Microfilm, when displayed on a microfilm reader (viewer) or reproduced on paper, must exhibit a high degree of legibility and readability.

(b) The quality of the contractor's record microfilming process is subject to periodic review by the administrative contracting officer.

Appendix G   Legal Group File Used to Prepare Figure 12.1

This Appendix presents the detailed legal considerations applied to produce Figure 12.1. In order to check the legal requirements for a specific record, first identify the Legal Group Code and then review the information following the code in this Appendix. Chapter 22 describes the preparation and use of the Legal Group File.

The chart consists of the following components:

Legal Group Code: the code used to group or classify a number of legal requirements related to the same or similar matter.

Subject: the subject names assigned to each Legal Group Code for quick identification and use.

Description: a brief description of the type of legal requirements included in the legal group with some typical records affected.

Retention Periods: the period of time identified in the legal requirements for records retention. Each retention period includes a typical citation from which the retention period was taken and any modifiers of the retention period.

Minimum: the minimum retention period identified for the legal group.
Maximum: the maximum retention period identified for the legal group.
Selected: the retention period selected for use in Figure 12.1. This period is always greater than the minimum retention period, but may be less than the maximum period based upon the discussion found in Part A to C.

The following records retention period abbreviations have been used in this appendix:

ACT: Active; while the matter is active. For example, while the contract is active or you own the property.
ACY: ACT+CY; active plus current year
ATX: ACT+TAX; active plus tax return filing date.
CY: Current year; all records created in the same year are treated as though they were created on December 31 of that year.
IND: Indefinite; the retention for certain records cannot be determined in advance so those records must be reviewed periodically to determine whether or not they can be destroyed.
MAINT: Maintain; law requires records to be maintained but no period stated. Generally, treat as retention of 3 years.
PROC: Procedure; follow procedural requirements specified in law.
SUP: Superseded; keep the records until they are replaced by more current ones.
TAX: Tax return filing date; all records created to document information in a tax return, including the tax return, are treated as though they were created on the day the tax return was filed.
+: Plus; some retention periods consist of two or more components. For example, general tax records should be kept for the current year plus four years (CY+4).

All records retention periods are in "years" unless months (M) or days (D) are specified. For convenience and to eliminate mistakes, **all records retention periods should start on the last day of the year in which the records were created (CY)**, unless otherwise indicated.

Code	Subject	Description / Legal Requirement / Citation		
ACC000	Accounting / Tax General	Includes tax assessment or specific tax requirements for accounts payable, accounts receivable, etc.		
		Minimum:	TAX+03	US: 26 CFR 301.6501(a)-1
		Maximum:	TAX+06	US: 26 CFR 301.6501(f)-1
		Selected:	CY+04	US: 26 CFR 301.6501(f)-1
ACC100	Accounting / Tax Capital Acquisitions	Includes depreciation, capital gains and losses, and repairs for capital property.		
		Minimum:	ATX+03	US: 26 CFR 301.6501(a)-1
		Maximum:	ATX+06	US: 26 CFR 301.6501(f)-1
		Selected:	ACY+04	US: 26 CFR 301.6501(f)-1
ACC300	Accounting / Tax Payroll	Includes records related to determination of payroll. Excludes time cards, work hours, etc. *See also* Employment.		
		Minimum:	04	US: 26 CFR 31.6001-1
		Maximum:	TAX+06	US: 26 CFR 301.6501(f)-1
		Selected:	CY+04	US: 26 CFR 301.6501(f)-1
ACC500	Accounting / Tax Loans / Credits	Includes tax information related to loans and payments.		
		Minimum:	TAX+03	US: 26 CFR 301.6501(a)-1
		Maximum:	TAX+06	US: 26 CFR 301.6501(f)-1
		Selected:	CY+04	US: 26 CFR 301.6501(f)-1
ADV000	Advertising Packaging / Labeling	Includes requirements related to promotions, introductory offers, and product size advantages.		
		Minimum:	CY+01	US: 16 CFR PART 502
		Maximum:	CY+01	US: 16 CFR PART 502
		Selected:	CY+01	US: 16 CFR PART 502
BUS000	Business Organization General Organization Documentation	Includes requirements for articles of incorporation, partnership documentation, etc. excludes meeting minutes, shareholder information, etc.		
		Minimum:	MAINT	CO: CRS 7-5-117
		Maximum:	IND	Legal consideration
		Selected:	IND	Legal consideration
BUS100	Business Organization Corporation Organization Documentation	Includes requirements for articles of incorporation, partnership documentation, etc. excludes meeting minutes, shareholder information, etc.		
		Minimum:	MAINT	CO: CRS 7-5-117
		Maximum:	IND	Legal consideration
		Selected:	IND	Legal consideration
BUS110	Business Organization Corporation Shareholder Records	Includes stock transactions, shareholder addresses, etc.		
		Minimum:	MAINT	CO: CRS 7-5-117
		Maximum:	IND	Legal consideration
		Selected:	ACT+03	Legal consideration
BUS120	Business Organization Corporation Meetings	Includes minutes and notices from board, shareholder, and committee meetings.		
		Minimum:	MAINT	CO: CRS 7-5-117
		Maximum:	IND	Legal consideration
		Selected:	10	Legal consideration

Code	Subject	Description / Legal Requirement / Citation
CON000	Contracts General	Includes documentation for general written contracts. excludes actual work products, deliverable products, or accounting.

		Minimum:	ACT+03	NC: GSNC 1-52
		Maximum:	ACT+20	IN: IC 34-1-2-2
		Selected:	ACT+06	WA: RCWA 4.16.040

Code	Subject	Description
CON010	Contracts General Compliance / Work Products	Includes proof of compliance or work products provided under written contracts. excludes contract documentation.

		Minimum:	03	NC: GSNC 1-52
		Maximum:	20	IN: IC 34-1-2-2
		Selected:	06	WA: RCWA 4.16.040

CON100	Contracts Sales	Includes documentation of written sales contracts under the uniform commercial code. excludes proof of compliance, work products or accounting.

		Minimum:	ACT+03	CO: CRS 13-80-101
		Maximum:	ACT+06	WI: WSA 402.725
		Selected:	ACT+04	NY: CLNY-UCC 2-725

CON110	Contracts Sales Compliance / Work Products	Includes proof of compliance or delivery of work products. excludes contract documentation.

		Minimum:	03	CO: CRS 13-80-101
		Maximum:	06	WI: WSA 402.725
		Selected:	04	NY: CLNY-UCC 2-725

CON300	Contracts Improvements, Real Property	Includes documentation for written contracts related to improvements to real property. excludes actual work products, deliverable products, or accounting.

		Minimum:	ACT+04	NC: NCGS 1-50
		Maximum:	ACT+20	MD: MCA-CJP 5-108
		Selected:	ACT+10	CA: CCP 337.15

CON310	Contracts Improvements, Real Property Compliance / Work Products	Includes proof of compliance or work products provided under written contracts for improvements to real property. excludes contract documentation.

		Minimum:	04	NC: NCGS 1-50
		Maximum:	20	MD: MCA-CJP 5-108
		Selected:	10	CA: CCP 337.15

CON500	Contracts Government	Includes documentation for written government contracts. excludes records related to cost accounting, pay administration, or procurement.

		Minimum:	ACT+03	US: 48 CFR 4.703
		Maximum:	ACT+03	US: 48 CFR 4.703
		Selected:	ACT+03	US: 48 CFR 4.703

CON510	Contracts Government Compliance / Work Products	Includes proof of compliance or work products under government contracts not otherwise specified in the federal acquisition regulations.

		Minimum:	ACT+03	US: 48 CFR 4.703
		Maximum:	ACT+03	US: 48 CFR 4.703
		Selected:	ACT+03	US: 48 CFR 4.703

Code	Subject	Description / Legal Requirement / Citation		

CON520	Contracts Government Cost Accounting	Includes accounting records allocating costs to federal government contracts. See also ACC000.		
		Minimum:	04	US: 48 CFR 4.705
		Maximum:	04	US: 48 CFR 4.705
		Selected:	04	US: 48 CFR 4.705
CON521	Contracts Government Procurement / Production	Includes records of procurement and production under government contracts specified in the federal acquisition regulations.		
		Minimum:	04	US: 48 CFR 4.705
		Maximum:	04	US: 48 CFR 4.705
		Selected:	04	US: 48 CFR 4.705
CON530	Contracts Government Time Cards / Pay	Includes selected records related to time cards and pay receipts such as canceled checks for allocating cost to government contracts. See also ACC000.		
		Minimum:	02	US: 48 CFR 4.705
		Maximum:	02	US: 48 CFR 4.705
		Selected:	02	US: 48 CFR 4.705
EMP000	Employment General	Includes wage rates, job descriptions, work schedules, employment practices and other employment requirements not included elsewhere.		
		Minimum:	02	US: 29 CFR 516.6
		Maximum:	03	US: 5 CFR 1320.6
		Selected:	03	US: 5 CFR 1320.6
EMP100	Employment Benefits / Pensions Reporting / Contributions	Includes requirements for contributions to and reporting for pension and benefit plans.		
		Minimum:	03	US: 29 USC 1113
		Maximum:	06	US: 29 USC 1113
		Selected:	06	US: 29 USC 1113
EMP110	Employment Benefits / Pensions Plans	Includes the actual pension and benefit plans in force.		
		Minimum:	ACT+01	US: 29 CFR 1627.3
		Maximum:	ACT+06	US: 29 USC 1113
		Selected:	ACT+06	US: 29 USC 1113
EMP120	Employment Benefits / Pensions Summary Data	Includes summary of contributions, years of service, benefit accrued, and other information need to implement the benefit and pension plans.		
		Minimum:	03	US: 5 CFR 1320.6
		Maximum:	IND	US: 29 USC 1113 + Legal consideration
		Selected:	IND	US: 29 USC 1113 + Legal consideration
EMP300	Employment Employment Actions	Includes requirements related to detailed employee personnel actions such as hiring, firing, promotion, work schedules, etc. Keep summary data separately.		
		Minimum:	01	US: 29 CFR 1627.3
		Maximum:	03	US: 29 CFR 1620.33
		Selected:	03	US: 29 CFR 1627.3

Code	Subject	Description / Legal Requirement / Citation		

EMP310   Employment   Employment Actions   Summary Records

Includes requirements related to summary employee personnel actions such as hiring, firing, promotion, work schedules, etc. Keep detailed data separately.

Minimum:	01	US: 29 CFR 1627.3
Maximum:	03	US: 29 CFR 1620.33
Selected:	IND	Legal consideration

EMP500   Employment   Health and Safety   Hazardous Exposure

Includes requirements related to work-related exposure to hazardous substances.

Minimum:	ACT+30	US: 29 CFR 1910.1001
Maximum:	ACT+30	US: 29 CFR 1910.20
Selected:	ACT+30	US: 29 CFR 1910.20

EMP510   Employment   Health and Safety   Noise Exposure Measurements

Includes requirements related to measurement of noise in work environment.

Minimum:	02	US: 29 CFR 1910.95
Maximum:	02	US: 29 CFR 1910.95
Selected:	02	US: 29 CFR 1910.95

EMP511   Employment   Health and Safety   Audiometric Test Record

Includes requirements related to audiometric tests conducted for employees.

Minimum:	ACT	US: 29 CFR 1910.95
Maximum:	ACT	US: 29 CFR 1910.95
Selected:	ACT	US: 29 CFR 1910.95

EMP700   Employment   Health and Safety   Illness / Accident

Includes requirements related to work-related illness and accident, including workers compensation.

Minimum:	CY+05	US: 29 CFR 1904.6
Maximum:	CY+05	US: 29 CFR 1904.6
Selected:	CY+05	US: 29 CFR 1904.6

EMP710   Employment   Health and Safety   Emergency Action Plans

Includes requirements related to fire prevention plans and other emergency action plans.

Minimum:	ACT	US: 29 CFR 1910.38
Maximum:	ACT	US: 29 CFR 1910.38
Selected:	ACT	US: 29 CFR 1910.38

EMP711   Employment   Health and Safety   Fire Protection

Includes requirements related to testing of fire protection equipment.

Minimum:	01	US: 29 CFR 1910.157
Maximum:	01	US: 29 CFR 1910.157
Selected:	01	US: 29 CFR 1910.157

EMP900   Employment   Selection   General

Includes requirements related to advertising, interviewing, testing, selecting, and hiring.

Minimum:	01	US: 29 CFR 1627.3
Maximum:	01	US: 29 CFR 1627.3
Selected:	01	US: 29 CFR 1627.3

EMP910   Employment   Selection   Apprenticehsip Programs

Includes requirements related to advertising, interviewing, testing, selecting, and hiring for apprenticeship programs.

Minimum:	02	US: 29 CFR 1602.21
Maximum:	02	US: 29 CFR 1602.21
Selected:	02	US: 29 CFR 1602.21

Code	Subject	Description / Legal Requirement / Citation
ENV100	Environment Hazardous Substances General	Includes records related to the manufacture, transportation, use, testing and disposal of hazardous substances.

		Minimum:	30	US: 29 CFR 1910.20
		Maximum:	30	US: 29 CFR 1910.20
		Selected:	30	US: 29 CFR 1910.20

ENV110	Environment Hazardous Substances Transportation	Includes records related to the transportation of hazardous substances such as manifests.

		Minimum:	03	US: 40 CFR 263.20
		Maximum:	03	US: 40 CFR 263.20
		Selected:	IND	Legal Consideration

ENV120	Environment Hazardous Substances Waste Disposal Sites	Includes records related to operation and clean-up of hazardous waste disposal sites.

		Minimum:	ACT	40 CFR 264.73
		Maximum:	ACT	40 CFR 264.73
		Selected:	IND	Legal consideration

EVD000	Evidence Records - General	Includes requirements related to creating records for submission to court or administrative agencies.

		Minimum:	PROC	US: 28 USC APP 803
		Maximum:	PROC	US: 28 USC APP 803
		Selected:	PROC	US: 28 USC APP 803

EVD100	Evidence Microfilm	Includes requirements related to microfilming records for submission to court or administrative agencies.

		Minimum:	PROC	US: 28 USC 1732
		Maximum:	PROC	US: 28 USC 1732
		Selected:	PROC	US: 28 USC 1732

EVD300	Evidence Computer Records	Includes requirements related to creating computer records for submission to court or administrative agencies.

		Minimum:	PROC	US: 28 USC APP 1001
		Maximum:	PROC	US: 28 USC APP 1001
		Selected:	PROC	US: 28 USC APP 1001

FOR000	Foreign Trade General	Includes requirements related to foreign trade including import and export certifications and other license-related records.

		Minimum:	02	US: 15 CFR 768.2
		Maximum:	02	US: 15 CFR 768.2
		Selected:	02	US: 15 CFR 768.2

LEG000	Legal Compliance General	Include records of compliance with state and federal laws not specifically covered elsewhere.

		Minimum:	00	NONE
		Maximum:	IND	Legal consideration
		Selected:	03	US: 5 CFR 1320.6

Code	Subject	Description / Legal Requirement / Citation

LEG200 Legal Compliance
Business Licenses / Orders

Includes licenses and permits required to do business and regulatory orders governing the conduct of business.

Minimum: 00 NONE
Maximum: ACT Legal consideration
Selected: ACT Legal consideration

LIT000 Litigation / Claims
General

Includes litigation and claims documentation, including judgments.

Minimum: 00 NONE
Maximum: ACT Legal consideration
Selected: ACT Legal consideration

MAN000 Manufacturing
Product Liability

Includes records related to the design and manufacture of products for potential use in future product liability suits. In most states, litigation can start within 2 or 3 years after the injury, regardless of when the product was first purchased or used.

Minimum: 01 AL: AC 6-5-502
Maximum: IND Legal consideration
Selected: IND Legal consideration

NONE No legal period

No legal retention requirement identified after adequate legal research.

Minimum: 00 NONE
Maximum: 03 5 CFR 1320.6
Selected: 00 NONE

POL100 Policies / Procedures
Policies

Includes policies for areas such as employment, records management, accounting, purchasing, quality control, etc.

Minimum: 00 NONE
Maximum: IND Legal consideration
Selected: ACT+10 Legal consideration

POL200 Policies / Procedures
Procedures

Includes procedures implementing policies for areas such as employment, records management, accounting, purchasing, quality control, etc.

Minimum: 00 NONE
Maximum: IND Legal consideration
Selected: ACT+10 Legal consideration

PRO000 Professional Liability
General

Includes requirements related to services provided to clients or customers.

Minimum: 02 GA: OCGA 9-3-71
Maximum: 15 IN: IC 34-1-2-3
Selected: 06 HI: HRS 657-7.3

TRA100 Transportation
Driving, Highway
Driving Record

Includes requirements related to driving records for drivers of vehicles on public highways used in interstate commerce.

Minimum: ACT+03 US: 49 CFR 391.51
Maximum: ACT+03 US: 49 CFR 391.51
Selected: ACT+03 US: 49 CFR 391.51

TRA110 Transportation
Driving, Highway
Hours of Service

Includes requirements related to hours of service for drivers of vehicles on public highways used in interstate commerce.

Minimum: 06M US: 49 CFR 395.8
Maximum: 06M US: 49 CFR 395.8
Selected: 06M US: 49 CFR 395.8

Appendix H   Uniform Laws Related to Record Media and Recordkeeping Requirements

The following Uniform Laws were prepared by the National Conference of Commissioners on Uniform State Laws. Differences may exist between the original versions and the versions finally adopted by the states.

Source:	Uniform Business Records as Evidence Act.

§ 1. "Business" defined.

The term "business" shall include every kind of business, profession, occupation, calling or operation of institutions, whether carried on for profit or not.

§ 2. Business records as evidence.

A record of an act, condition or event, shall in so far as relevant, be competent evidence if the custodian or other qualified witness testifies to its identity and the mode of its preparation, and if it was made in the regular course of business, at or near the time of the act, condition or event, and if, in the opinion of the court, the sources of information, method and time of preparation were such as to justify its admission.

§ 3. Construction.

This chapter shall be so interpreted and construed as to effectuate its general purpose to make uniform the law of those states which enact it.

§ 4. Short title.

This chapter may be cited as The Uniform Business Records as Evidence Act.

The following states have adopted this Uniform Law:

Arizona	North Dakota
California	Ohio
Connecticut	Pennsylvania
Idaho	Rhode Island
Minnesota	South Carolina
Missouri	Tennessee
New Jersey	Vermont
New York	Washington

Source:	Uniform Photographic Copies of Business and Public Records as Evidence Act.

§ 1. Admissibility of reproduced records in evidence.

If any business, institution, member of a profession or calling, or any department or agency of government, in the regular course of business or activity has kept or recorded any memorandum, writing, entry, print, representation or combination thereof, of any act, transaction, occurrence or event, and in the regular course of business has caused any or all of the same to be recorded, copied or reproduced by any photographic, photostatic, microfilm, micro-card, miniature photographic, or other process which accurately reproduces or forms a durable medium for so reproducing the original, the original may be destroyed in the regular course of business unless held in a custodial or fiduciary capacity or unless its preservation is required by law. Such reproduction, when satisfactorily identified, is as admissible in evidence as the original itself in any judicial or administrative proceeding whether the original is in existence or not and an enlargement or facsimile of such reproduction is likewise admissible in evidence if the original reproduction is in existence and available for inspection under direction of court. The introduction of a reproduced record, enlargement or facsimile, does not preclude admission of the original.

§ 2. Interpretation.

This act shall be so interpreted and construed as to effectuate its general purpose of making uniform the law of those states which enact it.

§ 3. Short title.

This act may be cited as the Uniform Photographic Copies of Business and Public Records as Evidence Act.

The following have adopted this Uniform Law:

Alabama	Georgia
Arkansas	Idaho
California	Iowa
Colorado	Kansas
Connecticut	Kentucky

Maine	Rhode Island
Maryland	South Carolina
Massachusetts	South Dakota
Michigan	Tennessee
Minnesota	United States
Nebraska	Utah
New Hampshire	Vermont
New Jersey	Virgin Islands
New York	Virginia
North Carolina	Washington
North Dakota	West Virginia
Pennsylvania	Wisconsin

Source: **Uniform Preservation of Private Business Records Act.**

§ 1. Definitions.

As used in this Act:

"Business" includes every kind of private business, profession, occupation, calling or operation of private institutions, whether carried on for profit or not.

"Person" means an individual, partnership, corporation, or any other association.

"Records" or "Business Records" include books of account, vouchers, documents, cancelled checks, payrolls, correspondence, records of sales, personnel, equipment and production, reports relating to any or all of such records, and other business papers.

"Reproduction" means a reproduction or durable medium for making a reproduction obtained by any photographic, photostatic, microfilm, micro-card, miniature photographic or other process which accurately reproduces or forms a durable medium for so reproducing the original.

§ 2. Period of preservation.

Unless a specific period is designated by law for their preservation, business records which persons by the laws of this state are required to keep or preserve may be destroyed after the expiration of three years from the making of such records without constituting an offense under such laws. [This section does not apply to minute books of corporations nor to records of sales or other transactions involving weapons, poisions or other dangerous articles or substances capable of use in the commission of crimes.]

§ 3. Preservation of reproductions.

If in the regular course of business a person makes reproductions of original business records, the preservation of such reproductions constitutes compliance with any laws of this State requiring that business records be kept or preserved.

§ 4. Destruction of records by state officers.

Nothing in this Act shall be construed to diminish the authority of an officer of this State under existing law to permit the destruction of business records.

§ 5. Uniformity of interpretation.

This Act shall be so interpreted and construed as to effectuate its general purpose to make uniform the law of those states which enact it.

§ 6. Short title.

This act may be cited as the Uniform Preservation of Private Business Records Act.

The following have adopted this Uniform Law:

Colorado
Georgia
Illinois
Maryland
New Hampshire
Oklahoma
Texas

Source: **Uniform Rules of Evidence.**

Article VIII.   Hearsay.

Rule 801. Definitions.

The following definitions apply under this article:

(a) *Statement.* A "statement" is (1) an oral or written assertion or (2) nonverbal conduct of a person, if it is intended by him to be communicative.

(b) *Declarant.* A "declarant" is a person who makes a statement.

(c) *Hearsay.* "Hearsay" is a statement other than one made by the declarant while testifying at the trial or hearing, offered in evidence to prove the truth of the matter asserted.

Rule 802. Hearsay rule.

Hearsay is not admissible except as provided by law or by these rules.

Rule 803. Hearsay exceptions; availability of declarant immaterial.

The following are not excluded by the hearsay rule, even though the declarant is available as a witness:

* * * * *

(5) *Recorded recollection.* A memorandum or record concerning a matter about which a witness once had knowledge but now has insufficient recollection to enable him to testify fully and accurately, shown to have been made or adopted by the witness when the matter was fresh in his memory and to reflect that knowledge correctly. If admitted, the memorandum or record may be read into evidence but may not itself be received as an exhibit unless offered by an adverse party.

(6) *Records of regularly conducted business activity.* A memorandum, report, record, or data compilation, in any form, of acts, events, conditions, opinions, or diagnoses, made at or near the time by, or from information transmitted by, a person with knowledge, if kept in the course of a regularly conducted business activity, and if it was the regular practice of that business activity to make the memorandum, report, record, or data compilation, all as shown by the testimony of the custodian or other qualified witness, unless the source of information or the method or circumstances of preparation indicate lack of trustworthiness. The term "business" as used in this paragraph includes business, institution,

association, profession, occupation, and calling of every kind, whether or not conducted for profit.

(7) *Absence of entry in records kept in accordance with the provisions of paragraph (6).* Evidence that a matter is not included in the memoranda, reports, records, or data compilations, in any form, kept in accordance with the provisions or paragraph (6), to prove the nonoccurrence or nonexistence of the matter, if the matter was of a kind of which a memorandum, report, record, or data compilation was regularly made and preserved, unless the sources of information or other circumstances indicate lack of trustworthiness.

(8) *Public records and reports.* To the extent not otherwise provided in this paragraph, records, reports, statements, or data compilations in any form of a public office or agency setting forth its regularly conducted and regularly recorded activities, or matters observed pursuant to duty imposed by law and as to which there was a duty to report, or factual findings resulting from an investigation made pursuant to authority granted by law. The following are not within this exception to the hearsay rule: (i) investigative reports by police and other law enforcement personnel; (ii) investigative reports prepared by or for a government, a public office, or an agency when offered by it in a case in which it is a party; (iii) factual findings offered by the government in criminal cases; (iv) factual findings resulting from special investigation of a particular complaint, case, or incident; and (v) any matter as to which the sources of information or other circumstances indicate lack of trustworthiness.

(9) *Records of vital statistics.* Records or data compilations, in any form, of births, fetal deaths, deaths, or marriages, if the report thereof was made to a public office pursuant to requirements of law.

(10) *Absence of public record or entry.* To prove the absence of a record, report, statement, or data compilation, in any form, or the nonoccurrence or nonexistence of a matter of which a record, report, statement, or data compilation, in any form, was regularly made and preserved by a public office or agency, evidence in the form of a certification in accordance with Rule 902, or testimony, that diligent search failed to disclose the record, report, statement, or data compilation, or entry.

(11) *Records of religious organizations.* Statements of births, marriages, divorces, death, legitimacy, ancestry, relationship by blood or marriage, or other similar facts of personal or family history, contained in a regularly kept record of a religious organization.

(12) *Marriage, baptismal, and similar certificates.* Statements of fact contained in a certificate that the maker performed a marriage or other ceremony or administered a sacrament, made by a clergyman, public official, or other person authorized by the rules or practices of a religious organization or by law to perform the act certified, and purporting to have been issued at the time of the act or within a reasonable time thereafter.

(13) *Family records.* Statements of fact concerning personal or family history contained in family Bibles, genealogies, charts, engravings on rings, inscriptions on family portraits, engravings on urns, crypts, or tombstones, or the like.

(14) *Records of documents affecting an interest in property.* The record of a document purporting to establish or affect an interest in property, as proof of the content of the original recorded document and its execution and delivery by each person by whom it purports to have been executed, if the record is a record of a public office and an applicable statute authorizes the recording of documents of that kind in that office.

(15) *Statements in documents affecting an interest in property.* A statement contained in a document purporting to establish or affect an interest in property if the matter stated was relevant to the purpose of the document, unless dealings with the property since the document was made have been inconsistent with the truth of the statement or the purport of the document.

(16) *Statements in ancient documents.* Statements in a document in existence twenty years or more the authenticity of which is established.

(17) *Market reports, commercial publications.* Market quotations, tabulations, lists, directories, or other published compilations, generally used and relied upon by the public or by persons in particular occupations.

(18) *Learned treatises.* To the extent called to the attention of an expert witness upon cross-examination or relied upon by him in direct examination, statements contained in published treatises, periodicals, or pamphlets on a subject of history, medicine, or other science or art, established as a reliable authority by testimony or admission of the witness or by other expert testimony or by judicial notice. If admitted, the statements may be read into evidence but may not be received as exhibits.

* * * * *

Article IX. Authentication and Identification.

Rule 901. Requirements of Authentication or Identification.

(a) *General provision.* The requirement of authentication or identification as a condition precedent to admissibility is satisfied by evidence sufficient to support a finding that the matter in question is what its proponent claims.

(b) *Illustrations.* By way of illustration only, and not by way of limitation, the following are examples of authentication or identification conforming with the requirements of this rule:

* * * * *

(7) *Public records or reports.* Evidence that a writing authorized by law to be recorded or filed and in fact recorded or filed in a public office, or a purported public record, report, statement, or data compilation, in any form, is from the public office where items of this nature are kept.

(8) *Ancient documents or data compilation.* Evidence that a document or data compilation, in any form, (A) is in such condition as to create no suspicion concerning its authenticity, (B) was in a place where it, if authentic, would likely be, and (C) has been in existence 20 years or more at the time it is offered.

(9) *Process or system.* Evidence describing a process or system used to produce a result and showing that the process or system produces an accurate result.

Rule 902. Self-authentication.

Extrinsic evidence of authenticity as a condition precedent to admissibility is not required with respect to the following:

(1) *Domestic public documents under seal.* A document bearing a seal purporting to be that of the United States, or of any State, district, Commonwealth, territory, or insular possession thereof, or the Panama Canal Zone, or the Trust Territory of the Pacific Islands, or of a political subdivision, department, officer, or agency thereof, and a signature purporting to be an attestation or execution.

(2) *Domestic public documents not under seal.* A document purporting to bear the signature in his official capacity of an officer or employee of any entity included in paragraph (1) hereof, having no seal, if a public officer having a seal and having official duties

in the district or political subdivision of the officer or employee certifies under seal that the signer has the official capacity and that the signature is genuine.

(3) *Foreign public documents.* A document purporting to be executed or attested in his official capacity by a person authorized by the laws of a foreign country to make the execution or attestation, and accompanied by a final certification as to the genuineness of the signature and official position (A) of the executing or attesting person, or (B) of any foreign official whose certificate of genuineness of signature and official position relates to the execution or attestation or is in a chain of certificates of genuineness of signature and official position relating to the execution or attestation. A final certification may be made by a secretary of embassy or legation, consul general, consul, vice consul, or consular agent of the United States, or a diplomatic or consular official of the foreign country assigned or accredited to the United States. If reasonable opportunity has been given to all parties to investigate the authenticity and accuracy of official documents, the court may, for good cause shown, order that they be treated as presumptively authentic without final certification or permit them to be evidenced by an attested summary with or without final certification.

(4) *Certified copies of public records.* A copy of an official record or report or entry therein, or of a document authorized by law to be recorded or filed and actually recorded or filed in a public office, including data compilations in any form, certified as correct by the custodian or other person authorized to make the certification, by certificate complying with paragraph (1), (2), or (3) of this rule or complying with paragraph (1), (2), or (3) of this rule or complying with any Act of Congress or rule prescribed by the Supreme Court pursuant to statutory authority.

(5) *Official publications.* Books, pamphlets, or other publications purporting to be issued by public authority.

(6) *Newspapers and periodicals.* Printed materials purporting to be newspapers or periodicals.

(7) *Trade inscriptions and the like.* Inscriptions, signs, tags, or labels purporting to have been affixed in the course of business and indicating ownership control, or origin.

(8) *Acknowledged documents.* Documents accompanied by a certificate of acknowledgment executed in the manner provided by law by a notary public or other officer authorized by law to take acknowledgments.

(9) *Commercial paper and related documents.* Commercial paper, signatures thereon, and documents relating thereto to the extent provided by general commercial law.

(10) *Presumptions under Acts of Congress.* Any signature, document or other matter declared by Act of Congress to be presumptively or prima facie genuine or authentic.

Article X. Contents of Writings, Recordings, and Photographs.

Rule 1001. Definitions.

For purposes of this Article the following definitions are applicable:

(1) *Writings and recordings.* "Writings" and "recordings" consist of letters, words, sounds, or numbers, or their equivalent, set down by handwriting, typewriting, printing, photostating, photographing, magnetic impulse, mechanical or electronic recording, or other form of data compilation.

(2) *Photographs.* "Photographs" include still photographs, X-ray films, video tapes, and motion pictures.

(3) *Original.* An "original" of a writing or recording is the writing or recording itself or any counterpart intended to have the same effect by a person executing or issuing it. An "original" of a photograph includes the negative or any print therefrom. If data are stored in a computer or similar device, any printout or other output readable by sight, shown to reflect the data accurately, is an "original."

(4) *Duplicate.* A "duplicate" is a counterpart produced by the same impression as the original, or from the same matrix, or by means of photography, including enlargements and miniatures, or by mechanical or electronic rerecording, or by chemical reproduction, or by other equivalent techniques which accurately reproduces the original.

Rule 1002. Requirement of original.

To prove the content of a writing, recording, or photograph, the original writing, recording, or photograph is required, except as otherwise provided in these rules or by [rules adopted by the Supreme Court of this State or by] statute.

Rule 1003. Admissibility of duplicates.

A duplicate is admissible to the same extent as an original unless (1) a genuine question is raised as to the authenticity or continuing effectiveness of the original or (2) in the circumstances it would be unfair to admit the duplicate in lieu of the original.

Rule 1004. Admissibility of other evidence of contents.

* * * * *

(1) *Originals lost or destroyed.* All originals are lost or have been destroyed, unless the proponent lost or destroyed them in bad faith; or

(2) *Original not obtainable.* No original can be obtained by any available judicial process or procedure; or

(3) *Original in possession of opponent.* At a time when an original was under the control of the party against whom offered, he was put on notice, by the pleadings or otherwise, that the contents would be a subject of proof at the hearing, and he does not produce the original at the hearing; or

(4) *Collateral matters.* The writing, recording, or photograph is not closely related to a controlling issue.

Rule 1005. Public records.

The contents of an official record, or of a document authorized to be recorded or filed and actually recorded or filed, including data compilations in any form, if otherwise admissible, may be proved by copy, certified as correct in accordance with Rule 902 or testified to be correct by a witness who has compared it with the original. If a copy complying with the foregoing cannot be obtained by the exercise of reasonable diligence, other evidence of the contents may be admitted.

Rule 1006. Summaries.

The contents of voluminous writings, recordings, or photographs which cannot conveniently be examined in court may be presented in the form of a chart, summary, or calculation. The originals, or duplicates, shall be made available for examination or copying, or both, by other parties at a reasonable time and place. The court may order that they be produced in court.

The following have adopted this Uniform Law:

Alaska	New Jersey
Arizona	New Mexico
Arkansas	North Carolina
Colorado	North Dakota
Delaware	Ohio
Florida	Oklahoma
Hawaii	Oregon
Indiana	Puerto Rico
Iowa	Rhode Island
Kentucky	South Dakota
Louisiana	Tennessee
Maine	Texas
Michigan	United States
Minnesota	Utah
Mississippi	Vermont
Montana	Washington
Nebraska	West Virginia
Nevada	Wisconsin
New Hampshire	Wyoming

Appendix I Other State Laws Related to Record Media and Recordkeeping Requirements

State:	**Alabama**
Source:	**Code of Alabama**

TITLE 12. COURTS.

CHAPTER 21. EVIDENCE AND WITNESSES.

Citation:	**Ala. Code § 12-21-43**

§ 12-21-43. Writings or records made in regular course of business — Originals.

Any writing or record, whether in the form of an entry in a book or otherwise, made as a memorandum or record of an act, transaction, occurrence or event, shall be admissible in evidence in proof of said act, transaction or event if it was made in the regular course of any business and it was the regular course of the business to make such memorandum or record at the time of such act, transaction, occurrence or event, or within a reasonable time thereafter. All other circumstances of the making of such writing or record, including lack of personal knowledge by the entrant or maker, may be shown to affect its weight, but they shall not affect its admissibility. The term, "business" shall include a business, profession, occupation and calling of every kind.

§ 12-21-44. Same - Photostatic, photographic or microphotographic plate or film of originals, or prints thereof; rights thereto when original not available.

(a) Any writing or record, whether in the form of an entry in a book or otherwise, made as a memorandum or record of any act, transaction, occurrence or event, if it was made in the regular course of any business and it was in the regular course of the business to make such memorandum or record at the time of such act, transaction, occurrence or event, or within a reasonable time thereafter, may be photostated, or it may be photographed or microphotographed on plate or film; and such photostat, photographic or microphotographic plate or film, or print thereof, whether enlarged or not, shall be deemed to be an original record and shall be admissible in evidence in proof of said act, transaction, occurrence or event in all instances that the original record might have been admissible and shall be presumed to be a true and correct reproduction of the original record it purports to represent. All other circumstances of the making of such writing or record, or of such photostat, photographic or microphotographic plate or film or print thereof, whether enlarged or not, including lack of personal knowledge by the entrant or maker, may be shown to affect its weight, but they shall not affect its admissibility.

(b) Whenever any writing or record, whether in the form of an entry in a book or otherwise, made as a memorandum or record of any act, transaction, occurrence or event has been photostated, photographed or microphotographed on plate or film, any party having the right to have the original record preserved or to an inspection of the original writing or record, or other rights in connection therewith, shall have the same rights as to the photostat, photographic or microphotographic plate or film, or prints made therefrom, in the event the original is not available. The custodian of such plate or film shall provide for the ready location of particular records so reproduced on plate or film and shall provide a projector or other convenient means for viewing the records so reproduced by those entitled thereto, and said custodian shall furnish a legible print or copy of such plate or film to such persons as are entitled to a copy of the original record. Nothing contained in this subsection shall be construed to allow the destruction or other disposition of original records which by statutory enactment now are, or hereafter may be, required to be preserved for inspection or for other purposes.

(c) For the purposes of this section, the term "business" shall mean and include any private business, industry, profession, occupation or calling of any kind. The term "record" or "records" as used in this section shall mean and include any writing or record as described in subsection (a) of this section, heretofore made or which may be made after May 21, 1951.

State:	**Illinois**
Source:	**Illinois Revised Statutes**

CHAPTER 5. - GENERAL PROVISIONS

CHAPTER 805. BUSINESS ORGANIZATIONS.

ACT 410. UNIFORM PRESERVATION OF PRIVATE BUSINESS RECORDS ACT

Citation:	**805 Ill.Rev.Stat. § 410/1**

§ 410/1. Definitions.

1. As used in this Act,

"Business" includes every kind of private business, profession, occupation, calling or operation of private institutions, whether carried on for profit or not.

"Person" means an individual, partnership, corporation, or any other association.

"Records" or "Business Records" include books of account, vouchers, documents, canceled checks, payrolls, correspondence, records of sales, personnel, equipment and production, reports relating to any or all of such records, and other business papers.

"Reproduction" means a reproduction or durable medium for making a reproduction obtained by any photographic, photostatic, microfilm, microcard, miniature photographic or other process which accurately reproduces or forms a durable medium for so reproducing the original.

Citation:	**805 Ill.Rev.Stat. 410/3**

§ 410/3. Reproductions - Preservation - Inspection - Enlargement - Admissibility.

3. (a) If reproductions of original business records are made, the preservation of such reproductions constitutes compliance with any laws of this State requiring that business records be kept or preserved, subject to the following conditions:

(1) The reproductions shall be made in the regular course of business or pursuant to a general plan for making reproductions of records:

(2) Persons required to keep the records shall without expense to the State make the reproductions available during usual business hours to State officers or authorized employees entitled to inspect or examine the records by running or projecting the reproductions for the inspection or examination of such officers, or employees, and shall so run or project the reproductions as to make it possible for such officers or employees to make notes or copies thereof;

(3) Persons required to keep the records, upon the request of the State department or agency charged with the administration of the Act requiring the records to be kept, shall without expense to the State provide enlargements of the reproductions in approximately original size of any and all records to the possession of which the department or agency would be entitled if reproductions have not been made.

(b) A reproduction constituting compliance with laws requiring the keeping of records under subsection (a), or an enlargement of such reproduction, when satisfactorily identified, is admissible in evidence, in instances where the original record would be admissible, to prove the contents of the original record in any judicial or administrative proceeding concerned with the enforcement of the laws of this State.

State:	**Missouri**
Source:	**Missouri Revised Statutes**

TITLE 8. - PUBLIC OFFICERS, BONDS AND RECORDS.

CHAPTER 109. PUBLIC AND BUSINESS RECORDS.

TRANSCRIBING AND REBINDING

Citation:	**Mo.Rev.Stat. § 109.120**

§ 109.120. Records reproduced by photostatic process - cost- marginal releases prohibited.

1. The head of any business, industry, profession, occupation or calling, or the head of any state, county or municipal department, commission, bureau or board may cause any and all records kept by such official, department, commission, bureau, board or business to be photographed, microphotographed, photostated or transferred to other material using photographic, video, or electronic processes and the judges and justices of the several courts of record within this state may cause all closed case files more than five years old to be photographed, microphotographed, photostated or transferred to other material using photographic, video, or electronic processes.

Such reproducing material shall be of durable material and the device used to reproduce the records shall be such as to accurately reproduce and perpetuate the original records in all details.

2. The cost of reproduction of closed files of the several courts of record as provided herein shall be chargeable to the county and paid out of the county treasury wherein that court is situated.

3. When any recorder of deeds in this state is required or authorized by law to record, copy, file, recopy, replace or index any document, plat, map or written instrument, he may do so by photostatic, photographic, microphotographic, microfilm, or similar mechanical process which produces a clear, accurate and permanent copy of the original. The reproductions so made may be used as permanent records of the original. When microfilm or a similar reproduction is used as a permanent record by recorder of deeds, duplicate reproductions of all recorded documents, indexes and files required by law to be kept by him shall be made and one copy of each document shall be stored in a fireproof vault and the other copy shall be readily available in his office together with suitable equipment for viewing the filmed record by projection to a size not smaller than the original and for reproducing copies of the recorded or filmed documents for any person entitled thereto. In all cases where instruments are recorded under the provisions of this section by microfilm, any release, assignment or other instrument affecting a previously recorded instrument by microfilm may not be made by marginal entry but shall be filed and recorded as a separate instrument and shall be in a separate book, cross-indexed to the document which it affects.

§ 109.130. Reproduced records deemed original, when.

Such reproduction of the original records shall be deemed to be an original record for all purposes provided that the reproduction is equal in resolution to microfilm produced under those standards set forth in subsection 4 of section 109.241 and shall be admissible in evidence in all courts or administrative agencies. A facsimile, exemplification, or certified copy thereof shall, for all purposes recited in sections 109.120 and 109.140, be deemed to be a transcript, exemplification or certified copy of the original.

Glossary

Acquisition. The purchase of one business by another with control remaining with the business that made the purchase.

Active record. A record that is regularly referenced or required for current use.

Admissibility in evidence. The character of evidence that enables it to be introduced in a court proceeding.

Admission. A statement made by an adverse party in litigation which is against the interests of that party and presumed to be true.

Adverse inference. A finding by a court in litigation that information contained in documents or other evidence, inappropriately destroyed by a party, is unfavorable to that party, even though the full content of the records or evidence was never reviewed by the court.

Asbestosis. A form of cancer caused by exposure to asbestos.

Audit. A periodic examination of an organization to determine whether appropriate procedures and practices are being followed.

Authentication. The act or process of determining the genuineness, reliability, or trustworthiness of evidence, including records, submitted as evidence.

Bad debt. A tax term used to indicate an amount of money owed to an organization which cannot or will not be collected.

Beyond a reasonable doubt. The weight of evidence in a criminal matter that fully establishes or convinces the decision maker of the defendant's guilt.

Burden of proof. The duty of a party in litigation to affirmatively prove the disputed facts that support the party's claims.

Business. An activity performed with some continuity or regularity in pursuit of an organizational goal.

Business organization. The structure or form of a business such as corporation, partnership, limited partnership, or sole proprietorship.

Capital gain or loss. A tax term indicating the amount of gain or loss realized when the purchase price plus cost of improvements is deducted from the ultimate sale price of capital property.

Capital property. A form of property designed to be used or endure for long periods of time.

Civil case. A court proceeding, other than a criminal case, to determine and enforce rights between parties, prevent future violation of rights, and provide appropriate redress or compensation.

Computer output microfilm. An original record in microfilm format produced directly from computer data without an intermediate visible record. Abbreviation: *COM*

Computer record. A form of record generated by data stored in electronic form on computer storage media or a record which has been produced in its visible form from the computer data.

Contempt of court. A deliberate act to disobey or disregard a legitimate order of a court.

Contract. An agreement between two or more people that creates, modifies, or destroys their legal relationship through a promise made by one party and assented to by the other.

Corporation. A legal entity created by authority of state law that grants a group of people certain legal powers, rights, privileges, and liabilities, distinct from those of the individuals making up the group.

Criminal case. A type of court case relating to the defendant's alleged violation of the law. Conviction could result in fines, loss of rights, or imprisonment.

Custodial capacity. A relationship creating the responsibility to protect property in the possession of one party but owned by another.

Depreciation. The loss in value of property or equipment used over time for business purposes and which is the amount that can be deducted on a tax return for this purpose.

Destruction suspension. A term used in record retention programs to indicate the process or procedure implemented to stop the destruction of records when it has been determined that litigation, gov ernment investigation or audit is pending or imminent.

Digitized Record. A record produced from an original by electronic scanning techniques, stored on optical disk or other high-density storage media, and then displayed on a high resolution terminal or printed onto paper. Also see *Electronic imaging system.*

Discovery. The legal process, generally conducted near the beginning of litigation, which enables parties to the litigation to obtain relevant records and information from each other.

Doing business. The acts of an organization which place it under the jurisdiction or control of government, courts, or law.

Duplicate. A facsimile or replica "produced by the same impression as the original or from the same matrix as the original by means of photography, including enlargements and miniatures, or by mechanical or electronic re-recording, chemical reproduction, or other equivalent techniques which accurately reproduces the original." (Uniform Rules of Evidence)

Electronic imaging system. A computer-based technology for scanning, storing, and retrieving scanned images of records in which the image is maintained in a electronic form.

Employee. One who performs services for another under the condition that the other person has a right to control and direct the employee not only as to the results to be accomplished by the work but also as to the details and means by which the result is accomplished.

Employment actions. Decisions and actions by employers that affect employees in areas such as promotion, demotion, transfer, selection for training, layoffs, or recalls.

Expungement. The process of removing information from courts or law enforcement agencies and obliterating it by any method to make the information unreadable or unusable under any circumstances.

Fiduciary capacity. A relationship creating the responsibility to manage, with a high degree of care, the financial matters and records of another.

Foreseeable. The action or event has not yet occurred but there is a reasonable anticipation that the activity or event will occur in the future.

Hazardous substance. A material or chemical determined to be harmful to human health.

Hearsay. "A statement other than one made by the declarant while testifying at the trial or hearing, offered in evidence to prove the truth of the matter asserted." (Uniform Rules of Evidence)

Hold. A term used in record retention schedules to indicate that certain records cannot be destroyed even though the record retention period has concluded. See also *Audit hold* and *Legal hold.*

Identification. The process of proving that evidence, such as a record, is in fact what its proponents claim it to be.

Imminent. The action or event is about to happen or likely to happen without delay.

Inactive records. Records still needed by an organization but not for current operations.

Indefinite. A term used in records retention schedules to indicate that the retention period for certain records cannot be determined in advance and that these records must be reviewed periodically to determine whether they can be destroyed.

Independent contractor. One who performs work according to his own methods, without being subject to the control of another except as to the result of the work.

Inference. The truth or falsehood of any matter derived from a process of reasoning in the absence of actual certainty or fact, or used until a certainty or fact can be determined.

Jurisdiction. A location in which government, courts, or laws have authority.

Law. An obligation to act or not act legitimately imposed by statute, rule or regulation, local ordinance or resolution, or judicial decision.

Lawsuit. Same as *Litigation.*

Legal compliance. The process or procedure to ensure that the organization is following relevant laws.

Legal consideration. Information related to a law or legal action that has a bearing on the records retention period but which is not a legal requirement to act or not act.

Legal group file. A summary of legal requirements and legal considerations, in a simplified form, for use in a records retention schedule.

Legal hold. A term used in records retention programs to indicate that certain records cannot yet be destroyed, even if otherwise permitted by the records retention schedule, because they are subject to litigation or government investigation.

Legal requirements. The obligation under a law to act or not act in the specified manner.

Legal research. The process of identifying and locating legal requirements.

Legal research index. An index prepared during legal research for a records retention program to organize the relevant laws.

Limitation of action. See *Statute of limitations*.

Limitation of assessment. The period of time after a tax return is filed or the tax becomes due during which the government tax agency can determine or modify the amount of taxes owed.

Limited partnership. A special form of partnership consisting of general partners who operate the partnership and are liable for any debts or losses, and limited partners who contribute capital and share in profits, but are not liable for debts or losses of the partnership beyond the amount con tributed.

Litigation. A proceeding in a court of law to enforce a right. Same as *lawsuit*.

Litigation protection. The process or procedures followed, in accordance with laws, that places an organization in the best possible position in litigation.

Machine-sensible record. A term used by the Internal Revenue Service to indicate computer-readable data, a record that is not visible but is accessible with appropriate equipment.

Media. The material or substance on which information is recorded such as paper, microfilm, magnetic disk or tape, or optical disk. Same as *Record media* .

Merger. The combination of two or more businesses with control resting in the new combined entity.

Microfiche. A form of microfilm, approximately 4 x 6 inches, on which documents are photographed in a reduced size for convenience in storage.

Microfilm. Film, in any format, on which documents are photographed in a reduced size for convenience in storage. The images on film can be enlarged for viewing or printing onto paper. The term also commonly used for microfilm in roll format.

Negligence. The failure to act like a reasonable person guided by ordinary considerations which regulates human affairs, or the commission of an act which the same reasonable person would not perform. The performance of an act by someone not exercising the level of care expected of a reasonable or ordinary person.

Non-Record. Preliminary materials, publishished materials, and other materials that are not records and that does not reflect the position or business of an organization; includes drafts and word processing files used to produce final, official records. "Library and museum material made or acquired and preserved for reference or exhibition purposes, extra copies of documents preserved only for convenience of reference, and stocks fo publications and of processed documents are not included." (Federal Records Act, 44 U.S.C. 3301)

Obstruction of justice. A deliberate act designed to interfere with a government investigation or judicial proceeding.

Office of record. The group, department, or office in an organization responsible for maintaining the official records for the total records retention period.

One-time project. A project, such as the destruction or microfilming of records, conducted in a non-recurring manner.

Optical disk. A technology used to store great quantities of information on a special disk that can be encoded by a laser beam.

Ordinance. A law prepared by a local governing body

Original. The "writing or recording itself or any counterpart intended to have the same effect by a person executing or issuing it. If data are stored in a computer or similar device, any printout or other output readable by sight, shown to reflect the data accurately, is an *original*." (Uniform Rules of Evidence).

Parole evidence rule. A rule that prohibits the introduction of verbal testimony to modify the terms of a written contract in most circumstances.

Partnership. An association of people working together and sharing profits.

Pending. The action or activity is in progress but not yet completed.

Permanent. The continued preservation of information or other matter forever, without any limit in time. A term sometimes used in laws to mean *durable* rather than *forever*.

Personal records. Same as *Private records*.

Preponderance of the evidence. The weight of evidence in a civil matter presented by one party in court, when fairly considered, produces a stronger impression or is more convincing than the evidence provided by the opposing party.

Private records. Records belonging to an individual that have no content relevant to the organization or were not produced using resources of the organization. Same as *Personal records*.

Product liability. The legal responsibility of a manufacturer or seller to the purchaser or consumer of the product for the design, safety, and utility of the product.

Quasi-judicial authority. Authority granted to some regulatory agencies to conduct hearings like the judicial branch.

Purge. The act of selectively destroying one or more documents from a file.

Reasonable. A legal term that qualifies an action or state of mind as being just, proper, ordinary, usual, rational, or sensible, or in the alternative, not extreme, immoderate, or excessive.

Reckless. The commission of an act with no regard to the probability or possibility of adverse consequences, even when the consequences of the act were foreseeable. The performance of an act by someone who knew or should have known of the adverse consequences that may result but performed the act anyway.

Record. *Organization Definiton*: The result of recording or preserving information on any media with the intent to preserve information that reflects the position or business of an organization. *See also Non-Record. Court Definition:* "Letters, words, sounds, or numbers, or their equivalent, set down by handwriting, typewriting, printing, photostating, photographing, magnetic impulse, mechanical electronic recording, or other form of data compilation", including "still photographs, X–rays, X-ray films, video tapes, and motion pictures." (Uniform Rules of Evidence)

Record media. See *Media*.

Record series. A group of similar or related records, used or filed as a unit.

Record value. The importance or usefulness of a record for operational, legal, fiscal, historical or other purpose.

Recordkeeping requirements. The obligations of law related to the creation, maintenance and disposition of records.

Records destruction. The process of totally obliterating information on records by any method to make the information unreadable or unusable under any circumstances.

Records management. The systematic control of all records from creation or receipt through processing, distribution, maintenance and retrieval, to their ultimate disposition.

Records manager. An individual, knowledgeable in records managements, designated by an organization to control the records management program.

Records retention period. The period of time during which records must be maintained by an organization because they are needed for operational, legal, fiscal, historical or other purposes. Records should be destroyed after the termination of the retention period.

Records retention program. A component of the total records management program that determines the period of time for retaining records and controls the ultimate disposition of records at the appropriate time.

Records retention schedule. A document prepared as part of a records retention program that lists the period of time for retaining records.

Regular course of business. The transacting of business activities in a regular, recurring, ordered, customary, or habitual manner.

Regulation. A law prepared by a regulatory agency acting under authority granted by Congress or the state legislature.

Regulatory agency. A government entity authorized to issue laws in the form of rules or regulations, conduct investigations or quasi judicial hearings, or initiate enforcement proceedings for existing laws.

Self-serving. Acts or records that are created to support the interests of the author.

Sham. A program or action that appears to be legal but is fraudulent in reality.

Statute. A law prepared by the United States Congress or a state legislature.

Statute of limitations. A time period after an event during which a legal action or lawsuit may be initiated.

Subpoena. A court order requiring a witness to appear in court and provide testimony.

Subpoena duces tecum. A court order requiring a witness to appear in court, produce relevant records in his possession or control, and provide testimony.

Suit. See *Lawsuit*.

Systematic. The process of conducting activities or procedures conducted according to a system, method, or plan in a regular, orderly or methodical manner.

Tax audit. The review by a government tax agency of tax returns and tax records to determine whether the correct amount of tax was paid.

Tax hold. A term used in records retention schedules to indicate that certain records cannot yet be destroyed, even when otherwise permitted under the records retention program, because they are currently subject to audit or the audit period for those records has been extended.

Trustworthiness. The degree to which a court, a judge, or other decision maker can rely on evidence or other representations.

Visible record. A form of record for which the image is visible directly by sight or with the assistance of magnification.

Bibliography

Allen, Michael. "Cleaning House: U.S. Companies Pay Increasing Attention to Destroying Files." *The Wall Street Journal* (September 2, 1987):1.

American Bankers Association. *The Retention of Bank Records*. Washington, DC: 1987.

Association of Records Managers and Administrators, Inc. *Records Retention Scheduling*. Prairie Village, KS: 1980.

————. Canadian Legislative and Regulatory Affairs Committee. *Records Retention for Business*. Toronto: 1985.

————. *Developing and Operating a Records Retention Program*. Prairie Village, KS: 1986.

Austin, Robert B. and Skupsky, Donald S. "How to Determine Cost-Savings for a Records/Files Management Program." *Journal of Information and Image Management* (November 1983).

Austin, Robert B. "10,000,000 Reasons for Records Management." *Records Management Quarterly* (July 1985).

Barber, Donald T. and Langemo, Mark. *Filing Dynamics: Development in Color Coding for Filing Systems*. California: Marsdale Publishing Co., Ltd., 1987.

Black, Henry Campbell. *Black's Law Dictionary*. St. Paul: West Publishing Company, current edition.

Code of Federal Regulations. Washington, DC: Government Printing Office, updated annually.

Code of Federal Regulations: List of CFR Sections Affected. Washington, DC: Government Printing Office, monthly.

Coker, Kathy Roe. "Records Appraisal: Practice and Procedure." *Records Management Quarterly* (October 1985).

Diamond, Susan Z. *Records Management: A Practical Guide*. New York: American Management Association, 1983.

Dickenson, A. Litchard. "Retention Schedules – Valuable to Business, But Why Are So Many Ineffective?" *Records Management Quarterly* (October 1984).

Fedders, John M. and Guttenplan, Lauryn H. "Document Retention and Destruction: Practical, Legal, and Ethical Considerations," *The Notre Dame Lawyer* (October 1980).

Federal Register. Washington, DC: Government Printing Office, daily.

Financial Executives Institute. *Records Retention and Destruction in Canada: A Guidebook*. Toronto: 1980.

Guide to Record Retention Requirements. Washington, DC: Government Printing Office, 1986.

Guide to Record Retention Requirements: Supplement. Washington, DC: Government Printing Office, printed annually.

Guyman, Fred E. *Records Retention Directory*. Orem, UT: Eastwood Publishing Company, 1984.

————. *National & International Records Retention Standards*. Orem, UT: Eastwood Publishing Company, 1986.

Hayes, Kenneth V. "Three Approaches to Records Retention." *Records Management Quarterly* (April 1985).

————. "Using a Microcomputer for Retention Schedule Maintenance." *Records Management Quarterly* (April 1985).

Institute of Certified Records Managers. *Survey of Records and Information Retention and Disposal Practices*. Washington, DC: 1983.

Internal Revenue Service. *Revenue Rulings and Revenue Procedures*. Washington, DC: Government Printing Office, weekly.

Langemo, Mark. "How Long Must You Keep Your Business Records?". *Office Systems 88* (April 1988).

Morgan, Dennis F., Millican, Dennis D. "The Electronic Media Retention Schedule Program: Selling It to Management." *Records Management Quarterly* (October 1984).

――――. "A Records Manager's Blueprint for the Inventory and Retention Scheduling of Information in Electronic Form." *Records Management Quarterly"* (July 1984).

――――. "Retention Scheduling of Electronically Stored Records Generated by Personal Computers, Word Processors, Microcomputers, Minicomputers, and Electronic Mail Systems." *Records Management Quarterly* (January 1985).

The National Directory of State Agencies. Bethesda, MD: National Standards Association, Inc, updated annually.

Penn, Ira A., Pennix, Gail, and Coulson, Jim. *Records Management Handbook*. London: Gower, 1994.

Place, Irene and Hyslop, David J. *Records Management: Controlling Business Information*. Reston, VA: Reston Publishing Co., 1982.

Records Controls, Inc. *Retention and Preservation of Records with Destruction Schedules*, 11th Edition. Chicago, IL: 1984.

Ricks, Betty R. and Gow, Kay F. *Information Resources Management*. Cincinnati: South-Western Publishing Co., 1984.

Robek, Mary F., Brown, Gerald F. and Maedke, Wilmer O. *Information and Records Management*. Encino, CA: Glencoe Publishing Company, 1987

Skupsky, Donald S. *Legal Requirements for Business Records: Federal Requirements*. Denver: Information Requirements Clearinghouse, updated annually.

――――. *Legal Requirements for Business Records: State Requirements*. Denver: Information Requirements Clearinghouse, updated annually.

――――. *Legal Requirements for Microfilm, Computer and Optical Disk Records*. Denver: Information Requirements Clearinghouse, 1994.

――――. *Records Retention Procedures*. Denver: Information Requirements Clearinghouse, 1994.

――――. "Legal Issues in Records Retention and Disposition Programs." *Records Management Quarterly* (July 1984).

――――. "Researching the Legal Requirements for Your Records." *Records Management Quarterly* (October 1984).

――――. "The Legal Status of Microfilm and Other Duplicate Records." *Records Management Quarterly* (January 1985).

――――. "Legality of Computer and Computer Output Microfilm Records." *Records Management Quarterly* (April 1985).

――――. "Legality of Records in Evidence: Paper, Microfilm, and Magnetic Media." *Office Systems Magazine*, The Office Systems Cooperative (Spring 1985).

――――. "Some Considerations Related to Records Retention Requirements for Tax Records." *Records Management Quarterly* (July 1985).

――――. "Legal Requirements for Records Retention . . . The Three-Year Presumption!" *Records Management Quarterly* (October 1985).

――――. "The Legal Status of Optical Disk and Electronic Imaging Systems." *Records Management Quarterly* (January 1986).

――――. "Admissibility of Original Records in Evidence." *Records Management Quarterly* (April 1986).

――――. "Determining Litigation and Statutes of Limitation Requirements for Records Retention Programs." *Records Management Quarterly* (July 1986).

――――. "The Legal Status of Selected Records." *Records Management Quarterly* (October 1986).

――――. "Legislative Reform for Legal Requirements for Records and Information Management Programs." *Records Management Quarterly* (January 1987).

――――. "Legal Liability of the Records and Information Management Professional." *Records Management Quarterly* (April 1987).

――――. "Legal Requirements for Personnel Records." *Records Management Quarterly* (July 1987).

――――. "Organizing the Legal Research for your Records Retention Program" *Records Management Quarterly* (October 1987).

――――. "Legal and Operational Reasons for Eliminating the Authorization for Destruction Form." *Records Management Quarterly* (January 1988)

――――. "Legal Requirements for One-Time Projects to Destroy or Microfilm Records." *Records Management Quarterly* (April 1988).

――――. "Legal Requirements for Computer Records Containing Federal Tax Information: An Update." *Records Management Quarterly* (July 1988).

Skupsky, Donald S. and Montaña, John C. *Law, Records and Information Management: The Court Cases*. Denver: Information Requirements Clearinghouse, updated annually.

Stephen, David O. "The Records Retention Schedule: A Key Element in Legal Administration." *Legal Administrator* (Spring 1985).

————. "Making Records Retention Decisions: Practical and Theoretical Considerations." *Records Management Quarterly* (January 1988).

United States Code. Washington, DC: Government Printing Office, updated annually.

United States Code Annotated. St. Paul: West Publishing Company, updated monthly.

United States Code Service, Lawyers Edition. Rochester, NY: Lawyers Coop Publishing Company, updated monthly.

Wilds, Thomas. *Records Retention and Files Management: Seminar Workbook*.. New York: Thomas Wilds Associates, 1980.

Williams, Robert V. *The Legality of Microfilm*. Chicago: Cohasset Associates, updated annually.

————. *The Legality of Optical Disk*. Chicago: Cohasset Associates, updated annually.

Wrona, Eugene A. "The Pyramid: An Analytical Tool for Records Retention." *Records Management Quarterly* (July 1984).

Index

Notes

Notes

Notes

Notes

Notes

Notes

Other Publications and Services . . .

Records Retention Procedures

Your old, valueless records cost you space, time and money. Yet, you may suffer fines, penalties or other legal consequences if you do not keep your records long enough or you destroy them improperly. If you keep them too long, adverse parties may also subpoena your records during litigation — records that could and should have been destroyed legally in the regular course of business — to help them win *their* case against you!

Realistically, you have to make a decision. You can no longer decide *whether or not* to destroy records . . . only *when* to destroy them! Keeping records for too short a time may cause you problems! Keeping them too long could even be worse!

Records Retention Procedures gives you the solution! We show you how to establish a records retention program for destroying records at the right time. We show you the step-by-step *Skupsky Retention Method* — proven in actual use:

Step 1.   The Preliminary Procedures
Step 2.   The Legal Research
Step 3.   The Legal Research Index
Step 4.   The Legal Group File
Step 5.   The Records Retention Schedule
Step 6.   The Records with Retention Periods
Step 7.   The Concluding Procedures

Take the mystery out of records retention. The records nightmare can become a thing of the past! Clean old records out of your valuable storage areas.

Legal Requirements for Business Records

For those who need all the information, *Legal Requirements for Business Records* gives the full text of over 7,500 United States federal and state laws that affect recordkeeping. Our annual update service helps you comply with the new laws!

Legal Requirement for Microfilm, Comuter and Optical Disk Records: Evidence, Regulation, Government and International Requirements

When an organization develops an advanced records system utilizing technologies such as microfilm, computer and optical disk, legal question can be expected. Will courts permit their use? Can the original recors be destroyed aftery they have been reproduced? When a regulation speicifies the tcreation of particular records, must a particular for the the records be used?

This 500-page book provides you:
☐ Detailed legal analysis and recommendations.
☐ Full text of major United States federal and
      state laws and international laws .
☐ Text of Uniform Laws and Guidelines.
☐ Annual supplements to keep you informed.

Law, Records and Information Management: The Court Cases

Compliance with statutes and regulations is not enough. The courts interprete these laws and expect you to have a system in place to identify and retrieve records when presented with a subpoena in litigation.

This 600-page book provides you:
☐ Selected text from over 200 leading court cases.
☐ Detailed legal analysis of the important cases.
☐ Indexes, tables and cross reference to help you
      find relevant informaltion.
☐ Practical, procedural recommendations.
☐ Annual supplements to keep you informed.

Retention!

Our new software package gives you *The Skupsky Retention Method* in computer form. We also provide you with the basic data to help you develop a records retention schedule quickly and accurately, plus the text of the records retention laws in computer-readable form taken from *Legal Requirements for Business Records.*

Order Form

Please complete and send to:

Information Requirements Clearinghouse
5600 South Quebec Street, Suite 250C
Englewood, Colorado 80111
(303) 721-7500, FAX (303) 721-8849

Please complete this form to order additional books or request information.

Name _____ Title _____
Company _____
Address _____
City _____ State _____ Zip Code _____
Phone ( )_____

Orders

Number	Description	Price	Total
	Law, Records and Information Management: The Court Cases	$ 95.00	
	Legal Requirements for Microfilm, Computer and Optical Disk Records	$ 59.00	
	Records Retention Procedures	$ 39.00	
	Recordkeeping Requirements	$ 35.00	
	Subtotal		
	Tax (Colorado residents add sales tax). Hawaii and Alaska add $10.00 shipping		
	*Shipping and Handling: $5.00 for first book, plus $2.00 for each additional book		$ 5.00 $
	Total		

☐ Enclosed is $ _____ check or money order for payment in full.

☐ Charge to: ___ MasterCard ___ Visa   Date card expires: _____

Credit Card Number: |_|_|_|_|_|_|_|_|_|_|_|_|_|_|_|_|

Signature of card holder _____

☐ Send me information about your records retention software, *Retention!*.
☐ Send me information about *Legal Requirements for Business Records*.
☐ Send me information about your seminars and consulting services.

*International Orders. (Make check payable in U.S. Dollars drawn on a U.S. Bank)

Canada: Add $10.00 additional shipping and handing.
Other: Add $25.00 additional shipping and handling.

GUARANTEE: If you are dissatisfied with our publication for any reason, please return it in resalable condition with proof of purchase within 30 days of receipt. Information Requirements Clearinghouse will promptly refund your purchase price.